A Sweet Smelling Savor

Compiled and Edited by Douglas B. Whitley Jr.

Copyright © 2017 Douglas B. Whitley Jr.

All rights reserved.

ISBN:1544007876
ISBN-13:9781544007878

CONTENTS

Introduction p. 4

Scripture p. 6

Collected Prayers in Alphabetical Order p. 43

Index 317

About the Author 318

A Sweet Smelling Savor

ACKNOWLEDGMENTS

I would like to thank Drew Dickenson and the team at Carpenter's Code, Abide.is for starting me down this path of prayer.

A SWEET SMELLING SAVOR

"I return unto Thee, O Lord, O Lord Thou lover of man, Thou hast a golden censer; add me Thine incense unto this prayer for a sweet-smelling savour before Thy throne, and let the lifting up of hands be set forth for an evening sacrifice."

Bishop Lancelot Andrewes

(1555-1626 AD)

Introduction

Several years ago, I was asked by an organization to record some ancient and classical prayers "in character" from men of God who were pillars of the church in their time. The research took me down a path of learning about prayer in a way I had never done before. I portray E.M. Bounds and George Meuller on prayer in the characterizations in our ministry, "Preachers of the Past". Andrew Murray is also one of the men I portray who has written much about prayer. There are sermons by Dr. R.A. Torrey and Rev. C. H. Spurgeon on prayer I present regularly, but nothing I had encountered prepared me for the wonder and depth of these prayers I began to gather for the prayer app for Abide.is. and hope to share with you.

Prayer is one of those topics in Christendom that everyone believes is important. Most people I talk with would say they need to pray more (myself included). No one would argue the power of prayer and yet it is one of the most neglected aspects of our Christian walk and in the Church as a whole. We like to do something, share the gospel, help the poor, teach a Bible study, preach, teach, work in the nursery, the tech team, the children's ministry, the traffic control team, the chair stacking team and most importantly the coffee prep team. The reality is that none of these things should be entered into without prayer. It is the foundational element in any endeavor for Jesus Christ.

If you are like me prayer is for you a "last resort" in the most desperate of times or for mealtimes (lest you be swallowed up like the ungrateful Israelites during the Exodus), the beginning of sports events at Christian schools, Invocations (insert deep pious voice here) Prayer is for shut-ins, grandmothers, children, people who can't do anything else, but not for the doers. The reality of Prayer is that it is, it must be, the underlying practice for everything we do in our Christian lives. It must be first. Prayer calls upon the power of our Abba Father, the Lord God Almighty, the One in Whom All Power Dwells, the Alpha and the Omega, Jehovah Jireh, Jehovah Shammah, the I AM, to bless, to empower, to work, to do for us that which we are truly incapable of doing. It is through prayer, through pouring out our hearts to our Father that His strength is made complete in our weakness. It is through prayer that we realize how great God is and how small we are. It is prayer that causes us to be still and know that He is God ("and we are not" as one of my favorite T-shirts says.)

There is a great deal said and written about prayer. I find some of it creates more excuses and barriers to prayer than I see in these men and women of old. There are no right words or forms. There is actually no perfect position for prayer, although there are several mentioned in scripture. There is nothing to great or too small for which we may not pray. There is nothing too insignificant about which we may pray. The Father God who numbers the hairs of our heads, whose thoughts of us are "more in number than the sands of the sea" (Psalm 139:18) is intimately acquainted with our lives and longs for us to call on Him, to truly cast every care upon Him because it matters to Him what happens to us.

I freely confess thinking of some of the imprecatory prayers from King David in the Psalms when I hear or read of someone limiting or diminishing prayer and the power of prayer because I see the results in a weakened prayer life, a weakened daily walk with God or such confusion is created that people stop praying altogether. "God binds us to pray by the most solemn obligations," wrote E.M. Bounds. We forget the simple "ask, seek, knock" of the words of Christ in Matthew 7.

These are verses from the Bible. They are not exhaustive of the scripture about prayer, but they are a starting point to underline the importance of prayer to us and to the Lord God Almighty.

Scripture on Prayer

Psalm 4:1 Hear me when I call, O God of my righteousness: thou hast enlarged me when I was in distress; have mercy upon me, and hear my prayer.

Psalm 5:2, 3 Hearken unto the voice of my cry, my King, and my God: for unto Thee will I pray. My voice shalt thou hear in the morning, O LORD; in the morning will I direct my prayer unto Thee, and will look up.

Psalm 6:9 The LORD hath heard my supplication; the LORD will receive my prayer.

Psalm 17:1 Hear the right, O LORD, attend unto my cry, give ear unto my prayer, that goeth not out of feigned lips..

Psalm 32:6 For this shall every one that is godly pray unto Thee in a time when thou mayest be found: surely in the floods of great waters they shall not come nigh unto him.

Psalm 35:13 But as for me, when they were sick, my clothing was sackcloth: I humbled my soul with fasting; and my prayer returned into mine own bosom.

Psalm 39:12 Hear my prayer, O LORD, and give ear unto my cry; hold not Thy peace at my tears: for I am a stranger with Thee, and a sojourner, as all my fathers were.

Psalm 42:8 Yet the LORD will command his lovingkindness in the daytime, and in the night his song shall be with me, and my prayer unto the God of my life.

Psalm 54:2 Hear my prayer, O God; give ear to the words of my mouth.

Psalm 55:1 Give ear to my prayer, O God; and hide not Thyself from my supplication.

Psalm 55:17 Evening, and morning, and at noon, will I pray, and cry aloud: and He shall hear my voice.

Psalm 61:1 Hear my cry, O God; attend unto my prayer.

Psalm 64:1 Hear my voice, O God, in my prayer: preserve my life from fear of the enemy.

Psalm 65:2 O Thou that hearest prayer, unto Thee shall all flesh come.

Psalm 66:19, 20 But verily God hath heard me; He hath attended to the voice of my prayer. Blessed be God, which hath not turned away my prayer, nor His mercy from me.

Psalm 69:13 But as for me, my prayer is unto Thee, O LORD, in an acceptable time: O God, in the multitude of Thy mercy hear me, in the truth of Thy salvation.

Psalm 80:4 O LORD God of hosts, how long wilt Thou be angry against the prayer of Thy people?

Psalm 84:8 O LORD God of hosts, hear my prayer: give ear, O God of Jacob. Selah.

Psalm 86:1 Bow down Thine ear, O LORD, hear me: for I am poor and needy.

Psalm 86:6 Give ear, O LORD, unto my prayer; and attend to the voice of my supplications.

Psalm 88:2 Let my prayer come before Thee: incline Thine ear unto my cry;

Psalm 88:13 But unto Thee have I cried, O LORD; and in the morning shall my prayer prevent Thee.

Psalm 102:1 Hear my prayer, O LORD, and let my cry come unto Thee.

Psalm 102:17 He will regard the prayer of the destitute, and not despise their prayer.

Psalm 109:4 For my love they are my adversaries: but I give myself unto prayer.

Psalm 116:1-2 I love the Lord, because He hath heard my voice and my supplications. Because He hath inclined His ear unto me, therefore will I call upon Him as long as I live.

Psalm 122:6 Pray for the peace of Jerusalem: they shall prosper that love Thee.

Psalm 141:2 Let my prayer be set forth before Thee as incense; and the lifting up of my hands as the evening sacrifice.

Psalm 142:1 I cried unto the LORD with my voice; with my voice unto the LORD did I make my supplication.

Psalm 143:1 Hear my prayer, O LORD, give ear to my supplications: in Thy faithfulness answer me, and in Thy righteousness.

2 Samuel 22:4 I will call on the LORD, who is worthy to be praised: so shall I be saved from mine enemies.

1 Kings 8:28,29 Yet have thou respect unto the prayer of Thy servant, and to his supplication, O LORD my God, to hearken unto the cry and to the prayer, which Thy servant prayeth before Thee today: That thine eyes may be open toward this house night and day, even toward the place of which thou hast said, My name shall be there: that thou mayest hearken unto the prayer which Thy servant shall make toward this place.

1 Kings 8:38 What prayer and supplication soever be made by any man, or by all Thy people Israel, which shall know every man the plague of his own heart, and spread forth his hands toward this house:

1 Kings 8:43 Hear thou in heaven Thy dwelling place, and do according to all that the stranger calleth to Thee for: that all people of the earth may know Thy name, to fear Thee, as do Thy people Israel; and that they may know that this house, which I have builded, is called by Thy name.

1 Kings 8:45 Then hear thou in heaven their prayer and their supplication, and maintain their cause.

1 Kings 8:49 Then hear thou their prayer and their supplication in heaven Thy dwelling place, and maintain their cause,

1 Kings 8:54 And it was so, that when Solomon had made an end of praying all this prayer and supplication unto the LORD, he arose from before the altar of the LORD, from kneeling on his knees with his hands spread up to heaven.

1 Kings 9:3 And the LORD said unto him, I have heard Thy prayer and Thy supplication, that thou hast made before me: I have hallowed this house, which thou hast built, to put my name there forever; and mine eyes and mine heart shall be there perpetually.

1 Kings 18:24, 25 And call ye on the name of your gods, and I will call on the name of the LORD: and the God that answereth by fire, let him be God. And all the people answered and said, "It is well spoken." And Elijah said unto the prophets of Baal, "Choose you one bullock for yourselves, and dress it first; for ye are many; and call on the name of your gods, but put no fire under."

2 Kings 19:4 It may be the LORD Thy God will hear all the words of Rabshakeh, whom the king of Assyria his master hath sent to reproach the living God; and will reprove the words which the LORD Thy God hath heard: wherefore lift up Thy prayer for the remnant that are left.

2 Kings 20:5 Turn again, and tell Hezekiah the captain of my people, "Thus saith the LORD, the God of David Thy father, I have heard Thy prayer, I have seen Thy tears: behold, I will heal Thee: on the third day thou shalt go up unto the house of the LORD."

2 Chronicles 6:19, 20 Have respect therefore to the prayer of Thy servant, and to his supplication, O LORD my God, to hearken unto the cry and the prayer which Thy servant prayeth before Thee: That thine eyes may be open upon this house day and night, upon the place whereof thou hast said that thou wouldest put Thy name there; to hearken unto the prayer which Thy servant prayeth toward this place.

2 Chronicles 6:29 Then what prayer or what supplication soever shall be made of any man, or of all Thy people Israel, when everyone shall know his own sore and his own grief, and shall spread forth his hands in this house:

2 Chronicles 6:35 Then hear thou from the heavens their prayer and their supplication, and maintain their cause.

2 Chronicles 6:39, 40 Then hear thou from the heavens, even from Thy dwelling place, their prayer and their supplications, and maintain their cause, and forgive Thy people which have sinned against Thee. Now, my God, let, I beseech Thee, thine eyes be open, and let thine ears be attentive unto the prayer that is made in this place.

2 Chronicles 7:12 And the LORD appeared to Solomon by night, and said unto him, I have heard Thy prayer, and have chosen this place to myself for an house of sacrifice. .

2 Chronicles 30:27 Then the priests the Levites arose and blessed the people: and their voice was heard, and their prayer came up to his holy dwelling place, even unto heaven.

2 Chronicles 33:18,19 Now the rest of the acts of Manasseh, and his prayer unto his God, and the words of the seers that spake to him in the name of the LORD God of Israel, behold, they are written in the book of the kings of Israel. His prayer also, and how God was entreated of him, and all his sin, and his trespass, and the places wherein he built high places, and set up groves and graven images, before he was humbled: behold, they are written among the sayings of the seers.

Nehemiah 1:6 Let thine ear now be attentive, and thine eyes open, that thou mayest hear the prayer of Thy servant, which I pray before Thee now, day and night, for the children of Israel Thy servants, and confess the sins of the children of Israel, which we have sinned against Thee: both I and my father's house have sinned.

Nehemiah 1:11 O Lord, I beseech Thee, let now thine ear be attentive to the prayer of Thy servant, and to the prayer of Thy servants, who desire to fear Thy name: and prosper, I pray Thee, Thy servant this day, and grant him mercy in the sight of this man. For I was the king's cupbearer.

Nehemiah 4:9 Nevertheless we made our prayer unto our God, and set a watch against them day and night, because of them.

Job 16:17 Not for any injustice in mine hands: also my prayer is pure.

Job 22:27 Thou shalt make Thy prayer unto him, and he shall hear Thee, and thou shalt pay Thy vows.

Proverbs15:8 The sacrifice of the wicked is an abomination to the LORD: but the prayer of the upright is his delight.

Proverbs 15:29 The LORD is far from the wicked: but he heareth the prayer of the righteous.

Proverbs 28:9 He that turneth away his ear from hearing the law, even his prayer shall be abomination.

Isaiah 1:15 And when ye spread forth your hands, I will hide mine eyes from you: yea, when ye make many prayers, I will not hear: your hands are full of blood.

Isaiah 26:16 LORD, in trouble have they visited Thee, they poured out a prayer when Thy chastening was upon them.

Isaiah 37:4 It may be the LORD Thy God will hear the words of Rabshakeh, whom the king of Assyria his master hath sent to reproach the living God, and will reprove the words which the LORD Thy God hath heard: wherefore lift up Thy prayer for the remnant that is left.

Isaiah 38:5 Go, and say to Hezekiah, Thus saith the LORD, the God of David Thy father, I have heard Thy prayer, I have seen Thy tears: behold, I will add unto Thy days fifteen years.

Isaiah 56:7 Even them will I bring to my holy mountain, and make them joyful in my house of prayer: their burnt offerings and their sacrifices shall be accepted upon mine altar; for mine house shall be called an house of prayer for all people.

Jeremiah 7:16 Therefore pray not thou for this people, neither lift up cry nor prayer for them, neither make intercession to me: for I will not hear Thee.

Jeremiah 11:14 Therefore pray not thou for this people, neither lift up a cry or prayer for them: for I will not hear them in the time that they cry unto me for their trouble.

Lamentations 3:8 Also when I cry and shout, He shutteth out my prayer.

Lamentations 3:44 Thou hast covered Thyself with a cloud, that our prayer should not pass through.

Daniel 9:3 And I set my face unto the Lord God, to seek by prayer and supplications, with fasting, and sackcloth, and ashes:

Daniel 9:13 As it is written in the law of Moses, all this evil is come upon us: yet made we not our prayer before the LORD our God, that we might turn from our iniquities, and understand Thy truth.

Daniel 9:17 Now therefore, O our God, hear the prayer of Thy servant, and his supplications, and cause Thy face to shine upon Thy sanctuary that is desolate, for the Lord's sake.

Daniel 9:21 Yea, whilst I was speaking in prayer, even the man Gabriel, whom I had seen in the vision at the beginning, being caused to fly swiftly, touched me about the time of the evening oblation.

Joel 2:32 And it shall come to pass, that whosoever shall call on the name of the LORD shall be delivered: for in Mount Zion and in Jerusalem shall be deliverance, as the LORD hath said, and in the remnant whom the LORD shall call.

Jonah 2:7 When my soul fainted within me I remembered the LORD: and my prayer came in unto Thee, into thine holy temple.

Zechariah 7:2 When they had sent unto the house of God Sherezer and Regemmelech, and their men, to pray before the LORD

Zechariah 8:21, 22 And the inhabitants of one city shall go to another, saying, Let us go speedily to pray before the LORD, and to seek the LORD of hosts: I will go also. Yea, many people and strong nations shall come to seek the LORD of hosts in Jerusalem, and to pray before the LORD.

Zechariah 13:9 And I will bring the third part through the fire, and will refine them as silver is refined, and will try them as gold is tried: they shall call on my name, and I will hear them: I will say, 'It is my people: and they shall say, The LORD is my God.'

Malachi 1:9 And now, I pray you, beseech God that he will be gracious unto us: this hath been by your means: will he regard your persons? saith the LORD of hosts.

Matthew 5:44 But I say unto you, Love your enemies, bless them that curse you, do good to them that hate you, and pray for them which despitefully use you, and persecute you;

Matthew 17:21 Howbeit this kind goeth not out but by prayer and fasting.

Matthew 21:13 And said unto them, "It is written, My house shall be called the house of prayer; but ye have made it a den of thieves."

Matthew 21:22 And all things, whatsoever ye shall ask in prayer, believing, ye shall receive.

Mark 9:29 And he said unto them, This kind can come forth by nothing, but by prayer and fasting.

Mark 11:17 And he taught, saying unto them, Is it not written, My house shall be called of all nations the house of prayer? but ye have made it a den of thieves.

Luke 1:13 But the angel said unto him, Fear not, Zacharias: for Thy prayer is heard; and Thy wife Elisabeth shall bear Thee a son, and thou shalt call his name John.

Luke 6:12 And it came to pass in those days, that he went out into a mountain to pray, and continued all night in prayer to God.

Luke 18:1 And He spake a parable unto them, that men ought always to pray and not to faint.

Luke 19:46 Saying unto them, It is written, My house is the house of prayer: but ye have made it a den of thieves.

Luke 22:45 And when he rose up from prayer, and was come to his disciples, he found them sleeping for sorrow,

John 17:20 Neither pray I for these alone, but for them also which shall believe on me through their word;

Acts 1:14 These all continued with one accord in prayer and supplication, with the women, and Mary the mother of Jesus, and with his brethren.

Acts 2:21 And it shall come to pass, that whosoever shall call on the name of the Lord shall be saved.

Acts 3:1 Now Peter and John went up together into the temple at the hour of prayer, being the ninth hour.

Acts 6:4 But we will give ourselves continually to prayer, and to the ministry of the word.

Acts 8:22 Repent therefore of this Thy wickedness, and pray God, if perhaps the thought of thine heart may be forgiven Thee.

Acts 10:9 On the morrow, as they went on their journey, and drew nigh unto the city, Peter went up upon the housetop to pray about the sixth hour:

Acts 10:31 And said, Cornelius, Thy prayer is heard, and thine alms are had in remembrance in the sight of God.

Acts 12:5 Peter therefore was kept in prison: but prayer was made without ceasing of the church unto God for him.

Acts 16:13 And on the Sabbath we went out of the city by a river side, where prayer was wont to be made; and we sat down, and spake unto the women which resorted thither.

Acts 16:16 And it came to pass, as we went to prayer, a certain damsel possessed with a spirit of divination met us, which brought her masters much gain by soothsaying:

Romans 8:26 Likewise the Spirit also helpeth our infirmities: for we know not what we should pray for as we ought: but the Spirit itself maketh intercession for us

Romans 10:1 Brethren, my heart's desire and prayer to God for Israel is, that they might be saved

Romans 10:14 How then shall they call on him in whom they have not believed? and how shall they believe in him of whom they have not heard? and how shall they hear without a preacher..

Romans 12:12 Rejoicing in hope; patient in tribulation; continuing instant in prayer;

1 Corinthians 7:5 Defraud ye not one the other, except it be with consent for a time, that ye may give yourselves to fasting and prayer; and come together again, that Satan tempt you not for your incontinency.

2 Corinthians 1:11 Ye also helping together by prayer for us, that for the gift bestowed upon us by the means of many persons thanks may be given by many on our behalf.

2 Corinthians 9:14 And by their prayer for you, which long after you for the exceeding grace of God in you.

Ephesians 6:18 Praying always with all prayer and supplication in the Spirit, and watching thereunto with all perseverance and supplication for all saints;

Philippians 1:4 Always in every prayer of mine for you all making request with joy,

Philippians 1:19 For I know that this shall turn to my salvation through your prayer, and the supply of the Spirit of Jesus Christ,

Philippians 4:6 Be careful for nothing; but in everything by prayer and supplication with thanksgiving let your requests be made known unto God.

Colossians 4:2 Continue in prayer, and watch in the same with thanksgiving;

1 Timothy 4:5 For it is sanctified by the word of God and prayer.

James 5:15,16,17 And the prayer of faith shall save the sick, and the Lord shall raise him up; and if he have committed sins, they shall be forgiven him. Confess your faults one to another, and pray one for another, that ye may be healed. The effectual fervent prayer of a righteous man availeth much. Elias was a man subject to like passions as we are, and he prayed earnestly that it might not rain: and it rained not on the earth by the space of three years and six months.

1Peter 4:7 But the end of all things is at hand: be ye therefore sober, and watch unto prayer.

Prayers recorded in Scripture

II Chronicles 14:11

And Asa cried unto the LORD his God, and said, "LORD, it is nothing with Thee to help, whether with many, or with them that have no power: help us, O LORD our God; for we rest on Thee, and in Thy name we go against this multitude. O LORD, Thou art our God; let not man prevail against Thee."

Habakkuk 1:1-4

1 The burden which Habakkuk the prophet did see. 2 "O LORD, how long shall I cry, and thou wilt not hear! Even cry out unto Thee of violence, and thou wilt not save! 3 Why dost thou shew me iniquity, and cause me to behold grievance? For spoiling and violence are before me: and there are that raise up strife and contention.

4 Therefore the law is slacked, and judgment doth never go forth: for the wicked doth compass about the righteous; therefore wrong judgment proceedeth".

2 Kings 19:15-19

And Hezekiah prayed before the Lord and said, "O Lord, the God of Israel, who art enthroned above the cherubim, Thou art the God, Thou alone, of all the kingdoms of the earth. Thou hast made heaven and earth. Incline Thine ear, O Lord, and hear; open Thine eyes, O Lord, and see; and listen to the words of Sennacherib, which he has sent to reproach the living God. Truly, O Lord, the kings of Assyria have devastated the nations and their lands and have cast their gods into the fire, for they were not gods but the work of men's hands, wood and stone. So they have destroyed them. And now, O Lord our God, I pray, deliver us from his hand that all the kingdoms of the earth may know that Thou alone, O Lord, art God."

Jonah 2:1-9

1 Then Jonah prayed unto the LORD his God out of the fish's belly, 2 And said, "I cried by reason of mine affliction unto the LORD, and he heard me; out of the belly of hell cried I, and thou heardest my voice. 3 For thou hadst cast me into the deep, in the midst of the seas; and the floods compassed me about: all thy billows and thy waves passed over me. 4 Then I said, I am cast out of thy sight; yet I will look again toward thy holy temple.5

The waters compassed me about, even to the soul: the depth closed me round about, the weeds were wrapped about my head.6 I went down to the bottoms of the mountains; the earth with her bars was about me forever: yet hast thou brought up my life from corruption, O LORD my God.7 When my soul fainted within me I remembered the LORD: and my prayer came in unto Thee, into thine holy temple.8 They that observe lying vanities forsake their own mercy. 9 But I will sacrifice unto Thee with the voice of thanksgiving; I will pay that that I have vowed. Salvation is of the LORD."

Job 42:1-6

1 Then Job answered the LORD, and said, 2 " I know that thou canst do everything, and that no thought can be withholden from Thee. 3 Who is he that hideth counsel without knowledge? therefore have I uttered that I understood not; things too wonderful for me, which I knew not.4 Hear, I beseech Thee, and I will speak: I will demand of Thee, and declare thou unto me.5 I have heard of Thee by the hearing of the ear: but now mine eye seeth Thee.6 Wherefore I abhor myself, and repent in dust and ashes."

Numbers 27:15-17

Then Moses spoke to the Lord, saying, "May the Lord, the God of the spirits of all flesh, appoint a man over the congregation, who will go out and come in before them, and who will lead them out and bring them in, that the congregation of the Lord may not be like sheep which have no shepherd."

Nehemiah 1:4-11

4 And it came to pass, when I heard these words, that I sat down and wept, and mourned certain days, and fasted, and prayed before the God of heaven, 5 And said, "I beseech Thee, O LORD God of heaven, the great and terrible God, that keepeth covenant and mercy for them that love him and observe his commandments:

6 Let thine ear now be attentive, and thine eyes open, that thou mayest hear the prayer of thy servant, which I pray before Thee now, day and night, for the children of Israel thy servants, and confess the sins of the children of Israel, which we have sinned against Thee: both I and my father's house have sinned.7 We have dealt very corruptly against Thee, and have not kept the commandments, nor the statutes, nor the judgments, which thou commandedst thy servant Moses.8 Remember, I beseech Thee, the word that thou commandedst thy servant Moses, saying, If ye transgress, I will scatter you abroad among the nations:

9 But if ye turn unto me, and keep my commandments, and do them; though there were of you cast out unto the uttermost part of the heaven, yet will I gather them from thence, and will bring them unto the place that I have chosen to set my name there. 10 Now these are thy servants and thy people, whom thou hast redeemed by thy great power, and by thy strong hand. 11 O Lord, I beseech Thee, let now thine ear be attentive to the prayer of thy servant,"

I Kings 3:6-9

6 And Solomon said, "Thou hast shewed unto thy servant David my father great mercy, according as he walked before Thee in truth, and in righteousness, and in uprightness of heart with Thee; and thou hast kept for him this great kindness, that thou hast given him a son to sit on his throne, as it is this day.

7 And now, O LORD my God, thou hast made thy servant king instead of David my father: and I am but a little child: I know not how to go out or come in. 8 And thy servant is in the midst of thy people which thou hast chosen, a great people, that cannot be numbered nor counted for multitude. 9 Give therefore thy servant an understanding heart to judge thy people, that I may discern between good and bad: for who is able to judge this thy so great a people?"

Psalm 90

1 A Prayer of Moses the man of God. " Lord, thou hast been our dwelling place in all generations. 2 Before the mountains were brought forth, or ever thou hadst formed the earth and the world, even from everlasting to everlasting, thou art God.3 Thou turnest man to destruction; and sayest, Return, ye children of men.4 For a thousand years in thy sight are but as yesterday when it is past, and as a watch in the night. 5 Thou carriest them away as with a flood; they are as a sleep: in the morning they are like grass which groweth up 6 In the morning it flourisheth, and groweth up; in the evening it is cut down, and withereth.7 For we are consumed by thine anger, and by thy wrath are we troubled. 8 Thou hast set our iniquities before Thee, our secret sins in the light of thy countenance. 9 For all our days are passed away in thy wrath: we spend our years as a tale that is told. 10 The days of our years are threescore years and ten; and if by reason of strength they be fourscore years, yet is their strength labour and sorrow; for it is soon cut off, and we fly away. 11 Who knoweth the power of thine anger? even according to thy fear, so is thy wrath. 12 So teach us to number our days, that we may apply our hearts unto wisdom. 13 Return, O LORD, how long? and let it repent Thee concerning thy servants.14 O satisfy us early with thy mercy; that we may rejoice and be glad all our days.15 Make us glad according to the days wherein thou hast afflicted us, and the years wherein we have seen evil.

16 Let thy work appear unto thy servants, and thy glory unto their children. 17 And let the beauty of the LORD our God be upon us: and establish thou the work of our hands upon us; yea, the work of our hands establish thou it."

1Kings 8:43 Hear thou in heaven thy dwelling place, and do according to all that the stranger calleth to Thee for: that all people of the earth may know thy name, to fear Thee, as do thy people Israel; and that they may know that this house, which I have builded, is called by thy name."

Matthew 6:9

Pray, then, in this way: "Our Father who art in heaven, hallowed by Thy name. Thy kingdom come. They will be done, on earth as it is in heaven. Give us this day our daily bread. And forgive us our debts, as we also have forgiven our debtors. And do not lead us into temptation, but deliver us from evil. For Thine is the kingdom, and the power, and the glory, forever. Amen."

John 11:41-42

And so they removed the stone. And Jesus raised His eyes, and said, "Father, I thank Thee that Thou heardest Me. And I knew that Thou hearest Me always; but because of the people standing around I said it, that they may believe that Thou didst send Me."

John 17:1-26

1 These words spake Jesus, and lifted up his eyes to heaven, and said, Father, the hour is come; glorify thy Son, that thy Son also may glorify Thee: 2 As thou hast given him power over all flesh, that he should give eternal life to as many as thou hast given him. 3 And this is life eternal, that they might know Thee the only true God, and Jesus Christ, whom thou hast sent. 4 I have glorified Thee on the earth: I have finished the work which thou gavest me to do. 5 And now, O Father, glorify thou me with thine own self with the glory which I had with Thee before the world was. 6 I have manifested thy name unto the men which thou gavest me out of the world: thine they were, and thou gavest them me; and they have kept thy word. 7 Now they have known that all things whatsoever thou hast given me are of Thee. 8 For I have given unto them the words which thou gavest me; and they have received them, and have known surely that I came out from Thee, and they have believed that thou didst send me. 9 I pray for them: I pray not for the world, but for them which thou hast given me; for they are thine. 10 And all mine are thine, and thine are mine; and I am glorified in them. 11 And now I am no more in the world, but these are in the world, and I come to Thee. Holy Father, keep through thine own name those whom thou hast given me, that they may be one, as we are. 12 While I was with them in the world, I kept them in thy name: those that thou gavest me I have kept, and none of them is lost, but the son of perdition; that the scripture might be fulfilled.

13 And now come I to Thee; and these things I speak in the world, that they might have my joy fulfilled in themselves. 14 I have given them thy word; and the world hath hated them, because they are not of the world, even as I am not of the world. 15 I pray not that thou shouldest take them out of the world, but that thou shouldest keep them from the evil. 16 They are not of the world, even as I am not of the world. 17 Sanctify them through thy truth: thy word is truth. 18 As thou hast sent me into the world, even so have I also sent them into the world. 19 And for their sakes I sanctify myself, that they also might be sanctified through the truth. 20 Neither pray I for these alone, but for them also which shall believe on me through their word; 21 That they all may be one; as thou, Father, art in me, and I in Thee, that they also may be one in us: that the world may believe that thou hast sent me. 22 And the glory which thou gavest me I have given them; that they may be one, even as we are one: 23 I in them, and thou in me, that they may be made perfect in one; and that the world may know that thou hast sent me, and hast loved them, as thou hast loved me. 24 Father, I will that they also, whom thou hast given me, be with me where I am; that they may behold my glory, which thou hast given me: for thou lovedst me before the foundation of the world. 25 O righteous Father, the world hath not known Thee: but I have known Thee, and these have known that thou hast sent me. 26 And I have declared unto them thy name, and will declare it: that the love wherewith thou hast loved me may be in them, and I in them.

Abraham - for a son (Genesis 15:2) And Abram said, "O Lord God, what wilt Thou give me, since I am childless, and the heir of my house is Eliezer of Damascus?"

Abraham - for Ishmael (Genesis 17:18) And Abraham said to God, "Oh that Ishmael might live before Thee!"

Abraham – for Sodom (Genesis 18:23-24) And Abraham came near and said, "Wilt Thou indeed sweep away the righteous with the wicked? Suppose there are fifty righteous with the city; wilt Thou indeed sweep it away and not spare the place for the sake or the fifty righteous who are in it?"

Abraham - for Abimelech (Genesis 20:17) And Abraham prayed to God; and God healed Abimelech and his wife and his maids, so that they bore children.

Abraham's servant - for guidance (Genesis 24:12,14) And he said, "O Lord, the God of my master Abraham, please grant me success today, and show lovingkindness to my master Abraham….now may it be that the girl to whom I say, 'please let down your jar so that I may drink,' and who answers, 'Drink, and I will water your camels also';--may she be the one whom Thou hast appointed for Thy servant Isaac…"

Cain - for mercy (Genesis 4:13-14) And Cain said to the Lord, "My punishment is too great to bear! Behold, Thou hast driven me this day from the face of the ground; and from Thy face I shall be hidden, and I shall be a vagrant and a wanderer on the earth and it will come about that whoever finds me will kill me."

Centurion - for his servant (Matthew 8:5-6) "And when He had entered Capernaum, a centurion came to Him, entreating Him, and saying, 'Lord, my servant is lying paralyzed at home, suffering great pain.'"

Christian disciples for boldness (Acts 4:29-30) "And now, Lord, take note of their threats, and grant that Thy bond-servants may speak Thy word with all confidence, while Thou dost extend Thy hand to heal, and signs and wonders take place through the name of Thy holy servant Jesus."

Christians - for Peter (Acts 12:5) So Peter was kept in the prison, but prayer for him was being made fervently by the church to God.

Cornelius - for enlightenment (Acts 10:3-4) About the ninth hour of the day he clearly saw in a vision an angel of God who had just come in to him, and said to him, "Cornelius!" And fixing his gaze upon him and being much alarmed, he said, "What is it, Lord?" And he said to him, "Your prayers and alms have ascended as a memorial before God."

Thief at the cross - for salvation (Luke 23:42) And he was saying, "Jesus, remember me when You come in Your kingdom!"

Daniel - for dream interpretation (Daniel 2:17-18) Then Daniel went to his house and informed his friends, Hananiah, Mishael and Azariah, about the matter, in order that they might request compassion from the God of heaven concerning this mystery, so that Daniel and his friends might not be destroyed with the rest of the wise men of Babylon.

Daniel - for the Jews (Daniel 9:3-5) So I gave my attention to the Lord God and seek Him by prayer and supplications, with fasting, sackcloth, and ashes. And I prayed to the Lord my God and confessed and said, "Alas, O Lord, the great and awesome God, who keeps His covenant and lovingkindness for those who love Him and keep His commandments, we have sinned, committed iniquity, acted wickedly, and rebelled, even turning aside from Thy commandments and ordinances."

David - for blessing (2 Samuel 7:18) Then David the king went in and sat before the Lord, and he said, "Who am I, O Lord God, and what is my house, that Thou hast brought me this far?"

David - for direction (1 Samuel 23:10-13) Then David said, "O Lord God of Israel, Thy servant has heard for certain that Saul is seeking to come to Keilah to destroy the city on my account. Will the men of Keilah surrender me into his hand? Will Saul come down just as Thy servant has heard? O Lord God of Israel, I pray, tell Thy servant." And the Lord said, "He will come down." Then David said, "Will the men of Keilah surrender me and my men into the hand of Saul?" And the Lord said, "They will surrender you." Then David and his men, about six hundred, arose and departed from Keilah, and they went wherever they could go. When it was told Saul that David had escaped from Keilah, he gave up the pursuit."

David for repentance (Psalm 51:10-13) Create in me a clean heart, O God, and renew a steadfast spirit within me. Do not cast me away from Thy presence, and do not take Thy Holy Spirit from me. Restore to me the joy of Thy salvation, and sustain me with a willing spirit. Then I will teach transgressors Thy ways, and sinners will be converted to Thee.

Elijah - for drought and rain (James 5:17-18) Elijah was a man with a nature like ours, and he prayed earnestly that it might not rain; and it did not rain on the earth for three years and six months. And he prayed again, and the sky poured rain, and the earth produced its fruit. (See 1 Kings 17-19 for the original story.)

Elijah - raising the widow's son from the dead (1 Kings 17:20-22) And he called to the Lord and said, "O Lord my God, hast Thou also brought calamity to the widow with whom I am staying, by causing her son to die?" Then he stretched himself upon the child three times, and called to the Lord, and said, "O Lord my God, I pray Thee, let this child's life return to him." And the Lord heard the voice of Elijah, and the life of the child returned to him and he revived.

Elijah - for death (1 Kings 19:4) But he himself went a day's journey into the wilderness, and came and sat down under a juniper tree; and he requested for himself that he might die, and said, "It is enough; now, O Lord, take my life, for I am not better than my fathers."

Elisha - for sight and blindness (2 Kings 6:17-18) Then Elisha prayed and said, "O Lord, I pray, open his eyes that he may see." And the Lord opened the servant's eyes, and he saw; and behold, the mountain was full of horses and chariots of fire all around Elisha. And when they came down to him, Elisha prayed to the Lord and said, "Strike this people with blindness, I pray." So He struck them with blindness according to the word of Elisha.

Ezra - confession for the sins of Israel (Ezra 9:6) "O my God, I am ashamed and embarrassed to lift up my face to Thee, my God, for our iniquities have risen above our heads, and our guilt has grown even to the heavens."

Gideon for proof of God's call (Judges 6:36) Then Gideon said to God, "If Thou wilt deliver Israel through me, as Thou hast spoken, behold, I will put a fleece of wool on the threshing floor. If there is dew on the fleece only, and it is dry on all the ground, then I will know that Thou wilt deliver Israel through me, as Thou hast spoken."

Habakkuk - for justice (Habakkuk 1:2-4) How long, O Lord, will I call for help, and Thou wilt not hear? I cry out to Thee, "Violence!" yet Thou dost not save. Why dost Thou make me see iniquity, and cause me to look on wickedness? Yes, destruction and violence are before me; strife exists and contention arises. Therefore, the law is ignored and justice is never upheld. For the wicked surround the righteous; therefore, justice comes out perverted.

Habakkuk - for revival and deliverance (Habakkuk 3:2) Lord, I have heard the report about Thee and I fear. O Lord, revive Thy work in the midst of the years, In the midst of the years make it known; in wrath remember mercy.

Hannah - for a son (1 Samuel 10:11) And she, greatly distressed, prayed to the Lord and wept bitterly. And she made a vow and said, "O Lord of hosts, if Thou wilt indeed look on the affliction of Thy maidservant and remember me, and not forget Thy maidservant, but wilt give Thy maidservant a son, then I will give him to the Lord all the days of his life, and a razor shall never come on his head."

Hezekiah - for deliverance (2 Kings 19:15-19) And Hezekiah prayed before the Lord and said, "O Lord, the God of Israel, who art enthroned above the cherubim, Thou art the God, Thou alone, of all the kingdoms of the earth. Thou hast made heaven and earth. Incline Thine ear, O Lord, and hear; open Thine eyes, O Lord, and see; and listen to the words of Sennacherib, which he has sent to reproach the living God. Truly, O Lord, the kings of Assyria have devastated the nations and their lands and have cast their gods into the fire, for they were not gods but the work of men's hands, wood and stone. So they have destroyed them. And now, O Lord our God, I pray, deliver us from his hand that all the kingdoms of the earth may know that Thou alone, O Lord, art God."

Hezekiah - for health (2 Kings 20:3) "Remember now, O Lord, I beseech Thee, how I have walked before Thee in truth and with a whole heart, and have done what is good in Thy sight." And Hezekiah wept bitterly.

Isaac - for children (Genesis 25:21) And Isaac prayed to the Lord on behalf of his wife, because she was barren; and the Lord answered him and Rebekah his wife conceived.

Israelites - for deliverance (Exodus 2:23) Now it came about in the course of those many days that the king of Egypt died. And the sons of Israel sighed because of the bondage, and they cried out; and their cry for help because of their bondage rose up to God.

Jabez - for blessing (1 Chronicles 4:10) Now Jabez called on the God of Israel, saying, "Oh that Thou wouldst bless me indeed, and enlarge my border, and that Thy hand might be with me, and that Thou wouldst keep me from harm, that it may not pain me!" And God granted him what he requested.

Jacob - deliverance from Esau (Genesis 32:11) "Deliver me, I pray, from the hand of my brother, from the hand of Esau; for I fear him, lest he come and attack me, the mothers with the children.

Jeremiah - for mercy (Jeremiah 14:7) Although our iniquities testify against us, O Lord, act for Thy name's sake! Truly our apostasies have been many, we have sinned against Thee.

Jesus - revelation to children (Matthew 11:25) "I praise Thee, O Father, Lord of heaven and earth, that Thou didst hide these things from the wise and intelligent and didst reveal them to babes."

Jesus - for deliverance from the cross (Matthew 26:39) And He went a little beyond the, and fell on His face and prayed, saying, "My Father, if it is possible, let this cup pass from Me; yet not as I will, but as Thou wilt."

Jesus - forgiveness for his killers (Luke 23:34) But Jesus was saying, "Father, forgive them; for they do not know what they are doing."

Jesus - submission to God's plan (Luke 23:46**)** And Jesus, crying out with a loud voice, said, "Father, into Thy hands I commit My spirit." And having said this, He breathed His last.

Job - confession of surrender to God's sovereignty (Job 42:1-6) "'Therefore I retract, and I repent in dust and ashes.'"

Jonah - for deliverance from the fish (Jonah 2:1-9) Then Jonah prayed to the Lord his God from the stomach of the fish, and he said, "I called out of my distress to the Lord, and He answered me. I cried for help from the depth of Sheol; Thou didst hear my voice. "

Joshua - for help and mercy (Joshua 7:6-9) Then Joshua tore his clothes and fell to the earth on his face before the ark of the Lord until the evening, both he and elders of Israel; and they put dust on their heads. And Joshua said, "Alas, O Lord God, why didst Thou ever bring this people over the Jordan, only to deliver us into the hand of the Amorites, to destroy us? If only we had been willing to dwell beyond the Jordan! O Lord, what can I say since Israel has turned their back before their enemies? For the Canaanites and all the inhabitants of the land will hear of it, and they will surround us and cut off our name from the earth. And what wilt Thou do for Thy great name?"

Manoah - for guidance (Judges 13:8) Then Manoah entreated the Lord and said, "O Lord, please let the man of God whom Thou hast sent come to us again that he may teach us what to do for the boy who is to be born."

Moses - forgiveness for the sin of Israel (Exodus 32:31-32) Then Moses returned to the Lord, and said; "Alas, this people has committed a great sin, and they have made a god of gold for themselves. But now, if Thou wilt, forgive their sin-and it no, please blot me out from Thy book which Thou has written!"

Moses - for Miriam (Numbers 12:11-13) Then Aaron said to Moses, "Oh, my lord, I beg you, do not account this sin to us, in which we have acted foolishly and in which we have sinned. Oh, do not let her be like one dead, whose flesh is half eaten away when he comes from his mother's womb!" And Moses cried out to the Lord, saying, "O God, heal her, I pray!"

Moses - to see the Promised Land (Deuteronomy 3:23-25) I also pleaded with the Lord at that time, saying, "O Lord God, Thou hast begun to show Thy servant Thy greatness and Thy strong hand; for what god is there in heaven or on earth who can do such works and mighty acts as Thine? Let me, I pray, cross over and see the fair land that is beyond the Jordan, that good hill country and Lebanon."

Moses - for a successor (Numbers 27:15-17) Then Moses spoke to the Lord, saying, "May the Lord, the God of the spirits of all flesh, appoint a man over the congregation, who will go out and come in before them, and who will lead them out and bring them in, that the congregation of the Lord may not be like sheep which have no shepherd."

Nehemiah - for the Jews to return to their land (Nehemiah 1:4-11) Now it came about when I heard these words, I sat down and wept and mourned for days; and I was fasting and praying before the God of heaven. And I said, "I beseech Thee, O Lord God of heaven, the great and awesome God, who preserves the covenant and lovingkindness for those who love Him and keep His commandments, let Thine ear now be attentive and Thine eyes open to hear the prayer of Thy servant which I am praying before Thee now, day and night, on behalf of the sons of Israel Thy servants, confessing the sins of the sons of Israel which we have sinned against Thee; I and my father's house have sinned."

Paul - for the Ephesians (Ephesians 3:14-21) For this reason, I bow my knees before the Father, from whom every family in heaven and on earth derives its name, that He would grant you, according to the riches of His glory, to be strengthened with power through His Spirit in the inner man; so that Christ may dwell in your hearts through faith; and that you, being rooted and grounded in love, may be able to comprehend with all the saints what is the breadth and length and height and depth, and to know the love of Christ which surpasses knowledge, that you may be filled up to all the fullness of God. Now to Him who is able to do exceeding abundantly beyond all that we ask or think, according to the power that works within us, to Him be the glory in the church and in Christ Jesus to all generations forever and ever. Amen.

Samson - for water (Judges 15:18) Then he became very thirsty, and he called to the Lord and said, "Thou hast given this great deliverance by the hand of Thy servant, and now shall I die of thirst and fall into the hands of the uncircumcised?"

Samson - for strength (Judges 16:28) Then Samson called to the Lord and said, "O Lord God, please remember me and please strengthen me just this time, O God, that I may at once be avenged of the Philistines for my two eyes."

Samuel - for Israel (1 Samuel 7:5-6) Then Samuel said, "Gather all Israel to Mizpah, and I will pray to the Lord for you." And they gathered to Mizpah, and drew water and poured it out before the Lord, and fasted on that day, and said there, "We have sinned against the Lord." And Samuel judged the sons of Israel at Mizpah.

Solomon - for wisdom (1 Kings 3:6-9) The Solomon said, "Thou hast shown great lovingkindness to Thy servant David my father, according as he walked before Thee in truth and righteousness and uprightness of heart toward Thee; and Thou hast reserved for him this great lovingkindness, that Thou hast given him a son to sit on his throne, as it is this day. And now, O Lord my God, Thou hast made Thy servant king in place of my father David, yet I am but a little child; I do not know how to go out or come in. And Thy servant is in the midst of Thy people which Thou hast chosen, a great people who cannot be numbered or counted for multitude. So give Thy servant an understanding heart to judge Thy people to discern between good and evil. For who is able to judge this great people of Thine?"

Tax-gatherer - mercy (Luke 18:13) "But the tax-gatherer, standing some distance away, was even unwilling to lift up his eyes to heaven, but was beating his breast, saying, 'God, be merciful to me, the sinner!'"

Prayers

Aethelwold of Winchester *(c 908-984) Aethelwold was Bishop of Winchester England from 963 until his death in 984 AD. He was born in Winchester of noble parents and served in King Athelstan's court as a counselor and friend to the king. He later became dean of Glastonbury Abbey before being made Bishop. He was known for monastic reform. Legend has it that he was fierce to the unrepentant and gentle to the contrite.*

Our God, God of all men God of heaven and earth, seas and rivers, God of sun and moon, of all the stars, God of high mountain and lowly valley, God over heaven, and in heaven, and under heaven. He has a dwelling in heaven and earth and sea and in all things that are in them. He inspires all things, he quickens all things. He is over all things, he supports all things. He makes the light of the sun to shine, He surrounds the moon and the stars, He has made wells in the arid earth, Placed dry islands in the sea. He has a Son co-eternal with himself... And the Holy Spirit breathes in them; Not separate are the Father and the Son and the Holy Spirit.

Alcuin *(730-804) Alcuin of York was a scholar, theologian and intellectual who served in the court of Charlemagne. At one time he taught Charlemagne and his two sons. He advocated against the burning of pagans because they would not be baptized. "Faith is a free act of the will, not a forced act. We must appeal to the conscience, not compel it by violence. You can force people to be baptized, but you cannot force them to believe."*

Eternal Light, shine into our hearts, Eternal Goodness, deliver us from evil, Eternal Power, be our support, Eternal Wisdom, scatter the darkness of our ignorance, Eternal Pity, have mercy upon us; that with all our heart and mind and soul and strength we may seek thy face and be brought by thine infinite mercy to thy holy presence; through Jesus Christ our Lord. Amen.

Give me, O Lord, I beseech Thee, firm faith, unwavering hope, perfect charity. Pour into my heart the Spirit of wisdom and understanding, the Spirit of counsel and spiritual strength, the Spirit of knowledge and true godliness, and the Spirit of thy holy fear. Light eternal, shine in my heart. Power eternal, deliver me from evil. Wisdom eternal, scatter the darkness of my ignorance. Might eternal, pity me. Grant that I may ever seek thy face with all my heart and soul and strength; and, in thine infinite mercy, bring me at last to thy holy presence where I shall behold thy glory and possess thy promised joys. Amen.

Ambrose of Milan *(c. 340 – 397) He was born in Germany to Christian parents. After the death of his father Ambrose was educated in Rome and pursued a political career. He was governor of Liguria and Emilia. He resided in Milan. When the bishop died the crowd made him bishop by proclamation which was later ratified by Rome. He was sought after as a peace maker. He promoted the cause of the poor, donating his personal lands and at one time had the plate of the church melted down to meet needs. Ambrose promoted church music. He was a prolific writer. His advice to Augustine on ritual days of worship is the famous, "When you are at Rome, live in the Roman style; when you are elsewhere, live as they live elsewhere."*

Lord Jesus Christ, I approach your banquet table in fear and trembling, for I am a sinner, and dare not rely on my own worth, but only on your goodness and mercy. I am defiled by many sins in body and soul, and by my unguarded thoughts and words.

Gracious God of majesty and awe, I seek your protection, I look for your healing. Poor troubled sinner that I am, I appeal to you, the fountain of all mercy. I cannot bear your judgment, but I trust in your salvation. Lord, I show my wounds to you and uncover my shame before you.

I know my sins are many and great, and they fill me with fear, but I hope in your mercies, for they cannot be numbered. Lord Jesus Christ, eternal king, God and man, crucified for mankind, look upon me with mercy and hear my prayer, for I trust in you. Have mercy on me, full of sorrow and sin, for the depth of your compassion never ends. Praise to you, saving sacrifice, offered on the wood of the cross for me and for all mankind. Praise to the noble and precious blood, flowing from the wounds of Thee my crucified Lord Jesus Christ and washing away the sins of the whole world. Remember, Lord your creature, whom you have redeemed with your blood; I repent my sins, and I long to put right what I have done. Merciful Father, take away all my offenses and sins; purify me in body and soul, and make me worthy to taste the holy of holies. May your body and blood, which I intend to receive, although I am unworthy, be for me the remission of my sins, the washing away of my guilt, the end of my evil thoughts, and the rebirth of my better instincts. May it incite me to do the works pleasing to you and profitable to my health in body and soul, and be a firm defense against the wiles of my enemies. Amen.

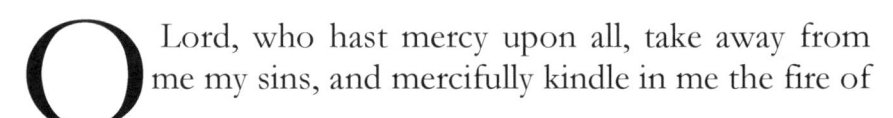

O Lord, who hast mercy upon all, take away from me my sins, and mercifully kindle in me the fire of thy Holy Spirit. Take away from me the heart of stone, and give me a heart of flesh, a heart to love and adore Thee, a heart to delight in Thee, to follow and enjoy Thee, for Christ's sake, Amen.

O great High-Priest, the true Pontiff, Jesus Christ, who didst offer Thyself to God the Father a pure and spotless Victim upon the Altar of the Cross for us miserable sinners, and didst give us Thy Flesh to eat and Thy Blood to drink, and didst ordain this Mystery in the power of Thy Holy Spirit, saying, "Do this for the commemoration of Me," I pray Thee, by the same Thy Blood, the great price of our salvation; I pray Thee, by that wonderful and unspeakable love wherewith Thou deignedst so to love us, miserable and unworthy, as to wash us from our sins in Thine own Blood: teach me, Thine unworthy servant, by Thy Holy Spirit, to approach so great a Mystery with that reverence and honour, that devotion and fear, which is due and fitting. Make me, through Thy grace, always so to believe and understand, to conceive and firmly to hold, to think and to speak, of that exceeding Mystery, as shall please Thee and be good for my soul. Let Thy Good Spirit enter my heart, and there be heard without utterance, and without the sound of words speak all truth. For Thy Mysteries are exceeding deep, and covered with a sacred veil. For Thy great mercy's sake, grant me to approach Thy Holy Mysteries with a clean heart and a pure mind. Free my heart from all defiling and unholy, from all vain and hurtful thoughts. Fence me round about with the holy and faithful guard and mighty protection of Thy Blessed Angels, that the enemies of all good may go away ashamed.

By the virtue of this mighty Mystery, and by the hand of Thy Holy Angel, drive away from me and from all Thy servants the hard spirit of pride and vainglory, of envy and blasphemy, of impurity and uncleanness, of doubt and mistrust. Let them be confounded that persecute us; let them perish who are bent upon our ruin. Amen.

I beg of you, O Lord, by this most holy mystery of Your Body and Blood, with which You daily nourish us in Your Church, that we may be cleansed and sanctified and made sharers in Your divinity. Grant to me Your holy virtues, which will enable me to approach Your altar with a clean conscience, so that this heavenly Sacrament may be a means of salvation and life to me, for You Yourself have said: "I am the living bread that has come down from heaven. If anyone eat of this bread, he shall live forever; and the bread that I will give is my flesh for the life of the world."

Most Sweet Bread, heal my heart, that I may taste the sweetness of Your love. Heal it from all weakness, that I may enjoy no sweetness but You. Most pure Bread, containing every delight which ever refreshes us, may my heart consume You and may my soul be filled with Your sweetness. Holy Bread, living Bread, perfect Bread, that has come down from heaven to give life to the world, come into my heart and cleanse me from every stain of body and soul. Enter into my soul; heal and cleanse me completely. Be the constant safeguard and salvation of my soul and body. Guard me from the enemies who lie in wait. May they flee from the protecting presence of Your power, so that, armed in soul and body by You, I may safely reach Your Kingdom.

There we shall see You, not as now as in mysteries, but face to face, when You will deliver the Kingdom to God the Father, and will reign as God over all. Then You, who with the same God the Father and the Holy Spirit, live and reign forever, will satisfy the hunger of my soul perfectly with Yourself, so that I shall neither hunger nor thirst again. Amen

Thee alone I follow, Lord Jesus, Who heals my wounds. For what shall separate me from the love of God, which is in Thee? Shall tribulation, or distress, or famine? I am held fast as though by nails, and fettered by the bonds of charity. Remove from me, O Lord Jesus, with Thy potent sword, the corruption of my sins. Secure me in the bonds of Thy love; cut away what is corrupt in me. Come quickly and make an end of my many, my hidden and secret afflictions. Open the wound lest the evil humor spread. With Thy new washing, cleanse in me all that is stained. Hear me, you earthly men, who in your sins bring forth drunken thoughts: I have found a Physician. He dwells in Heaven and distributes His healing on earth. He alone can heal my pains Who Himself has none. He alone Who knows what is hidden can take away the grief of my heart, the fear of my soul: Jesus Christ. Christ is grace! Christ is life! Christ is Resurrection! Amen.

O Lord teach me to seek you, and reveal yourself to me when I seek you. For I cannot seek you unless you first teach me, nor find you unless you first reveal yourself to me. Let me seek you in longing, and long for you in seeking. Let me find you in love, and love you in finding. Amen.

Lancelot Andrewes *(1555-1626 AD) Fellow of Pembroke College, Cambridge. Chief among the Compilers of the KJV Bible. Anglican Theologian and Bishop during Queen Elizabeth's reign and James I. He assisted in the coronation of James I.*

Glory be to Thee, O Lord, glory to Thee. Glory to Thee who givest me sleep to recruit my weakness, and to remit the toils of this fretful flesh. To this day and all days, a perfect, holy, peaceful, healthy, sinless course, Vouchsafe O Lord.

The Angel of peace, a faithful guide, guardian of souls and bodies, to encamp around me, and ever to prompt what is salutary, Vouchsafe O Lord. Pardon and remission of all sins and of all offences Vouchsafe O Lord. To our souls what is good and convenient, and peace to the world, Repentance and strictness for the residue of our life, and health and peace to the end, Vouchsafe O Lord. Whatever is true, whatever is honest, whatever just, whatever pure, whatever lovely, whatever of good report, if there be any virtue, if any praise, such thoughts, such deeds, Vouchsafe O Lord.

A Christian close, without sin, without shame, and, should it please Thee, without pain, and a good answer at the dreadful and fearful judgment-seat of Jesus Christ our Lord, Vouchsafe O Lord. Confession Essence beyond essence, Nature increate, Framer of the world, I set Thee, Lord, before my face, and I lift up my soul unto Thee. I worship Thee on my knees, and humble myself under Thy mighty hand. I stretch forth my hands unto Thee, my soul gaspeth unto Thee as a thirsty land. I smite on my breast and say with the Publican, God be merciful to me a sinner, the chief of sinners; to the sinner above the Publican, be merciful as to the Publican.

Father of mercies, I beseech Thy fatherly affection, despise me not an unclean worm, a dead dog, a putrid corpse, despise not Thou the work of Thine own hands, despise not Thine own image though branded by sin. Lord, if Thou wilt, Thou canst make me clean, Lord, only say the word, and I shall be cleansed. And Thou, my Savior Christ, Christ my Savior, Savior of sinners, of whom I am chief, despise me not, despise me not, O Lord, despise not the cost of Thy blood, who am called by Thy Name;

but look on me with those eyes with which Thou didst look upon Magdalene at the feast, Peter in the hall, the thief on the wood; that with the thief I may entreat Thee humbly. Remember me, Lord, in Thy kingdom; that with Peter I may bitterly weep and say, O that mine eyes were a fountain of tears that I might weep day and night; that with Magdalene I may hear Thee say, Thy sins be forgiven Thee, and with her may love much, for many sins yea manifold have been forgiven me. And Thou, All-holy, Good, and Life-giving Spirit, despise me not, Thy breath, despise not Thine own holy things; but turn Thee again, O Lord, at the last, and be gracious unto Thy servant.

Blessed art Thou, O Lord, Our God, the God of our Fathers; Who turnest the shadow of death into the morning; and lightenest the face of the earth; Who separatest darkness from the face of the light ; and banishest night and bringest back the day; Who lightenest mine eyes, that I sleep not in death; Who deliverest me from the terror by night, from the pestilence that walketh in darkness; Who drivest sleep from mine eyes, and slumber from mine eyelids; Who makest the outgoings of the morning and evening to praise Thee; because I laid me down and slept and rose up again, for the Lord sustained me; because I waked and beheld, and my sleep was sweet unto me. Blot out as a thick cloud my transgressions, and as a cloud my sins; grant me to be a child of light, a child of the day, to walk soberly, holily, honestly, as in the day, vouchsafe to keep me this day without sin. Thou who upholdest the falling and liftest the fallen, let me not harden my heart in provocation, or temptation or deceitfulness of any sin. Moreover, deliver me to-day from the snare of the hunter and from the noisome pestilence; from the arrow that flieth by day, from the sickness that destroyeth in the noon day.

Defend this day against my evil, against the evil of this day defend Thou me. Let not my days be spent in vanity, nor my years in sorrow. One day telleth another, and one night certifieth another. O let me hear Thy loving-kindness betimes in the morning, for in Thee is my trust; shew Thou me the way that I should walk in, for I lift up my soul unto Thee.

Deliver me, O Lord, from mine enemies, for I flee unto Thee. Teach me to do the thing that pleaseth Thee, for Thou art my God: let Thy Loving Spirit lead me forth into the land of righteousness. Quicken me, O Lord, for Thy Name's sake, and for Thy righteousness' sake bring my soul out of trouble: remove from me foolish imaginations, inspire those which are good and pleasing in Thy sight. Turn away mine eyes lest they behold vanity: let mine eyes look right on, and let mine eyelids look straight before me.

Hedge up mine ears with thorns lest they incline to undisciplined words. Give me early the ear to hear, and open mine ears to the instruction of Thy oracles.

Set a watch, O Lord, before my mouth, and keep the door of my lips. Let my word be seasoned with salt, that it may minister grace to the hearers. Let no deed be grief unto me nor offence of heart. Let me do some work for which Thou wilt remember me, Lord, for good, and spare me according to the greatness of Thy mercy. Into Thine hands I commend my spirit, soul, and body, which Thou hast created, redeemed, regenerated, O Lord, Thou God of truth: and together with me all mine and all that belongs to me. Thou hast vouchsafed them to me, Lord, in Thy goodness.

Guard us from all evil, guard our souls, I beseech Thee, O Lord. Guard us without falling, and place us immaculate in the presence of Thy glory in that day. Guard my going out and my coming in henceforth and forever. Prosper, I pray Thee, Thy servant this day, and grant him mercy in the sight of those who meet him.

O God, make speed to save me, 0 Lord, make haste to help me. O turn Thee then unto me, and have mercy upon me; give Thy strength unto Thy servant, and help the son of Thine handmaid. Show some token upon me for good, that they who hate me may see it and be ashamed, because Thou, Lord, hast holpen me and comforted me.

The day is gone, and I give Thee thanks, O Lord. Evening is at hand, make it bright unto us. As day has its evening so also has life; the even of life is age, age has overtaken me, make it bright unto us.

Cast me not away in the time of age; forsake me not when my strength faileth me. Even to my old age be Thou He, and even to hoar hairs carry me; do Thou make, do Thou bear, do Thou carry and deliver me. Abide with me, Lord, for it is toward evening, and the day is far spent of this fretful life. Let Thy strength be made perfect in my weakness. Day is fled and gone, life too is going, this lifeless life. Night cometh, and cometh death, the deathless death. Near as is the end of day, so too the end of life. We then, also remembering it, beseech of Thee for the close of our life, that Thou wouldest direct it in peace, Christian, acceptable, sinless, shameless, and, if it please Thee, painless, Lord, O Lord, gathering us together under the feet of Thine Elect, when Thou wilt, and as Thou wilt, only without shame and sins. Remember we the days of darkness, for they shall be many, lest we be cast into outer darkness.

Remember we to outstrip the night doing some good thing. Near is judgment; a good and acceptable answer at the dreadful and fearful judgment-seat of Jesus Christ vouchsafe to us, O Lord. By night I lift up my hands in the sanctuary, and praise the Lord. The Lord hath granted His loving-kindness in the day time; and in the night season did I sing of Him, and made my prayer unto Thee God of my life.

As long as I live will I magnify Thee on this manner, and lift up my hands in Thy Name. Let my prayer be set forth in Thy sight as the incense, and let the lifting up of my hands be an evening sacrifice. Blessed art Thou, 0 Lord, our God, the God of our fathers, who hast created the changes of days and nights, who givest songs in the night, who hast delivered us from the evil of this day who hast not cut off like a weaver my life, nor from day even to night made an end of me.

Lord, as we add day to day, so sin to sin. The just falleth seven times a day; and I, an exceeding sinner, seventy times seven; a wonderful, a horrible thing, O Lord. But I turn with groans from my evil ways, and I return into my heart, and with all my heart I turn to Thee, O God of penitents and Saviour of sinners; and evening by evening I will return in the innermost marrow of my soul; and my soul out of the deep crieth unto Thee. I have sinned, O Lord, against Thee, heavily against Thee; alas, alas, woe is me! for my misery. I repent, O me! I repent, spare me, O Lord, I repent, O me, I repent, help Thou my impenitence. Be appeased, spare me, O Lord; be appeased, have mercy on me ; I said, Lord, have mercy upon me, heal my soul, for I have sinned against Thee. Have mercy upon me, O Lord, after Thy great goodness, according to the multitude of Thy mercies do away mine offences.

Remit the guilt, heal the wound, blot out the stains, clear away the shame, rescue from the tyranny, and make me not a public example.

O bring Thou me out of my trouble, cleanse Thou me from secret faults, keep back Thy servant also from presumptuous sins. My wanderings of mind and idle talking lay not to my charge. Remove the dark and muddy flood of foul and wicked thoughts. 0 Lord, I have destroyed myself; whatever I have done amiss, pardon mercifully. Deal not with us after our sins, neither reward us after our iniquities. Look mercifully upon our infirmities; and for the glory of Thy All-holy Name, turn from us all those ills and miseries, which by our sins, and by us through them, are most righteously and worthily deserved.

To my weariness, O Lord, vouchsafe Thou rest, to my exhaustion renew Thou strength. Lighten mine eyes that I sleep not in death. Deliver me from the terror by night, the pestilence that walketh in darkness. Supply me with healthy sleep, and to pass through this night without Fear. O Keeper of Israel, who neither slumberest nor sleepest, guard me this night from all evil, guard my soul, 0 Lord. Visit me with the visitation of Thine own, reveal to me wisdom in the visions of the night. If not, for I am not worthy, not worthy, at least, O loving Lord, Let sleep be to me a breathing time as from toil, so from sin. Yea, O Lord, nor let me in my dreams imagine what may anger Thee, what may defile me. Let not my loins be filled with illusions, yea, let my reins chasten me in the night season, yet without grievous terror. Preserve me from the black sleep of sin; all earthly and evil thoughts put to sleep within me. Grant to me light sleep, rid of all imaginations fleshly and satanical.

Lord, Thou knowest how sleepless are mine unseen foes, and how feeble my wretched flesh, Who madest me; shelter me with the wing of Thy pity; awaken me at the fitting time, the time of prayer; and give me to seek Thee early, for Thy glory and for Thy service. Into Thy hands, 0 Lord, I commend myself, my spirit, soul, and body: Thou didst make, and didst redeem them; and together with me, all my friends and all that belongs to me. Thou hast vouchsafed them to me, Lord, in Thy goodness. Guard my lying down and my rising up, from henceforth and forever.

Let me remember Thee on my bed, and search out my spirit; let me wake up and be present with Thee; let me lay me down in peace, and take my rest: for it is Thou, Lord, only that makest me dwell in safety.

O Lord, as days unto days, so withal do we add sins to sin. The just man stumbleth seven times a day, but I, a singular great sinner, seventy times seven. Nay but I return unto Thee, O Lord, O Lord Thou lover of man, Thou hast a golden censer; add me thine incense unto this prayer for a sweet-smelling savor before thy throne, and let the lifting up of hands be set forth for an evening sacrifice. Lord, the Almighty, all our works Thou hast wrought in us; if we have gotten any good success, receive it favorably, O Lord abundant in goodness and very pitiful: but so many things as we have done amiss, pardon graciously, for our destruction cometh of ourselves.

Deliver me, O Lord, from the terror by night, from the pestilence that walketh in darkness. Give me to seek Thee early, even for thy praise and service. Preserve my lying down and my uprising from this time forth even for evermore. Discover me my mind for meditation by night, so as to remember Thee upon my bed; in the night to commune with mine own heart and to search out my spirit: and to keep my spirit: but if not this (for I am not worthy, I am not worthy, O Lord) yet at leastwise, O Lord Thou lover of man, let my sleep be to me a respite, as from toiling, so from sinning withal. Yea, O Lord, I beseech Thee, look upon me, and put to sleep in me every earthly and evil thought.

The sleeplessness of mine unseen foes, Thou wottest, O Lord : the slackness of my wretched flesh Thou knowest, which didst form me. Let the wing of thy goodness shelter me: lighten mine eyes that I never sleep in death. Give me, O Lord, a good life, a good death, and deathlessness: for I know not, I know not, O Lord, how soon is the off of my tabernacle.

Wherein grant me, O Lord, that the end of life be Christian, sinless, shameless, and, if it like Thee, painless; and a good defense at the appalling and fearful judgment-seat of Jesus Christ; that I may hear the most sweet voice. Come ye blessed, and that I may enter into thy joy and get fruition of the vision of our Father which is in heaven. Grant me sleep, O Lord, for repose of weakness and for relief of the toils of this travailing flesh. Into thy hands, O

Lord, I commend myself and all things mine: preserve me, o Lord, Thou that art the keeper of Israel, that didst neither slumber nor sleep ever yet.

Blessing, thanksgiving and doxology Blessed art Thou, O Lord God of our fathers, that didst create changes of days and nights, that hast delivered us from the evil of this day, that hast bestowed on us occasions of songs in the evening and to get us through the night fearlessly in hope: for Thou art our light, salvation and strength of life of whom then shall we be afraid?

Glory be to Thee, O Lord, glory be to Thee, for all thy divine perfections, for thine inexpressible and unimaginable goodness and mercy, unto sinners and unworthy, and to me sinner, of all most unworthy yea, O Lord, glory and praise and blessing and thanksgiving by the voices and concert of voices as well of angels as of men and of all thy saints in heaven and of all thy creation withal on earth, and under their feet of me the sinner unworthy and wretched, world without end. On going to bed Let me think upon thy name in the night season, and keep thy law; Let the evening prayer go up unto Thee, and thy pity come down unto us, O Thou which givest songs in the night, Which makest the outgoings of the morning and evening to praise Thee, Which givest thy beloved wholesome sleep.

Psalm 5:7 Psalm 28:2 As for me, I will come into Thy house, even upon the multitude of Thy mercy; and in Thy fear will I worship towards Thy holy Temple. O Lord, hear the voice of my humble petitions, when I cry unto Thee; when I hold up my hands toward the mercy-seat of Thy holy Temple. We wait for Thy loving-kindness, O God, in the midst of Thy Temple. Psalm 48:8.

Be mindful of the brethren who are present, and join together in prayer with us now: Remember their devotion and their zeal. Be mindful of them also who upon good cause are absent: And have mercy upon them and us, according to the multitude of Thy mercies, O Lord. We bless Thee or our (Godly Princes, Orthodox Prelates,) and for the founders of this Thy holy habitation. Glory be to Thee, O Lord, glory be to Thee; glory be to Thee, because Thou hast glorified them; for and with whom we glorify Thee.

Let Thine eyes be open, and Thine ears graciously attend, to hear the prayer which Thy servant prayeth in this place, wherein Thy Name is called upon. 2 Chronicles 6: 20, 33, 40. Woe is me, I have sinned against Thee, O Lord, I have sinned against Thee: O how evilly have I done; And yet Thou hast not requited me, according to my sins. Job 33:27. But I am ashamed, And turn from my wicked ways, And return to my own heart, And with all my heart I return to Thee, And seek Thy face; And pray unto Thee: saying, I have sinned, I have done perversely, I have committed wickedness; Lord, I know the plague of my own heart, and, behold, I return unto Thee with all my heart, and with all my might.

And now, O Lord, in Thy dwelling place, the glorious throne of Thy kingdom in heaven, hear the prayer and supplication of Thy servant. (King Solomon's Prayer at the Dedication of the Temple, 1Kings 8. & 2Chron.6)

And be merciful unto Thy servant, and heal his soul. Psalm. 41:4. I dare not so much as lift up mine eyes unto heaven, but standing afar off, I smite upon my breast, And say with the publican, God be merciful to me a sinner. Luke 18: 13 To me, a greater sinner than the publican, be merciful as to the publican. The earnest desire of man shall be to Thy praise, and the continuance of that desire shall hold a festival to Thee.

Angela di Foligno *(1248 – 4 January 1309) Angela was born into a wealthy family in Foligno, Umbria, Italy. She was married at a young age and gave birth to a number of children. Her mother passed away followed shortly by Angela's husband and children. She renounced the world and her possessions to follow a life given to God. She dictated her memoires and thoughts about following God in her work <u>Il Libro della Beata Angela da Forligno.</u>*

O my God! make me worthy to understand something of the mystery of the burning charity which is in You, which impelled You to effect the sublime act of the Incarnation! which brings to man, with the outpouring of love, the assurance of salvation. How ineffable is this charity! Truly there is no greater than this, that the Word was made flesh in order to make me like unto God! You became nothing in order to make me something; You clothed Yourself like the lowliest slave to give me the garments of a King and a God!

Although You took the form of a slave, You did not lessen Your substance, nor injure Your divinity, but the depths of Your humility pierce my heart and make me cry out: O incomprehensible One, made comprehensible because of me! O uncreated One, now created! O Thou who art inaccessible to mind and body, become palpable to thought and touch, by a prodigy of Thy power! Amen.

Ohappy fault! not in itself, but by the power of divine mercy. O happy fault, which has disclosed the sacred, hidden depths of the abyss of love! Truly a higher form of charity cannot be imagined… O ineffable love! Sublime, transforming love! Blessed art Thou, O Lord, because Thou teachest me that Thou wert born for me! To feel this is indeed a delight and the joy of joys!… O admirable God, how marvelous are Thy mercies! O uncreated God, make me worthy to know the depths of Thy love and the abyss of Thy mercy! Make me worthy to understand Thy ineffable charity, which was transmitted to us when the Father gave Jesus Christ to us in the Incarnation." Amen.

Anselm of Canterbury *c. 1033 – 21 April 1109 Also called Anselm of Aosta after his birthplace and Anselm of Bec after his monastery, was a Benedictine monk, philosopher, and prelate of the Church, who held the office of Archbishop of Canterbury from 1093 to 1109. Called the founder of scholasticism, he is a major influence in Western theology and is the originator of the argument for the existence of God and the satisfaction theory of atonement.*

Oheavenly Father, look, I beseech Thee, upon the ever flowing fountain of Thy compassion, which, as a flood of cleansing, a flood precious beyond all price, and full of life, gushed from Thy dearest and only-begotten Son for the cleansing of the world; by the death of Whom Thy goodness has been even pleased to give us life, and also to wash us with His Blood.

Nay more; Thou hast consigned Thy dearest Son to men as a shield of Thy good-will a shield wherewith to shelter themselves from Thy wrath; He receiving in Himself the death they fear, He presented as a shield to Thy justice and Thy all-just anger. Nor only so; it pleased Thy mercy that not only should He bear the brunt of Thy wrath, but endure our death as well. 'Twas so indeed; Thy Son, Thine Only-begotten, has alone borne our death.

Remember, O Lord, Thy bowels of compassion, and Thy mercies that are from the beginning of the world' (Ps. 24: 6) and stretch out Thy hand to Thy creature that stretches forth to Thee. Help the weakness of him that struggles after Thee. Draw me; for Thou knowest that I cannot come to Thee, except Thou, the Father, draw me with the cords of love and desire. Make me a servant acceptable and pleasing unto Thee; for Thou knowest that I cannot please Thee else. Give me, I pray Thee, those holy gifts with which alone to please Thee,

Thou that givest good gifts to them that ask Thee. Grant, I pray Thee, that my sole love and sole desire may be Thyself; my sole love and only fear, Thyself.

Take me wholly for Thine own, Thou who knowest that to Thee I owe all that I am, all that I have, all that I know, and all my powers. Convert me wholly to Thy praise and glory, I that owe myself wholly to Thy praise.

Deliver not, I pray Thee, Thy creature to Thy enemies; keep me for Thyself, whose alone I am entirely; and perfect in every part what Thou hast begun, and confirm what Thou hast wrought.

Hear my prayer, I beseech Thee, Thou who givest and inspirest it even ere I thought to call to Thee. Look upon Thy suppliant, Thou Who when I had a mind to pray didst even then deign to look upon me. Not in vain, O Lord of mercy, didst Thou deign to inspire that my prayer, not for nothing didst Thou give it me.

Nay, for this very end didst Thou deign to give it, that Thou mightest listen to me; for this didst Thou grant it to me, that I might implore Thee to have mercy on me a sinner. So thus having given me an earnest of Thy mercy, give me the rest. Rescue me, O Lord my God, and snatch me out of the hands of my enemies; for they too are Thine, they are the subjects of Thy almighty power; and they hate nothing of good works in me except what Thou hast given me. There is nothing in me that they hate, but only that I love Thee. And they scheme with all their endeavors, with all their might, with all their craft, to prevent my loving Thee, glorifying Thee, and ever seeking Thee.

Therefore let not the enemies of Thy glory be too strong for me; but let them be the more confounded as they see that I, bent on praising Thee and glorifying Thee, am seeking with all best endeavors that peace and glory of Thine, which they are intent upon diminishing.

O Lord, let not, I beseech Thee, their so unholy and execrable design concerning me, nay, against me, be brought to pass; but enlarge Thou my soul, O Lord, for telling forth Thy praise and heralding Thy glory, that I may henceforth live altogether according to Thy great glory, and that my whole life may glorify Thee; and do Thou by my example invite and incite many of Thy predestined to glorify Thee. Let the presence of Thy light, and the sweetness of Thy glory, a glory which they cannot bear, drive away from me the vile, unclean, and hateful spirits of darkness. O break my chains asunder, and take me out of durance, out of the horrible, black, and gloomy prison, out of the lake of misery and the mire of dregs, out of the abyss of death and darkness; and lead me forth into liberty and Thy marvelous light.

Enlighten me with Thy saving faith; gladden and strengthen me with Thy joyful and never-faltering hope; quicken me with Thy mighty and all-holy love. Subdue and humble me, and guard me with Thy strongest, securest, and most invincible fear. Fill me with wholesome shame from Thy all-lovely and all-glorious Self. And whensoever I present anything before Thine eyes that may offend them, break me, chastise me with pain greater than a woman's, and medicine me, after Thine own sweet fashion, with most efficacious compunction from Thyself, that I go not out from Thy mercy's presence empty and confounded;

but obtain whatsoever by Thy bidding, by Thy gift, by Thy inspiration, I may ask, and whatsoever Thou hast promised unto them that ask.

Let me find, O compassionate and merciful Lord, that not in vain do men fly for refuge to Thy mercy; that Thou art very close to all who seek Thee, helping them to find Thee; and that I can never faint or fail so long as I am with Thee, the Fountain of Compassion, O Thou who hast snatched me from the pit, and lavished on me Thou knowest how much, Thou knowest what. Ay, with what uneffort of omnipotence, of wisdom, and of goodness, wherewith Thou saidst and all things were made, with a like uneffort of compassion Thou canst speak, and all my deformities can be corrected and restored to sightliness.

And now, almighty and merciful Father, behold I have enumerated so many and so great Thy benefits which I have received from Thee; I have recounted the ills, so many and so great, which I have repaid Thee for Thy goodness. O wretched I, O thankless I, that for all so many and so great ills await and overhang me, yet appear before Thee with a heart obdurate and stolid, and dead and cold; and still am not ashamed. Detected in misdeeds so many and grievous, with no better prospect in the future than a gibbet in hell, still I am neither palsied with fright, nor tortured with grief, nor confounded with shame: no, nor set on fire with love of Thy so gentle and so long-forbearing goodness.

What, art Thou waiting, dearest Father, and delaying to look on me and pity me, until, according to the measure of Thy mercy, I shall have become fit to appear in Thy Presence, and present in Thy Presence something fit to ask of Thee, and say something fit for Thee to listen to?

See, see, it is a corpse that I have brought Thee; a corpse swarming with worms, and three days dead, is what comes to Thee, Thou Giver of life. See, see; what I present to Thy almighty mercy is one blind, to be illuminated; one sick, to be made whole; one involved in, O how many and how great debts, to be set free; stark-naked and poverty-stricken, to be enriched. For easy it is to Thee to enrich a beggar in a moment. Nor can I otherwise, most clement God, than offer Thee myself, just as I am; show Thee my death and wounds, my nakedness and poverty, and my debts, for which I fear the dungeon of everlasting death.

Do Thou, then, show me Thine Eyes of mercy; if, indeed, Thou canst be turned and canst forgive, and canst pour upon me of Thy grace and bliss. For turn myself to Thee I cannot; I am wounded with too many and too deep wounds; I am borne down by sicknesses and even death, and am become altogether helpless.

But do Thou, O merciful Father, convert me, and I shall be converted to Thee. Convert me to Thee, and bruise and crush my heart, and implant in me the sensibilities of a quickening grief. For there is no fountain of blessings besides Thee; there is none from whom to receive love and fear, and grief and shame, wherewith to appear in Thy sight and be found worthy of Thy mercy, unless Thou, from the vast reservoir of Thy mercy, pour out grace on me, so all unworthy of Thy grace. O Lord, if Thou give me this, I shall be happy.

If Thou vouch safe to chastise my offences and my crimes according to Thy judgment and thy justice, O happy I; not so, if Thou correct me in Thy fury, the fury which in the end overtakes and seizes all who rebel against and dare Thy mercy.

And this, O merciful Father, is Thy judgment and Thy justice; even this, that fear, love, shame, and grief work in the hearts of all who truly repent and return to Thy goodness, that they may gain Thy mercy. Pierce, then, this thief with Thy holy fear, and burn this rebel with the fire of Thy love and charity; pierce, O Lord, this malefactor with life-giving and most wholesome sorrow from Thee; confuse this unblushing sinner with shame from thy glorious Self; nail, nail this miscreant to his cross of penal anguish, and let that anguish conciliate Thy mercy.

Make me hunger for Thee with all my heart, and thirst for Thee with all my bowels; make me serve only Thee with all my inward parts, and with all my energies pursue what is well-pleasing in Thy sight. And so to Thee, with Jesus Christ, Thine only-begotten Son and our Lord, and with the Holy Ghost, the Paraclete, Thy most holy Gift, be all honor and glory for ever and ever. Amen.

Love our only possible return to Christ for His sufferings.] And as for Thee, O Lord Jesus, Lord of almighty zeal, what due return, what worthy thanks, can I ever pay Thee, mortal that I am, dust and ashes, and worthless clay? For what was there that it behooved Thee to do for my salvation, and Thou hast not done it!

From the sole of Thy foot to the crown of Thy head Thou didst plunge Thy whole Self in the waters of suffering, that all that is of me might be extricated from them; and so the waters came in even unto Thy soul. For Thou gavest up Thy soul to death to give back my lost soul to me; and so Thou hast bound me in a double debt, in that Thou gavest what Thou didst, and in that Thou didst freely give it up for my sake. Either way I am Thy debtor.

And yet again, since Thou hast twice given me life, once in creating, and once in redeeming; that life, surely, is the very best return that I could ever pay Thee. But when I think of Thine own precious Soul so tortured, I know not what due return could be by mortal ever paid to Thee. For could I pay Thee in return for it all heaven, all earth, and all the bravery of heaven and earth, yet even so I should not attain to the measure of my obligation. Nay, the very giving Thee what I have and what I can, is in itself Thy gift. I must love Thee, I must love Thee, Lord, with all my heart, all my soul, all my mind, all my strength, and follow as best I can Thy footsteps, who didst deign to die for me. And how shall all this be done in me, unless Thou do it? O let my soul cling to Thee; for all its strength comes from Thee.

And now, O Lord Jesus, my Redeemer, I adore Thee as very God; I believe in Thee, I hope in Thee, and I sigh after Thee with all possible desires; O, help my imperfection. I bow down my whole self before the glorious insignia of Thy Passion, wherewith Thou didst accomplish my salvation. The royal standard of Thy Victorious Cross; in Thy Name, O Christ, do I adore it. The thorny diadem; the nails glistening with Thy Blood; the lance plunged into Thy sacred Side; Thy Wounds; Thy Blood; Thy Death; Thy Burial; Thy triumphant Resurrection, and Thy Glory,

O Christ, I suppliantly adore and glorify them. For the balm of life breathes forth on me from all of them. By their life-giving odor revive and raise my spirit from the death of sin. Shield me by their virtue from the crafts of Satan; and comfort me, O Lord, that the yoke of Thy commandments may be sweet to me, and that the burden of the cross which Thou biddest me carry after Thee may be light and portable to the shoulders of my soul. For what courage have I for bearing up according to Thy precepts against the so many and so manifold oppressions of the world? Are my feet like hart's feet that I should be able to follow after Thee in Thy fleet passage through the thorns and roughnesses of Thy sufferings? But hear my voice, I pray Thee, and bend over Thy servant that sweet Cross of Thine, which is a tree of life to all that lay hold on it; and then will I run with alacrity, even as I hope to do; then will I carry after Thee without fainting and unweariedly the Cross Thine enemies have given Thee. Lay that divinest Cross, I pray Thee, on my shoulders; whose breadth is charity spreading over all creation; whose length, eternity; whose height, omnipotence; whose depth, unfathomable wisdom. And fasten my hands to it, and my feet; and clothe me from head to foot with the impress and the likeness of Thy Passion.

Grant me, I implore Thee, to abstain from deeds of the flesh, which Thou hatest, and to do justice, which Thou lovest; and either way to seek Thy glory. So shall I deem my left hand to have been fastened with the nail of temperance, and my right hand with the nail of justice, to that lofty Cross of Thine. Let my mind meditate in Thy law continually, and direct its every thought to Thee continually; and so by the nail of prudence fasten Thou my right foot to the same tree of life.

Let not the joyless joy of this fleeting life dissipate the senses, which should only minister to the spirit, nor yet its jocund joylessness waste and diminish the rewards of the life eternal laid up in store for me; and so shall my left foot also be nailed to the Cross by the nail of fortitude.

But, that some likeness may appear in me even to the thorns on Thy Head, let the compunction of a saving penance be impressed in my mind, and compassion for the miseries of others, and a penetrating zeal urging and pricking me to what is right in Thine eyes; and so shall I in my griefs be conformed to Thee, so shall the threefold wreath of thorn be fastened on me.

I would also have Thee put to my lips the sponge upon the reed, and make me taste the vinegar and its harshness; for I would have Thee, through Thy Scriptures, make my reason taste and see to see how like a sponge is all the hollow glory of the world, and how much more sour than vinegar is all the concupiscence of the world. So, Father, may it be brought to pass in me that the golden cup of Babylon that makes all the earth drunk may not seduce me with its worthless glitter, nor intoxicate me with its treacherous sweetness, as it does those who think darkness light, and light darkness, who think bitter sweet, and sweet bitter.

And as to the wine mingled with myrrh, I suspect it, for Thou wouldest not drink of it; because, perhaps, it indicated the too great bitterness of Thy crucifiers. And let Thy servant not only share Thy sufferings, let him also be made conformable to Thy life-giving death, by working this in me, that I may die after the flesh to sin, and live after the spirit to justice.

But that I may glory in bearing the perfect image of the Crucified, I pray Thee to express in me what the insatiable malice of sinners wrought in Thee even after Thou hadst died. Let Thy word wound my heart, Thy word living and effectual, more penetrating than the sharpest lance, and reaching even to the inmost parts of the soul; and let it draw forth from it, as though it were from my right side, in place of blood and water, love of Thee and love of my brethren. And last of all, wrap my spirit in the clean linen of the first robe; and in it let me rest, going in to Thee into the place of Thy wonderful tabernacle, and there hide me until Thy indignation pass away. But on the third day, the day of toil and the day of single glory overpast, on the first early morning of the week that shall see no end, do Thou revive me and raise me up, unworthy though I be, that in my flesh I may see Thy beauty, and be filled to the full with the joy of Thy countenance, O my Saviour and my God. Come, come the day, O my Saviour and my God; speed, speed the time; that what now I believe in I may then behold at last with unveiled eye; that what now I hope for and salute from afar, I may apprehend; that what now I desire with all my powers, I may clasp in my soul's embrace and rapturously greet; and be all swallowed up in Thy love's abyss, O my Saviour and my God! But now meanwhile, O thou my soul, bless thou thy Saviour; and magnify His Name, for it is holy and full of holiest delights.

O how good and sweet Thou art, Lord Jesus, to the soul that seeks Thee, Jesus, Redeemer of the captives; Saviour of the lost; Hope of the exiles; Strength of those that labor; Repose of the anxious spirit; dear Solace and sweet Refreshment of the tearful soul that runs toiling after Thee;

Crown of them that conquer; sole Reward and only Joy of the citizens above; full Fountain overflowing with all graces; glorious Offspring of great God; Thyself great God. Great God, let all things that are in heaven above and in earth beneath bless Thee, for Thou art great and great is Thy Name.

O unfading Beauty of the most high God, and purest Brightness of Eternal Light; O Life enlivening all life, O Light enlightening all light, and sustaining in eternal splendor the thousand thousand thousands of lights that blaze before the Throne of Thy Divine Majesty, on from the distant dawn of their first early shining. O Thou welling Fountain, hidden from mortal sight in the eternal and exhaustless outgushing of Thy fresh limpid floods, Whose springs have no beginning, Whose deeps are deep and infinitely deep, Whose height attains no limit, Whose breadth broadens onwards marginless forever, Whose purity is unruffled through eternity! The Bosom of unfathomable God pours Thee forth from the unsearchable abyss of His own profound, Life begetting Life, Light begetting Light, God begetting God, eternal God begetting eternal God, infinite God, God infinite and in all things coequal with Himself. And, Of Thy fullness we have all received. Thee too, all-plentiful Spring of every good, priceless Light of sevenfold grace, Thee, O most merciful Spirit, I implore to vouchsafe to illuminate me by Thy visitation, whereinsoever, by reason of my frailty, I have too feebly grasped the truth of Thy majesty and grandeur, and whatsoever of all that I have understood of Thy Divine precepts I have by carnal wantonness disesteemed; so may I correct what is amiss, and, helped by Thee, whom, voyaging over this life's sea of perils, I have invoked to my assistance, may I be guided without shipwreck to the harbor of eternal peace.

Thee, too, I entreat, all-pitiful Father, that, as Thou didst first make me and then re-make by the Passion of Thy only-begotten Son, so Thou wouldst give me to think and love whatsoever tends to Thy glory. I am frail and unequal to my undertaking, but do Thou grant me by diligent confession to attain the grace of redemption and salvation. And whatever work I undertake henceforth, make it tend altogether, by Thy grace, through Thy grace, and in Thy grace, to Thine only praise. Keep me henceforth from sin, teach me to be more constant and courageous in good works; and so long as I live in this body, let me show myself some way Thy servant. And so grant me, after my soul's exit from the flesh, to obtain pardon of all my sins and reap life everlasting. Through Him who with Thee liveth and reigneth for ever and ever. Amen.

I am not trying, O Lord, to penetrate your loftiness, for I cannot begin to match my understanding with it, but I desire in some measure to understand your truth, which my heart believes and loves. For I do not seek to understand in order to believe, but I believe in order to understand. For this too I believe, that 'unless I believe, I shall not understand. Teach me to seek you, and reveal yourself to me as I seek: For unless you instruct me I cannot seek you, and unless you reveal yourself I cannot find you. Let me seek you in desiring you: let me desire you in seeking you. Let me find you in loving you: let me love you in finding you. My God, I pray that I may so know you and love you that I may rejoice in you. And if I may not do so fully in this life let me go steadily on to the day when I come to that fullness ...Let me receive That which you promised through your truth that my joy may be full Remember, O just, O holy, O bountiful God, that Thou art merciful, and hast made me and re-made me.

Therefore remember not, good Lord, Thy justice against Thy sinner, but be mindful of Thy condescension to Thy creature; remember not Thy fury against the guilty, but be mindful of Thy mercy to the miserable. True it is that my conscience and sense of guilt deserves damnation, and that my penance is not enough for satisfaction; but yet it is certain that Thy mercy out strips all Thy resentment.

Spare, therefore, Thou good Lord, to whom salvation belongeth, and who desirest not the death of the sinner, spare my sinful soul; for it flies, frightened by Thy frightening justice, to Thy consoling mercy; that so, since the treasure of his marred virginity is now—O grief!—irrecoverable, yet the punishment due to fornication may not be inevitable to the penitent; for 'tis neither impossible to Thy omnipotence, nor ill-becoming to Thy justice, nor unwonted to Thy mercy; since Thou art good, and since Thy mercy reaches to eternity, Thou who art blessed for ever more. Amen.

Suffer me therefore, O Lord Jesus Christ, to gaze on Thy unspeakable mercy, and to tell abroad Thy sweetness and goodness towards the sinful and the wretched. I have said it already, but O, it delights me much, whenever fit occasion offers, to make remembrance of Thy sweetness and Thy grace to sinners, and to say how great they are. For, out of love for sinners and for their redemption not merely sinners who are sinners more or less, but sinners who are sinful beyond measure, if only they repent—Thou earnest down from the Bosom of the Father, Thou didst enter the Virgin's womb, didst take true flesh of her, and living in the world didst call all sinners to penance, at last didst endure the gibbet of the Cross for them,

and dying thus according to the flesh, didst restore to them the life which by their sin they had justly lost. Therefore, when I consider the evil deeds that I have done, I am sure that I shall be lost, if Thou shouldest please to judge me according to my deserts; but, when I consider that death of Thine which Thou didst undergo for the redemption of sinners, I do not despair of Thy mercy.

Why; the thief who for his sins was crucified by Thy side lived on in sin, to the very passing away of his soul in death; and yet, in the very hour of his dissolution, because he confessed his faults and proclaimed his guilt, found mercy and was that very day with Thee in Paradise. And I, beholding Thee, as I do, dead for the redemption of sinners, Thy Hands and Thy Feet fastened by the nails, Thy Side opened by the soldier's lance, the river of Blood and Water flowing from that dear Side of Thine, am I to despair? One thing, and one thing only, dost Thou desire; that is, that we're pent of our wickednesses, and endeavor to amend as best we may. If we do this, we are safe; for if our last day finds us thus—since we have the instance of the thief who thus in his last hour merited to be saved—confiding in the unspeakable mercy of our Lord Jesus Christ, we may have little or no fear of the accusation of the enemy.

Having, therefore, before our eyes the price of our redemption, the Death, that is to say, of our Redeemer, and His Blood which was shed for us; having, besides, the example of the thief and of many who, having been entangled in many and great sins, have been mercifully forgiven by Him, the Fountain of Mercy, Jesus Christ, let us not despair, but fly, sure of the remission of our sins, to Him the Fountain of Mercy, in whom we see and know that so many and so great sinners have been washed clean;

and let us be sure that we in like manner shall be cleansed by the same Fountain of Mercy, if we abstain from our wickednesses and our sins, and, as far as we can, have a care to do what is right. But, to abstain from evil and do good, is what we cannot compass by our own strength and without His help.

Let us, therefore, implore His unspeakable compassion, whose care it was to create us when we were not, that He would grant us thus in this life, before we go forth hence, to amend our faults; that, this life ended, we may have strength to travel home to Him in a straight unfettered flight, and so may dwell with Him in everlasting glory, joined with the angelic choirs who now enjoy it, rejoicing in unending bliss.

O Holy Father, Thou didst not therefore entrust those precious talents of Thine to me, as to have me yield Thee for usury so hateful an offence. Thou didst not therefore shed so many and so great benefits upon me, that Thou shouldest reap no better fruit from the seed sown than worthless weeds and thorns and thistles. Thou didst not therefore fill me and enrich me with so many and so great benefits, that I should turn them into weapons against Thee my God. It was not the design of Thy loving-kindness to give me arms against Thyself, nor to increase the devil's power by arms of Thy giving. And now behold me. See, see, I am stricken with all these wounds, these fearful wounds, yet I do not suffer. Ah, surely, I am blind; for with all their foulnesses and this utter nakedness, yet I am not ashamed. Yes, yes indeed; I am senseless and dull of heart, not to grieve over the so many and the so sad losses that I have suffered; not even to have spirit left in me to bewail the death that I am dying.

Yes, yes indeed; my heart must be of stone, that I am so hardened as not even now and then upon occasion to dread the eternal torments that overhang me.

Yes, yes indeed; this heart is a rock of ice, for all the fires of my all-pitiful Father's love and His love's blessings do not avail to warm it. Yes, yes indeed; I take shame to myself and chide myself, for the trumpet-cry of preaching and the thunders of Thy threatenings are alike in effectual to arouse me. Where is the piercing grief of which they tell, the grief of compunction, with which to crush and fling away all this hell-inspired hardness, and annihilate all the stone, the stubbornness, the rebellion? Where, my God, is the shame that should cover me with confusion before Thine eyes and the eyes of all the whole court of heaven?

Where is the dread of Thy vengeance, that should make me tremble through and through before Thee? Where is the love, and the desire of recovering Thy peace and love and grace, that ought to burn within me? Where are the torrents of tears with which I should wash away my stains and my defilements from before Thee?

Where is the prayerful devotion by which I should strive to appease and propitiate Thee? Whither shall I turn, O tender and compassionate Father, having, as I have, nothing worthy of Thy regard that I can offer to Thy majesty? Whither shall I fly, most merciful Father, I that am empty of all good; nay, that stand displayed full of all evil; beneath the gaze of Thy saints and the holy armies of Thy celestial hosts?

O heavenly Father, look, I beseech Thee, upon the ever flowing fountain of Thy compassion, which, as a flood of cleansing, a flood precious beyond all price, and full of life, gushed from Thy dearest and only-begotten Son for the cleansing of the world; by the death of Whom Thy goodness has been even pleased to give us life, and also to wash us with His Blood. Nay more; Thou hast consigned Thy dearest Son to men as a shield of Thy good-will a shield wherewith to shelter themselves from Thy wrath; He receiving in Himself the death they fear, He presented as a shield to Thy justice and Thy all-just anger.

Nor only so; it pleased Thy mercy that not only should He bear the brunt of Thy wrath, but endure our death as well. 'Twas so indeed; Thy Son, Thine Only-begotten, has alone borne our death. Remember, O Lord, Thy bowels of compassion, and Thy mercies that are from the beginning of the world' and stretch out Thy hand to Thy creature that stretches forth to Thee. Help the weakness of him that struggles after Thee. Draw me; for Thou knowest that I cannot come to Thee, except Thou, the Father, draw me with the cords of love and desire. Make me a servant acceptable and pleasing unto Thee; for Thou knowest that I cannot please Thee else.

Give me, I pray Thee, those holy gifts with which alone to please Thee, Thou that givest good gifts to them that ask Thee. Grant, I pray Thee, that my sole love and sole desire may be Thyself; my sole love and only fear, Thyself. Take me wholly for Thine own, Thou who knowest that to Thee I owe all that I am, all that I have, all that I know, and all my powers. Convert me wholly to Thy praise and glory, I that owe myself wholly to Thy praise. Deliver not, I pray Thee, Thy creature to Thy enemies; keep me for Thyself, whose alone I am entirely; and perfect in every part what Thou hast begun, and confirm what Thou hast wrought. Hear my prayer, I beseech Thee, Thou who givest and inspirest it even ere I thought to call to Thee. Look upon Thy suppliant, Thou Who when I had a mind to pray didst even then deign to look upon me. Not in vain, O Lord of mercy, didst Thou deign to inspire that my prayer, not for nothing didst Thou give it me. Nay, for this very end didst Thou deign to give it, that Thou mightest listen to me; for this didst Thou grant it to me, that I might implore Thee to have mercy on me a sinner. So thus having given me an earnest of Thy mercy, give me the rest.

Rescue me, O Lord my God, and snatch me out of the hands of my enemies; for they too are Thine, they are the subjects of Thy almighty power; and they hate nothing of good works in me except what Thou hast given me. There is nothing in me that they hate, but only that I love Thee. And they scheme with all their endeavors, with all their might, with all their craft, to prevent my loving Thee, glorifying Thee, and ever seeking Thee. Therefore let not the enemies of Thy glory be too strong for me; but let them be the more confounded as they see that I, bent on praising Thee and glorifying Thee, am seeking with all best endeavors that peace and glory of Thine, which they are intent upon diminishing.

O Lord, let not, I beseech Thee, their so unholy and execrable design concerning me, nay, against me, be brought to pass; but enlarge Thou my soul, O Lord, for telling forth Thy praise and heralding Thy glory, that I may henceforth live altogether according to Thy great glory, and that my whole life may glorify Thee; and do Thou by my example invite and incite many of Thy predestined to glorify Thee.

Let the presence of Thy light, and the sweetness of Thy glory, a glory which they cannot bear, drive away from me the vile, unclean, and hateful spirits of darkness. O break my chains asunder, and take me out of durance, out of the horrible, black, and gloomy prison, out of the lake of misery and the mire of dregs, out of the abyss of death and darkness; and lead me forth into liberty and Thy marvelous light.

Enlighten me with Thy saving faith; gladden and strengthen me with Thy joyful and never-faltering hope; quicken me with Thy mighty and all-holy love. Subdue and humble me, and guard me with Thy strongest, securest, and most invincible fear. Fill me with wholesome shame from Thy all-lovely and all-glorious Self. And whensoever I present anything before Thine eyes that may offend them, break me, chastise me with pain greater than a woman's, and medicine me, after Thine own sweet fashion, with most efficacious compunction from Thyself, that I go not out from Thy mercy's presence empty and confounded; but obtain whatsoever by Thy bidding, by Thy gift, by Thy inspiration, I may ask, and whatsoever Thou hast promised unto them that ask.

Let me find, O compassionate and merciful Lord, that not in vain do men fly for refuge to Thy mercy; that Thou art very close to all who seek Thee, helping them to find Thee; and that I can never faint or fail so long as I am with Thee, the Fountain of Compassion, O Thou who hast snatched me from the pit, and lavished on me Thou knowest how much, Thou knowest what. Ay, with what uneffort of omnipotence, of wisdom, and of goodness, wherewith Thou saidst and all things were made, with a like uneffort of compassion Thou canst speak, and all my deformities can be corrected and restored to sightliness.

O Sovereign and almighty Lord, bless all thy people, and all thy flock. Give thy peace, thy help, thy love unto us thy servants, the sheep of thy fold, that we may be united in the bond of peace and love, one body and one spirit, in one hope of our calling, in thy divine and boundless love. Lord, be with us this day, Within us to purify us; Above us to draw us up; Beneath us to sustain us; Before us to lead us; Behind us to restrain us; Around us to protect us.

Antiochus of Palestine (*600s AD*) *The information about him is limited. He is thought to have been born in Ankara, Turkey. He* *was a monk and later an abbot. When his monastery was destroyed he was asked to write a compilation of scripture and an account of the slaughter of 44 monks from the monastery of St. Sabbas by Bedouins, Pandects.*

O Holy Spirit, most merciful Comforter: You proceed from the Father in a manner beyond our understanding. Come, I beseech You, and take up your abode in my heart. Purify and cleanse me from all sin, and sanctify my soul.

Cleanse it from every impurity, water its dryness, melt its coldness, and save it from its sinful ways. Make me truly humble and resigned, that I may be pleasing to You, and that You might abide with me forever. Most Blessed Light, most Amiable Light, enlighten me. O Rapturous Joy of Paradise, Fount of Purest Delight, My God, give yourself to me and kindle in my innermost soul the fire of Your love. My Lord, instruct, direct, and defend me in all things. Give me strength against all immoderate fears and against despondency. Bestow upon me a true faith, a firm hope, and a sincere and a perfect love. Grant that I always do Thy Most Gracious Will. Amen

O Only-Begotten Word of the Father, Jesus Christ, who alone are perfect: according to the greatness of your mercy, do not abandon me, your servant, but ever rest in my heart. O Sweet Jesus, Good Shepherd of Your flock, deliver me from the attacks of The Enemy. Do not allow me to become the prey of Satan's evil intent, even though I have within me the seed of eternal damnation. Instead, O Lord Jesus Christ, Adorable God, Holy King, while I sleep, protect me by Your Holy spirit, through Whom You sanctified Your Apostles. Enlighten my mind by the light of the Holy Gospel, my soul by the love of Your Cross, my heart by the purity of Your teaching. Protect my body by Your sacred passion, my senses by Your humility, and awaken me in due time for Your glorification. For You, above all, are adorable, together with Your eternal Father, and the Holy Spirit, now and ever, and forever. Amen.

O All-Ruler, Word of the Father, Jesus Christ, Thou Who art perfect, never in Thy great mercy leave me, but ever abide in me, Thy servant. O Jesus, Good Shepherd of Thy sheep, deliver me not to the revolt of the serpent and leave me not to the will of Satan, for the seed of corruption is in me. Lord, adorable God, Holy King, Jesus Christ, guard me asleep by the unwaning light, Thy Holy Spirit, by Whom Thou didst sanctify Thy disciples. O Lord, grant me, Thy unworthy servant, Thy salvation on my bed. Enlighten my mind with the light of understanding of Thy Holy Gospel. Enlighten my soul with the love of Thy Cross. Enlighten my heart with the purity of Thy Word. Enlighten my body with Thy passionless Passion. Keep my thoughts in Thy humility. And rouse me in good time to glorify Thee, for Thou art supremely glorified, with Thy eternal Father, and Thy most Holy Spirit forever. Amen.

THOMAS AQUINAS (*1225 – 7 March 1274AD) Tommaso d'Aquino was born in Italy of nobility. Against his parent's wishes he joined the Dominican Order. His parents had him kidnapped on his way to join the order and kept him prisoner in his family castle for a year. One story tells of his brothers hiring a prostitute to seduce him. He is acknowledged as a scholar, theologian and jurist. He believed that God reveals himself through nature, so to study nature is to study God. His theological writings and his analysis of Aristotle are some of the pillars of Western thought and philosophy.*

Almighty and everlasting God, behold I come to the Sacrament of Thine only-begotten Son, our Lord Jesus Christ: I come as one infirm to the physician of life, as one unclean to the fountain of mercy, as one blind to the light of everlasting brightness, as one poor and needy to the Lord of heaven and earth. Therefore I implore the abundance of Thy measureless bounty that Thou wouldst vouchsafe to heal my infirmity, wash my uncleanness, enlighten my blindness, enrich my poverty and clothe my nakedness, that I may receive the Bread of Angels, the King of kings, the Lord of lords, with such reverence and humility, with such sorrow and devotion, with such purity and faith, with such purpose and intention as may be profitable to my soul's salvation. Grant unto me, I pray, the grace of receiving not only the Sacrament of our Lord's Body and Blood, but also the grace and power of the Sacrament.

O most gracious God, grant me so to receive the Body of Thine only-begotten Son, our Lord Jesus Christ, which He took from the Virgin Mary, as to merit to be incorporated into His mystical Body, and to be numbered amongst His members.

O most loving Father, give me grace to behold forever Thy Beloved Son with His face at last unveiled, whom I now purpose to receive under the sacramental veil here below. Amen.

I give thanks to Thee, O Lord, most holy, Father almighty, eternal God, that Thou hast vouchsafed, for no merit of mine own, but out of Thy pure mercy, to appease the hunger of my soul with the precious body and blood of Thy Son, Our Lord Jesus Christ. Humbly I implore Thee, let not this holy communion be to me an increase of guilt unto my punishment,

but an availing plea unto pardon and salvation. Let it be to me the armor of faith and the shield of good will. May it root out from my heart all vice; may it utterly subdue my evil passions and all my unruly desires. May it perfect me in charity and patience; in humility and obedience; and in all other virtues. May it be my sure defense against the snares laid for me by my enemies, visible and invisible. May it restrain and quiet all my evil impulses, and make me ever cleave to Thee Who art the one true God. May I owe to it a happy ending of my life.

And do Thou, O heavenly Father, vouchsafe one day to call me, a sinner, to that ineffable banquet, where Thou, together with Thy Son and the Holy Ghost, art to Thy saints true and unfailing light, fullness of content, joy for evermore, gladness without alloy, consummate and everlasting happiness. Through the same Christ our Lord. Amen.

LORD, Father all-powerful, and ever-living God, I thank Thee, for even though I am a sinner, Thy unprofitable servant, not because of my worth, but in the kindness of Thy mercy, Thou hast fed me with the precious Body and Blood of Thy Son, our Lord Jesus Christ. I pray that this holy communion may not bring me condemnation and punishment but forgiveness and salvation. May it be a helmet of faith and a shield of good will. May it purify me from evil ways and put an end to my evil passions. May it bring me charity and patience, humility and obedience, and growth in power to do good. May it be my strong defense against all my enemies, visible and invisible, and the perfect calming of all my evil impulses, bodily and spiritual.

May it unite me more closely to Thee, the one true God and lead me safely through death to everlasting happiness with Thee. And I pray that Thou willest lead me, a sinner to the banquet where Thou with Thy Son and Holy Spirit, are true and perfect light, total fulfillment, everlasting joy, gladness without end, and perfect happiness to Thy saints. Grant this through Christ our Lord. Amen.

Come, Holy Spirit, Divine Creator, true source of light and fountain of wisdom! Pour forth your brilliance upon my dense intellect, dissipate the darkness which covers me, that of sin and of ignorance. Grant me a penetrating mind to understand, a retentive memory, method and ease in learning, the lucidity to comprehend, and abundant grace in expressing myself. Guide the beginning of my work, direct its progress, and bring it to successful completion.

This I ask through Jesus Christ, true God and true man, living and reigning with You and the Father, forever and ever. Amen.

Creator of all things, true Source of light and wisdom, lofty origin of all being, graciously let a ray of Your brilliance penetrate into the darkness of my understanding and take from me the double darkness in which I have been born, an obscurity of both sin and ignorance. Give me a sharp sense of understanding, a retentive memory, and the ability to grasp things correctly and fundamentally. Grant me the talent of being exact in my explanations, and the ability to express myself with thoroughness and charm. Point out the beginning, direct the progress, and help in completion; through Christ our Lord. Amen.

O ineffable Creator, Who, out of the treasure of Thy wisdom, hast ordained three hierarchies of Angels, and placed them in wonderful order above the heavens, and hast most wisely distributed the parts of the world; Thou, Who are called the true fountain of light and wisdom, and the highest beginning, vouchsafe to pour upon the darkness of my understanding, in which I was born, the double beam of Thy brightness, removing from me all darkness of sin and ignorance. Thou, Who makest eloquent the tongue of the dumb, instruct my tongue, and pour on my lips the grace of Thy blessing.

Give me quickness of understanding, capacity of retaining, subtlety of interpreting, facility in learning, and copious grace of speaking. Guide my going in, direct my going forward, accomplish my going forth; through Christ our Lord. Amen.

Grant me grace, O merciful God, to desire ardently all that is pleasing to Thee, to examine it prudently, to acknowledge it truthfully, and to accomplish it perfectly, for the praise and glory of Thy name. Amen.

Grant me, O Lord my God, a mind to know you, a heart to seek you, wisdom to find you, conduct pleasing to you, faithful perseverance in waiting for you, and a hope of finally embracing you. Amen.

I Thank You Holy Lord I thank you, O holy Lord, almighty Father, eternal God, who have deigned, not through any merits of mine, but out of the condescension of Your goodness, to satisfy me a sinner,

Your unworthy servant, with the precious Body and Blood of Your Son, our Lord Jesus Christ.

I pray that this Holy Communion be not a condemnation to punishment for me, but a saving plea to forgiveness. May it be to me the armor of faith and the shield of a good will. May it be the emptying out of my vices and the extinction of all lustful desires; an increase of charity and patience, of humility and obedience, and all virtues; a strong defense against the snares of all my enemies, visible and invisible; the perfect quieting of all my evil impulses of flesh and spirit, binding me firmly to You, the one true God; and a happy ending of my life.

I pray too that You will deign to bring me, a sinner, to that ineffable banquet where You with Your Son and the Holy Spirit, are to Your Saints true light, fulfillment of desires, eternal joy, unalloyed gladness, and perfect bliss. Through the same Christ our Lord. Amen.

Lord, Father all-powerful and ever-living God, I thank You, for even though I am a sinner, your unprofitable servant, not because of my worth but in the kindness of your mercy, You have fed me with the Precious Body & Blood of Your Son, our Lord Jesus Christ.

I pray that this Holy Communion may not bring me condemnation and punishment but forgiveness and salvation. May it be a helmet of faith and a shield of good will. May it purify me from evil ways and put an end to my evil passions. May it bring me charity and patience, humility and obedience, and growth in the power to do good. May it be my strong defense against all my enemies, visible and invisible, and the perfect calming of all my evil impulses, bodily and spiritual. May it unite me more closely to you, the One true God, and lead me safely through death to everlasting happiness with You. And I pray that You will lead me, a sinner, to the banquet where you, with Your Son and holy Spirit, are true and perfect light, total fulfillment, everlasting joy, gladness without end, and perfect happiness to your saints. grant this through Christ our Lord, Amen.

Francis of Assisi *(1181-October 3, 1226 AD) Born Giovanni di Pietro di Bernardone to a wealthy Italian silk merchant. He pursued life as a soldier until being captured and spending a year as a prisoner of war. After that time, Francesco, as his father called him, began to reevaluate his life and priorities. He never became a monk or priest. He lived a simple life seeking to follow Christ's command in Matthew 10:9 to preach the Kingdom of God. Eventually he founded two religious orders given to poverty with this as the rule: "To follow the teachings of our Lord Jesus Christ and to walk in his footsteps"*

Lord, make me an instrument of your peace; where there is hatred, let me sow love; where there is injury, pardon: where there is doubt, faith; where there is despair, hope where there is darkness, light where there is sadness, joy. O divine Master, grant that I may not so much seek to be consoled as to console; to be understood, as to understand; to be loved, as to love;

for it is in giving that we receive, it is in pardoning that we are pardoned, and it is in dying that we are born to Eternal Life.

AUGUSTINE of HIPPO *Augustine Aurelius (13 November 354 – 28 August 430AD) Augustine was a Berber from North Africa. He was a gifted student and orator. At the age of 19 he took a lover for 15 years. She bore him a son who died young. He* *became a convert to Christianity at age 31. He abandoned worldly pursuits, gave his money to charity and turned his family home into a monastery. He became bishop of Hippo in what is now Algeria in 395 AD. Augustine was a prolific writer and was instrumental in formulating many of what we now consider foundational doctrines of the Church.*

O thou, who art the light of the minds that know Thee, the life of the souls that love Thee, and the strength of the wills that serve Thee; help us so to know Thee that we may truly love Thee; so to love Thee that we may fully serve Thee, whom to serve is perfect freedom. Watch, dear Lord, with those who wake, or watch, or weep tonight, and let your angels protect those who sleep. Tend the sick. Refresh the weary. Sustain the dying. Calm the suffering. Pity the distressed. We ask this for the sake of your love.

Lord Jesus, our Savior, let us come to you. Our hearts are cold; Lord, warm them with your selfless love. Our hearts are sinful; cleanse them with your precious blood. Our hearts are weak; strengthen them with our joyous Spirit. Our hearts are empty; fill them with your divine presence. Lord Jesus, our hearts are yours; possess them always and only for yourself. I beg of You, my God, let me know You and love You so that I may be happy in You. And though I cannot do this fully in this life,

yet let me improve from day to day till I may do so to the full. Let me know You more and more in this life, that I may know You perfectly in heaven.

Let me know You more and more here, so that I may love you perfectly there, so that my joy may be great in itself here, and complete in heaven with You.

O Truthful God, let me receive the happiness of heaven which You promise so that my joy may be full. In the meantime, let my mind think of it, let my tongue talk of it, let my heart long for it, let my mouth speak of it, let my soul hunger after it, let my flesh thirst after it, let my whole being desire it, until such time as I may enter through death into the joy of my Lord, there to continue forever, world without end. Amen.

Look upon us, O Lord, and let all the darkness of our souls vanish before the beams of thy brightness. Fill us with holy love, and open to us the treasures of thy wisdom. All our desire is known unto Thee, therefore perfect what thou hast begun, and what thy Spirit has awakened us to ask in prayer. We seek thy face, turn thy face unto us and show us thy glory. Then shall our longing be satisfied, and our peace shall be perfect. We beseech Thee, Master, to be our helper and protector. Save the afflicted among us; have mercy on the lowly; raise up the fallen; appear to the needy; heal the ungodly; restore the wanderers of thy people; feed the hungry; ransom our prisoners; raise up the sick; comfort the faint-hearted. Lord Jesus, let me know myself and know you, and desire nothing, save only you. Let me hate myself and love you. Let me do everything for the sake of you. Let me humble myself and exalt you. Let me think of nothing except you. Let me accept whatever happens as from you. Let me banish self and follow you, And ever desire to follow you. Let me fly from myself and take refuge in you, That I may deserve to be defended by you. Let me fear for myself, let me fear you, And let me be among those who are chosen by you. Let me be willing to obey for the sake of you. Let me cling to nothing, save only to you, And let me be poor because of you. Look upon me, that I may love you. Call me, that I may see you, And forever enjoy you. Amen

Basil of Caesarea *(c329-January 379 AD) Basil came from a wealthy Turkish family. His grandfather was martyred before the reign of Constantine I. Basil received a formal education. He traveled widely and was impressed by the dedication of those in monastic life. He wrote of his conversion,* "I had wasted much time on follies and spent nearly all of my youth in vain labors, and devotion to the teachings of a wisdom that God had made foolish. Suddenly, I awoke as out of a deep sleep. I beheld the wonderful light of the Gospel truth, and I recognized the nothingness of the wisdom of the princes of this world." Basil, Ep. 223, 2, as quoted in Quasten (1986), p. 205 *He gave away much of his personal wealth and established a monastery in his family home with rooms for the poor and a public soup kitchen. He was an able administrator. He became a bishop. He is known for his support of the Nicene Creed and his writings,* <u>On the Holy Spirit</u> *and his* <u>Refutation of the Apology of the Impious Eunomius</u>. *He also left many homilies, written lectures and over three hundred letters.*

Almighty Lord, God of the Powers and of all flesh, Who livest in the highest and carest for the humble, Who searchest our hearts and affections, and clearly foreknowest the secrets of men; eternal and ever living Light, in Whom is no change nor shadow of variation; O Immortal King, receive our prayers which at the present time we offer to Thee from unclean lips, trusting in the multitude of Thy mercies.

Forgive all sins committed by us in thought, word or deed, consciously or unconsciously, and cleanse us from all defilement of flesh and spirit. Grant us to pass the night of the whole present life with wakeful heart and sober thought, ever expecting the coming of the radiant day of the appearing of Thy only-begotten Son, our Lord and

God and Saviour, Jesus Christ, when the Judge of all will come with glory to render to each according to their deeds.

May we not be found fallen and idle, but awake and alert for action, ready to accompany Him into the joy and divine palace of His glory, where there is the ceaseless sound of those keeping festival and the unspeakable delight of those who behold the ineffable beauty of Thy Face. For Thou art the true Light that enlightens and sanctifies all, and all creation sings to Thee throughout the ages. Amen.

We bless Thee, O most high God and Lord of mercy, Who art ever doing numberless great and inscrutable things with us, glorious and wonderful; Who grantest to us sleep for rest from our infirmities, and repose from the burdens of our much toiling flesh. We thank Thee that Thou hast not destroyed us with our sins, but hast loved us as ever, and though we are sunk in despair, Thou hast raised us up to glorify Thy power. Therefore we implore Thy incomparable goodness, enlighten the eyes of our understanding and raise up our mind from the heavy sleep of indolence; open our mouth and fill it with Thy praise, that we may be able undistracted to sing and confess Thee, Who art God glorified in all and by all, the eternal Father, with Thy only-begotten Son, and Thy all-holy and good and life-giving Spirit, now and ever, and to the ages of ages. Amen.

Benedict of Nursia *(March 2, 480-547AD) Benedict is the son of a Roman noble. He grew up in Rome. He is traditionally to be thought the twin brother of Scholastica. He founded twelve monasteries during his lifetime and is best known for his Rule of St. Benedict which governs the majority of Roman Catholic Monasteries around the world.*

Gracious and holy Father, please give me: intellect to understand you; reason to discern you; diligence to seek you; wisdom to find you; a spirit to know you; a heart to meditate upon you; ears to hear you; eyes to see you; a tongue to proclaim you; a way of life pleasing to you; patience to wait for you; and perseverance to look for you. Grant me: a perfect end, your holy presence. A blessed resurrection, and life everlasting.

John Calvin *(1509-1564AD) Jehan Cauvin was born in France. He first studied to be a monk, adopting the tonsure at a young age, later left the church and under the direction of his parents studied law and became a humanist lawyer in France. He left the Roman Catholic Church at the age of 21. He is best known as a theologian, a pastor, and a reformer. His primary work is his <u>Institutes of Christian Religion.</u>*

Lord, save us from being self-centered in our prayers and teach us to remember to pray for others. May we be so bound up in love with those for whom we pray, that we may feel their needs as acutely as our own, and interceded for them with sensitivity, with understanding and with imagination. Grant, Almighty God, that as thou hast once adopted us, and continue to confirm this thy favor by calling us unceasingly to thyself, and dost not only severely chastise us, but also gently and paternally invite us to thyself, and exhort us at the same time to repentance, -

O grant that we may not be so hardened as to resist Thy goodness, nor abuse this Thine incredible forbearance, but submit ourselves in obedience to Thee; that whenever Thou mayest severely chastise us, we may bear Thy corrections with genuine submission of faith, and not continue untamable and obstinate to the last, but return to

Thee the only fountain of life and salvation, that as thou has once begun in us a good work, so Thou mayest perfect it to the day of our Lord. Amen.

Grant, Almighty God, that as Thou hast not only of late adopted us as thy children, but before we were born, and as Thou hast been pleased to sign us, as soon as we came forth from our mother's womb, with the symbol of that holy redemption, which has been obtained for us by the blood of Thy only begotten Son, Though we have by our ingratitude renounced so great a benefit, - O grant, that being mindful of our defection and unfaithfulness, of which eve are all guilty, and for which Thou hast justly rejected us, we may now with true humility and obedience of faith embrace the grace of Thy gospel now again offered to us, by which Thou reconciles Thyself to us; and grant that we may steadfastly persevere in pure faith, so as never to turn aside from the true obedience of faith, but to advance more and more in the knowledge of Thy mercy, that having strong and deep roots, and being firmly grounded in the confidence of sure faith, we may never fall away from the true worship of Thee, until Thou at length receives us in to that eternal kingdom, which has been procured for us by the blood of Thy only Son. Amen.

Grant, Almighty God, that inasmuch as we are so dull and slothful, that though often admonished, we yet consider not our sins, yea, though chastised by Thy hand, we yet return not immediately to a right mind, - O grant, that we may hereafter profit more under thy rod, and not be refractory and intractable; but as soon as Thou raises Thy hand, may each of us mourn, know our own evils, and then, with one consent, surrender ourselves to be ruled by Thee; and may we, in the meantime, patiently and calmly endure Thy chastisements, and never murmur against Thee, but ever aspire to the attainment of true repentance, until, having at length put off all the vices and corruptions of our flesh, we attain to the fulness of righteousness, and to that true and blessed glory which has been prepared for us in heaven by Jesus Christ. Amen.

Grant, Almighty God, that as we set up against Thee so many obstacles through the depravity of our flesh and natural disposition, that we seem as it were to be designedly striving to close up the door against Thy goodness and paternal favor, O grant, that our hearts may be so softened by Thy Spirit, and the hardness which has hitherto prevailed may be so corrected, that we may submit ourselves to Thee with genuine docility, especially as Thou dost so kindly and tenderly invite us to Thyself, that being allured by Thy sweet invitation, we may run, and so run as not to be weary in our course, until Christ shall at length bring us together to Thee, and, at the same time, lead us to Thee for that eternal life, which He has obtained for us by His own blood. Amen.

Grant, Almighty God, that as we are in this life subject to so many miseries, and in the meantime grow insensible in our sins, - O grant that we may learn to search ourselves and consider one sins, that we may be really humbled before Thee, and ascribe to ourselves the blame of all our evils, that we may be thus led to a genuine feeling of repentance, and so strive to be reconciled to Thee in Christ, that we may wholly depend on Thy paternal love, and thus ever aspire to the fulness of eternal felicity, through Thy goodness and that immeasurable kindness which Thou testifies is ready and offered to all those, who with a sincere heart worship Thee, call upon Thee, and flee to Thee, through Christ our Lord. Amen.

Grant, Almighty God, that as Thou often dost justly hide thy face from us, so that on every side we see nothing but evidences of thy dreadful judgment, - O grant, that we, with minds raised above the scene of this world, may at the same time cherish the hope which Thou constantly settest before us, so that we may feel fully persuaded that we are loved by Thee, however severely Thou mayest chastise us and may this consolation so support and sustain our souls, that patiently enduring whatever chastisements Thou mayest lay upon us, we may ever hold fast the reconciliation which Thou hast promised to us in Christ thy Son. Amen.

Grant, Almighty God, that as Thou dost train us up with so much diligence and assiduous care, and regard us as dear and precious like an hereditary vine, - O grant, that we may not bring forth wild grapes, and that our fruit may not be bitter and unpleasant to Thee, but that we may strive so to form our whole life in obedience to Thy law, that all our actions and thoughts may be pleasant and sweet fruits to Thee. And as there is ever some sin mixed up with our works, even when we desire to serve Thee sincerely and from the heart, grant that all stains in our works may be so cleansed and washed away by the sacrifice of thy Son, that they may be to Thee sacrifices of sweet odor, through the same, even Christ Jesus, Who has so reconciled us to Thee, as to obtain pardon even for our works. Amen.

Grant, Almighty God, that as Thou hast once appeared in the person of thy only-begotten Son, and hast rendered in Him Thy glory visible to us, and as Thou dost daily set forth to us the same Christ in the glass of Thy gospel, - O grant, that we, fixing our eyes on Him, may not go astray, nor be led here and there after wicked inventions, the fallacies of Satan, and the allurements of this world: but may we continue firm in the obedience of faith and persevere in it through the whole course of our life, until we be at length fully transformed into the image of Thy eternal glory, which now in part shines in us, through the same Christ our Lord. Amen.

Grant, Almighty God, that as we remain yet in our own wickedness, though often warned and sweetly invited by Thee, and as Thou prevailest not with us by thy daily instruction, -

O grant, that we may, in a spirit of meekness, at length turn to Thy service, and fight against the hardness and obstinacy of our flesh, till we render ourselves submissive to Thee, and not wait until Thou puttest forth thy hand against us, or at least so profit under thy chastisements, as not to constrain Thee to execute extreme vengeance against us, but to repent without delay; and that we may indeed, without hypocrisy, plough under Thy yoke, and so enjoy Thy special blessings, that Thou mayest show Thyself to us not only as our Lord, but also as our Father, full of mercy and kindness, through Christ our Lord. Amen.

Grant, Almighty God, that as Thou hast deigned to choose us before the foundations of the world were laid, and included us in Thy free adoption when we were the children of wrath and doomed to utter ruin, and afterwards embraced us even from the womb, and hast at length favored us with a clearer proof of Thy love, in calling us by Thy gospel into a union and communion with Thy only-begotten Son, - O grant, that we may not be unmindful of so many and so singular benefits, but respond to Thy holy calling, and labor to devote ourselves wholly to Thee, and labor, not for one day, but for the whole time designed for us here, both to live and to die according to Thy good pleasure, so that we may glorify Thee to the end, through our Lord Jesus Christ. Amen.

Grant, Almighty God, that since we are too secure and torpid in our sins, thy dread majesty may come to our minds, to humble us, and to remove our fear, that we may learn anxiously to seek reconciliation through Christ, and so abhor ourselves for our sins, that Thou mayest then be prepared to receive us:

and that unbelief may not shut the door against us, enable us to regard Thee to be such as Thou hast revealed thyself, and to acknowledge that Thou art not like us, but the fountain of all mercy, that we may thus be led to entertain a firm hope of salvation, and that, relying on the Mediator, Thy only-begotten Son, we may know Him as the throne of grace, full of compassion and mercy. O grant, that we may thus come to Thee, that through Him we may certainly know that Thou art our Father, so that the covenant Thou hast made with us may never fail through our fault, even this, that we are Thy people, because Thou hast once adopted us in Thy only-begotten Son, our Lord Jesus Christ. Amen.

Grant, Almighty God, that inasmuch as Thou slowest Thyself to us at this day so kindly as a Father, having presented to us a singular and an invaluable pledge of Thy favor in Thy only begotten Son, - O grant, that we may entirely devote ourselves to Thee, and truly render Thee that free service and obedience which is due to a Father, so that we may have no other object in life but to confirm that adoption, with which Thou hast once favoured us, until we at length, being gathered into Thy eternal kingdom, shall partake of its fruit, together with Christ Jesus thy Son. Amen.

Grant, Almighty God, that as Thou appearest not now to us in shadows and types, as formerly to the holy fathers, but clearly and plainly in Thy only-begotten Son, - O grant, that we may be wholly given to the contemplation of Thine image, which thus shines before us; and that we may in such a manner be transformed into it, as to make increasing advances, until at length, having put off all the filth of our flesh, we be fully conformed to that pure and perfect holiness which dwells in Christ, as in him dwells the fulness of all blessings and thus obtain at last a participation of that glory which our Lord has procured for us by his resurrection. Amen.

Grant, Almighty God, that as we have not only been created by Thee, but when Thou hast placed us in this world, Thou hast also enriched us with abundance of all blessings, - O grant, that we may not transfer to others the glory duo to Thee, and that especially since we are daily admonished by Thy word, and even severely reproved, we may not with an iron hardness resist, but render ourselves pliable to Thee, and not give ourselves up to our own devices, but follow with true docility and meekness, that rule which Thou hast prescribed in thy word, until at length having put off all the remains of errors, we shall enjoy that blessed light, which Thou hast prepared for us in heaven, through Jesus Christ our Lord. Amen.

Grant, Almighty God, that as Thou dost so kindly call on us daily by Thy voice, meekly and calmly to offer ourselves to be ruled by Thee, and since Thou hast exalted us to a high degree of honor by freeing us from the dread of the devil, and from that tyranny which kept us in miserable fear, and hast also favored us with the Spirit of adoption and of hope, - O grant, that we, being mindful of these benefits, may ever submit ourselves to Thee, and desire only to raise our voice for this end, that the whole world may submit itself to Thee, and that those who seem now to rage against Thee may at length be brought, as well as we, to render Thee obedience, so that Thy Son Christ may be the Lord of all, to the end that Thou alone mayest be exalted, and that we may be made subject to Thee, and be at length raised up above, and become partakers of that glory which has been obtained for us by Christ our Lord. Amen.

Grant, Almighty God, that as Thou hast given us Thy only begotten Son to rule us, and hast by Thy good pleasure consecrated him a King over us, that we may be perpetually safe and secure under his hand against all the attempts of the devil and of the whole world, - O grant, that we may suffer ourselves to be ruled by his authority, and so conduct ourselves, that he may ever continue to watch for our safety: and as Thou hast committed us to him, that he may be the guardian of our salvation, so also suffer us not either to turn aside or to fall, but preserve us ever in his service, until we be at length gathered into that blessed and everlasting kingdom, which has been procured for us by the blood of Thy only Son. Amen.

Grant, Almighty God, that as we now carry about us this mortal body, yea, and nourish through sin a Thousand deaths within us, - O grant, that we may ever by faith direct our eyes towards heaven, and to that incomprehensible power, which is to be manifested at the last day by Jesus Christ our Lord, so that in the midst of death we may hope that twilt be our Redeemer, and enjoy that redemption, which He completed when He rose from the dead; and not doubt but that the fruit which he then brought forth by His Spirit will come also to us, when Christ himself shall come to judge the world; and may we thus walk in the fear of Thy name, that we may be really gathered among His members, to be made partakers of that glory, which by His death He has procured for us. Amen.

Grant, Almighty God, that as we are so miserable as soon as Thou withdrawest Thy favor from us, - O grant, that we may deeply feel this conviction, and thus learn to be humble before Thee, and to hate our own selves, and that we may not in the mean lime deceive ourselves by such allurements as commonly prevail, to put our hope in creatures or in this world, but raise our minds upwards to Thee, and fix on Thee our hearts, and never doubt, but that when Thou embraces us with Thy paternal love, nothing shall be wanting to us. And in the meantime, may we suppliantly flee to Thy mercy, and with true and genuine confession, acknowledge this to be our only protection – that Thou deign to receive us into favor, and to abolish our sins, into which we not only daily fall, but by which we also deserve eternal death, so that we may daily rise through Thy free pardon, till at length our Redeemer Christ Thy Son shall appear to us from heaven. Amen.

Catherine of Genoa *(1447 – 15 September 1510) Caterina Fieschi Adorno was of the noble Fieschi family. She spent much of her life and money helping the sick, especially during the plague in Genoa in 1497 and 1501. She published her biography and thoughts in her work, <u>Life and Doctrine of Saint Catherine of Genoa.</u> Catherine was married in a political union to bring two feuding families together. The first ten years of the marriage were unhappy until her husband came to Christ. They lived in the hospital and served the sick together until her death in 1510.*

How this devout soul, praising and thanking GOD, made a prayer for the Holy Church. Then this soul, as if inebriated, tormented, and on fire with love, her heart wounded with great bitterness, turned herself to the Supreme and Eternal Goodness, saying: "Oh! Eternal God! oh! Light above every other light, from whom issues all light! Oh! Fire above every fire, because You are the only Fire who burn without consuming, and consume all sin and self-love found in the soul, not afflicting her, but fattening her with insatiable love, and though the soul is filled she is not sated, but ever desires You, and the more of You she has, the more she seeks - and the more she desires, the more she finds and tastes of You - Supreme and Eternal Fire, Abyss of Charity.

Oh! Supreme and Eternal Good, who has moved You, Infinite God, to illuminate me, Your finite creature, with the light of Your Truth? You, the same Fire of Love are the cause, because it is always love which constrained and constrains You to create us in Your image and similitude, and to do us mercy, giving immeasurable and infinite graces to Your rational creatures.

Oh! Goodness above all goodness! You alone are He who is Supremely Good, and nevertheless You gave the Word, Your only-begotten Son, to converse with us filthy ones and filled with darkness. What was the cause of this? Love. Because You loved us before we were. Oh! Good! oh! Eternal Greatness! You made Yourself low and small to make man great.

On whichever side I turn I find nothing but the abyss and fire of Your charity. And can a wretch like me pay back to You the graces and the burning charity that You have shown and show with so much burning love in particular to me beyond common charity, and the love that You show to all Your creatures? No, but You alone, most sweet and amorous Father, are He who will be thankful and grateful for me, that is, that the affection of Your charity itself will render You thanks, because I am she who is not, and if I spoke as being anything of myself, I should be lying by my own head, and should be a lying daughter of the Devil, who is the father of lies, because You alone are He who is. And my being and every further grace that You have bestowed upon me, I have from You, who give them to me through love, and not as my due.

"Oh! sweetest Father, when the human race lay sick through the sin of Adam, You sent it a Physician, the sweet and amorous Word - Your Son; and now, when I was lying infirm with the sickness of negligence and much ignorance, You, most soothing and sweet Physician, Eternal God, have given a soothing, sweet, and bitter medicine, that I may be cured and rise from my infirmity.

You have soothed me because with Your love and gentleness You have manifested Yourself to me, Sweet above all sweetness, and have illuminated the eye of my intellect with the light of most holy faith, with which light, according as it has pleased You to manifest it to me, I have known the excellence of grace which You have given to the human race, administering to it the entire God- Man in the mystic body of the holy Church. And I have known the dignity of Your ministers whom You have appointed to administer You to us. I desired that You would fulfill the promise that You made to me, and You gave much more, more even than I knew how to ask for. Wherefore I know in truth that the heart of man knows not how to ask or desire as much as You can give, and thus I see that You are He who is the Supreme and Eternal Good, and that we are they who are not.

And because You are infinite, and we are finite, You give that which Your rational creature cannot desire enough; for she cannot desire it in itself, nor in the way in which You can and will satisfy the soul, filling her with things for which she does not ask You. Moreover, I have received light from Your Greatness and Charity, through the love which You have for the whole human race, and in particular for Your anointed ones, who ought to be earthly angels in this life. You have shown me the virtue and beatitude of these Your anointed ones who have lived like burning lamps, shining with the Pearl of Justice in the holy Church. And by comparison with these I have better understood the sins of those who live wretchedly.

Wherefore I have conceived a very great sorrow at Your offense and the harm done to the whole world, for they do harm to the world, being mirrors of sin when they ought to be mirrors of virtue. And because You have manifested and grieved over their iniquities to me - a wretch who am the cause and instrument of many sins - I am plunged in intolerable grief.

"You, oh! Inestimable love, have manifested this to me, giving me a sweet and bitter medicine that I might wholly arise out of the infirmity of my ignorance and negligence, and have recourse to You with anxious and solicitous desire, knowing myself and Your goodness and the offenses which are committed against You by all sorts of people, so that I might shed a river of tears, drawn from the knowledge of Your infinite goodness, over my wretched self and over those who are dead in that they live miserably. Wherefore I do not wish, oh! Eternal Father, ineffable Fire of Love, that my heart should ever grow weary, or my eyes fail through tears, in desiring Your honor and the salvation of souls, but I beg of You, by Your grace, that they may be as two streams of water issuing from You, the Sea Pacific.

Thanks, thanks to You, oh! Father, for having granted me that which I asked You and that which I neither knew nor asked, for by thus giving me matter for grief You have invited me to offer before You sweet, loving, and yearning desires, with humble and continual prayer. Now I beg of You that You will do mercy to the world and to the holy Church. I pray You to fulfill that which You caused me to ask You.

Alas! what a wretched and sorrowful soul is mine, the cause of all these evils. Do not put off any longer Your merciful designs towards the world, but descend and fulfill the desire of Your servants."Ah me! You cause them to cry in order to hear their voices! Your truth told us to cry out, and we should be answered; to knock, and it would be opened to us; to beg, and it would be given to us. Oh! Eternal Father, Your servants do cry out to Your mercy; do You then reply. I know well that mercy is Your own attribute, wherefore You cannot destroy it or refuse it to him who asks for it. Your servants knock at the door of Your truth, because in the truth of Your only-begotten Son they know the ineffable love which You have for man, wherefore the fire of Your love ought not and cannot refrain from opening to him who knocks with perseverance. Wherefore open, unlock, and break the hardened hearts of Your creatures, not for their sakes who do not knock, but on account of Your infinite goodness, and through love of Your servants who knock at You for their sakes. Grant the prayer of those, Eternal Father who, as You see, stand at the door of Your truth and pray. For what do they pray? For with the Blood of this door - Your truth have You washed our iniquities and destroyed the stain of Adam's sin. The Blood is ours, for You have made it our bath, wherefore You cannot deny it to anyone who truly asks for it. Give, then, the fruit of Your Blood to Your creatures. Place in the balance the price of the blood of Your Son, so that the infernal devils may not carry off Your lambs.

You are the Good Shepherd who, to fulfill Your obedience, laid down His life for Your lambs, and made for us a bath of His Blood. "That Blood is what Your hungry servants beg of You at this door, begging You through it to do mercy to the world, and to cause Your holy Church to bloom with the fragrant flowers of good and holy pastors, who by their sweet odor shall extinguish the stench of the putrid flowers of sin.

You have said, Eternal Father, that through the love which You have for Your rational creatures, and the prayers and the many virtues and labors of Your servants, You would do mercy to the world, and reform the Church, and thus give us refreshment; wherefore do not delay, but turn the eye of Your mercy towards us, for You must first reply to us before we can cry out with the voice of Your mercy. Open the door of Your inestimable love which You have given us through the door of Your Word. I know indeed that You open before even we can knock, for it is with the affection of love which You have given to Your servants, that they knock and cry to You, seeking Your honor and the salvation of souls. Give them then the bread of life, that is to say, the fruit of the Blood of Your only-begotten Son, which they ask of You for the praise and glory of My name and the salvation of souls. For more glory and praise will be Yours in saving so many creatures, than in leaving them obstinate in their hardness of heart.

To You, Eternal Father, everything is possible, and even though You have created us without our own help, You will not save us without it. I beg of You to force their wills, and dispose them to wish for that for which they do not wish; and this I ask You through Your infinite mercy. You have created us from nothing; now, therefore, that we are in existence, do mercy to us, and remake the vessels which You have created to Your image and likeness. Re-create them to Grace in Your mercy and the Blood of Your Son sweet Christ Jesus." Amen

CATHERINE OF SIENA *(March 25, 1347 – April 29, 1380) Caterina di Giacomo di Benincasa was unmarried, but not a nun in the strictest sense. She continued to live unmarried in her family home. Caterina frequently fasted and abstained from water. This probably led to her early death. She was very active in writing letters and advocating reform of the clergy and advising people that repentance and renewal could be done through "the total love for God. She left home and traveled extensively. Caterina wrote* <u>The Dialogue of Divine Providence.</u>

Lord, take me from myself and give me to yourself. – Amen.

O Supreme Physician! O unspeakable Love of my soul! I have recourse to Thee. O infinite and eternal Trinity, I, though unworthy, ardently sigh for Thee! I turn to Thee in the mystical body of Thy holy Church, so that Thou mayest wash away with Thy grace all stains of my soul. I beseech Thee through the merits of St. Peter, to whom Thou hast committed the care of Thy Bark, to delay no longer to help Thy Spouse, who hopes in the fire of Thy charity and in the abyss of Thy admirable wisdom. Despise not the desires of Thy servants, but do Thou Thyself guide Thy holy Bark. O Thou, the Author of peace, draw unto Thyself all the faithful; dispel the darkness of the storm, so that the dawn of Thy light may shine upon the Head of Thy Church, and pour down upon him zeal for the salvation of souls. O eternal and merciful Father, Thou hast given us the means of restraining the arms of Thy justice in the humble prayer and ardent desires of Thy devoted servants, whom Thou hast promised to hear when they ask Thee to have mercy upon the world.

O powerful and eternal God, I thank Thee for the peace which Thou wilt grant to Thy Spouse! I will enter into Thy gardens, and there I will remain until I see the fulfilment of Thy promises, which never fail. Wash away our sins, O Lord, and purify our souls in the blood which Thy only-begotten Son shed for us, so that with joyful countenances and pure hearts we may return love for love, and, dying to ourselves, live for Him alone. Amen.

In Your nature, eternal Godhead,
I shall come to know my nature.
And what is my nature, boundless love?

It is fire, because You are nothing but a fire of love. And You have given humankind a share in this nature, for by the fire of love You created us. And so with all other people and every created thing; You made them out of love. O ungrateful people! What nature has your God given you? His very own nature!

Are you not ashamed to cut yourself off from such a noble thing through the guilt of deadly sin? O eternal Trinity, my sweet love! You, light, give us light. You, wisdom, give us wisdom. You, supreme strength, strengthen us. Today, eternal God, let our cloud be dissipated so that we may perfectly know and follow Your Truth in truth, with a free and simple heart. God, come to our assistance! Lord, make haste to help us! Amen.

Holy Spirit, come into my heart; draw it to Thee by Thy power, O my God, and grant me charity with filial fear. Preserve me, O ineffable Love, from every evil thought; warm me, inflame me with Thy dear love, and every pain will seem light to me. My Father, my sweet Lord, help me in all my actions. Jesus, love, Jesus, love. Amen.

Precious Blood, Ocean of Divine Mercy: Flow upon us! Precious Blood, Most pure Offering: Procure us every Grace! Precious Blood, Hope and Refuge of sinners: Atone for us! Precious Blood, Delight of holy souls: Draw us! Amen.

I see that you have endowed your Vicar by nature with a fearless heart; so I humbly, imploringly beg you to pour the light beyond nature into the eye of his understanding. For unless this light, acquired through pure affection for virtue, is joined with it, a heart such as his tends to be proud. Today again let every selfish love be cut away from those enemies of Yours and from the Vicar and from us all, so that we may be able to forgive those enemies when You bend their hardness. For them, that they may humble themselves and obey this Lord of ours, I offer you my life from this moment and for whenever you wish me to lay it down for your glory. Amen

Clement of Alexandria *.(c. 150 – c. 215AD) Titus Flavius Clemens known as Clement of Alexandria to distinguish him from the earlier Clement of Rome, was a classically trained Christian theologian who taught at Alexandria. He defined prayer as "keeping company with God." Three of Clement's major works have survived in full, and they are collectively referred to as the trilogy; the Protrepticus (Exhortation) – written c. 195, the Paedagogus (Tutor) – written c. 198, the Stromata (Miscellanies) – written c. 198 – c. 203*

O Lord, who hast mercy upon all, take away from me my sins, and mercifully kindle in me the fire of thy Holy Spirit. Take away from me the heart of stone, and give me a heart of flesh, a heart to love and adore Thee, a heart to delight in Thee, to follow and to enjoy Thee, for Christ's sake. The radiance of the Father's splendor, the Father's visible image, Jesus Christ our God, peerless among counselors, Prince of Peace, Father of the world to come, the model after which Adam was formed, for our sakes became like a slave: in the womb of Mary the virgin, without assistance from any man, he took flesh....Enable us, Lord, to reach the end of this luminous feast in peace,

forsaking all idle words, acting virtuously, shunning our passions, and raising ourselves above the things of this world. Bless your church, which you brought into being long ago and attached to yourself through your own life-giving blood. Help all orthodox pastors, heads of churches, and doctors [theologians].Bless your servants, whose trust is all in you; bless all Christian souls, the sick, those tormented by evil spirits, and those who have asked us to pray for them. Show yourself as merciful as you are rich in grace; save and preserve us; enable us to obtain those good things to come which will never know an end. May we celebrate your glorious birth, and the Father who sent you to redeem us, and your Spirit, the Giver of life, now and forever, age after age. Amen.

You, Lord, through your works have revealed the everlasting structure of the world. You, Lord, created the earth. You are faithful throughout all generations, righteous in your judgments, marvelous in strength and majesty, wise in creating and prudent in establishing what exists, good in all that is observed and faithful to those who trust in you, merciful and compassionate; forgive us our sins and our injustices, our transgressions and our shortcomings. Do not take into account every sin of your servants, but cleanse us with the cleansing of your truth, and "direct our steps to walk in holiness and righteousness and purity of heart," and "to do what is good and pleasing in your sight" and in the sight of our rulers. Yes, Lord, "let your face shine upon us" in peace "for our good," that we may be sheltered "by your mighty hand" and delivered from every sin "by your uplifted arm"; deliver us as well from those who hate us unjustly. Give harmony and peace to us and to all who dwell on the earth, just as you did to our fathers when they reverently "called upon you in faith and trust," that we may be saved, while we render obedience to your almighty and most excellent name, and give harmony and peace to our rulers and governors on earth.

As I rise from sleep I thank Thee, O Holy Trinity, for through Thy great goodness and patience Thou wast not angered with me, an idler and sinner, nor hast Thou destroyed me in my sins, but hast shown Thy usual love for men, and when I was prostrate in despair, Thou hast raised me to keep the morning watch and glorify Thy power. And now enlighten my mind's eye and open my mouth to study Thy words and understand Thy commandments and do Thy will and sing to Thee in heartfelt adoration and praise Thy Most Holy Name of Father, Son and Holy Spirit, now and ever, and to the ages of ages. Amen.

Columba, *(c. December 7, 521 – 597 AD) Columba was an Irish born abbot who became a missionary to Scotland. He was of noble birth. He was a scholar and diplomat often called upon to resolve Clan conflicts in Scotland. He is credited with translation and authorship of over 300 books. He founded numerous churches and monasteries in Scotland and Ireland. It is recorded that he slept on a stone for a pillow.*

Lord, thou hast given us thy Word for a light to shine upon our path; Grant us so to meditate on that Word, and to follow its teaching, That we may find in it the light that shines more and more until the Perfect day; through Jesus Christ our Lord.

John Chrysostom *(c. 349 – 407AD) Born in Antioch, raised by his widowed mother, he was educated by a pagan teacher. He spent the earliest days of his ministry as an ascetic hermit. It damaged his health for the rest of his life. During a local rebellion against the*

Roman emperor he preached to the town and encouraged the crowds to see that God is sovereign. He rose quickly in the church because of his outspoken preaching. In his sermons, he denounced abortion, prostitution, gluttony, the theater, and swearing. It was this which drove him into exile that led to his sickness and death.

Lord, deprive me not of Thy heavenly joys. Lord, deliver me from eternal torments. Lord, if I have sinned in mind or thought, in word or deed, forgive me. Lord, deliver me from all ignorance, forgetfulness, cowardice and stony insensibility. Lord, deliver me from every temptation. Lord, enlighten my heart which evil desires have darkened. Lord, I being human have sinned, but Thou being the generous God, have mercy on me, knowing the sickness of my soul. Lord, send Thy grace to my help, that I may glorify Thy holy Name.

Lord Jesus Christ, write me Thy servant in the Book of Life, and grant me a good end. O Lord my God, even though I have done nothing good in Thy sight, yet grant me by Thy grace to make a good start. Lord, sprinkle into my heart the dew of Thy grace. Lord of heaven and earth remember me, Thy sinful servant, shameful and unclean, in Thy Kingdom. Amen.

O Lord, accept me in penitence. O Lord, leave me not. O Lord, lead me not into temptation. O Lord, grant me good thoughts. O Lord, grant me tears and remembrance of death and compunction. O Lord, grant me the thought of confessing my sins. O Lord, grant me humility, chastity and obedience. O Lord, grant me patience, courage and meekness. O Lord, plant in me the root of all blessings, the fear of Thee in my heart. O Lord, grant me to love Thee with all my mind and soul, and always to do Thy will. O Lord, protect me from certain people, and demons, and passions, and from every other harmful thing. O Lord, Thou knowest that Thou actest as Thou wilt; may Thy will be also in me, a sinner, for blessed art Thou forever. Amen.

JOHN DONNE *(22 January 1572 – 31 March 1631) Dean of St. Paul's Cathedral, London Royal Chaplain to James I. He comes from a long line of recusants. His early life was wanton and he is known as one of the metaphysical poets. He married, became an Anglican and gave himself to serving God. He was a member of Parliament. He became vicar of St Dunstan-in-the-West and later Dean of St. Paul's. He was known for his preaching and writings.*

Bring us, O Lord God, at our last awakening into the house and gate of heaven to enter into that gate and dwell in that house, where there shall be no darkness nor dazzling, but one equal light; no noise nor silence, but one equal music; no fears nor hopes, but one equal possession; no ends nor beginnings, but one equal eternity; in the habitations of thy glory and dominion, world without end.

FROM DEVOTIONS UPON EMERGENT OCCASIONS *Dr. Donne believed he was dying. No physician could diagnose his illness and in what he believed were the last days of his life, John Donne wrote these prayers each day to focus his mind on God.*

Prayer I

O eternal and most gracious God, who, considered in Thyself, art a circle, first and last, and altogether; but, considered in thy working upon us, art a direct line, and leadest us from our beginning, through all our ways, to our end, enable me by thy grace to look forward to mine end, and to look backward too, to the considerations of thy mercies afforded me from the beginning; that so by that practice of considering thy mercy, in my beginning in this world, when thou plantedst me in the Christian church, and thy mercy in the beginning in the other world, when thou writest me in the book of life, in my election, I may come to a holy consideration of thy mercy in the beginning of all my actions here: that in all the beginnings, in all the accesses and approaches, of spiritual sicknesses of sin, I may hear and hearken to that voice, O thou man of God, there is death in the pot, and so refrain from that which I was so hungrily, so greedily flying to.

A faithful ambassador is health, says thy wise servant Solomon. Thy voice received in the beginning of a sickness, of a sin, is true health. If I can see that light betimes, and hear that voice early, then shall my light break forth as the morning, and my health shall spring forth speedily.

Deliver me therefore, O my God, from these vain imaginations; that it is an over-curious thing, a dangerous thing, to come to that tenderness, that rawness, that scrupulousness, to fear every concupiscence, every offer of sin, that this suspicious and jealous diligence will turn to an inordinate dejection of spirit, and a diffidence in thy care and providence; but keep me still established, both in a constant assurance, that thou wilt speak to me at the beginning of every such sickness, at the approach of every such sin; and that, if I take knowledge of that voice then, and fly to Thee, thou wilt preserve me from falling, or raise me again, when by natural infirmity I am fallen. Do this, O Lord, for his sake, who knows our natural infirmities, for he had them, and knows the weight of our sins, for he paid a dear price for them, thy Son, our Saviour, Christ Jesus. Amen.

Prayer II

O most gracious God, who pursuest and perfectest thine own purposes, and dost not only remember me, by the first accesses of this sickness, that I must die, but inform me, by this further proceeding therein, that I may die now; who hast not only waked me with the first, but called me up, by casting me further down, and clothed me with Thyself, by stripping me of my self, and by dulling my bodily senses to the meats and eases of this world, hast whet and sharpened my spiritual senses to the apprehension of Thee; by what steps and degrees soever it shall please Thee to go, in the dissolution of this body, hasten, O Lord, that pace, and multiply, O my God, those degrees, in the exaltation of my soul toward Thee now, and to Thee then.

My taste is not gone away, but gone up to sit at David's table, to taste, and see, that the Lord is good. My stomach is not gone, but gone up, so far upwards toward the supper of the Lamb, with thy saints in heaven, as to the table, to the communion of thy saints here in earth. My knees are weak, but weak therefore that I should easily fall to and fix myself long upon my devotions to Thee. A sound heart is the life of the flesh; and a heart visited by Thee, and directed to Thee, by that visitation is a sound heart. There is no soundness in my flesh, because of thine anger.

Interpret thine own work, and call this sickness correction, and not anger, and there is soundness in my flesh. There is no rest in my bones, because of my sin; transfer my sins, with which thou art so displeased, upon him with whom thou art so well pleased, Christ Jesus, and there will be rest in my bones.

And, O my God, who madest Thyself a light in a bush, in the midst of these brambles and thorns of a sharp sickness, appear unto me so that I may see Thee, and know Thee to be my God, applying Thyself to me, even in these sharp and thorny passages. Do this, O Lord, for his sake, who was not the less the King of heaven for thy suffering him to be crowned with thorns in this world.

Prayer III

O most mighty and most merciful God, who, though thou have taken me off of my feet, hast not taken me off of my foundation, which is Thyself; who, though thou have removed me from that upright form in which I could stand and see Thy throne, the heavens, yet hast not removed from me that light by which I can lie and see Thyself; who, though thou have weakened my bodily knees, that they cannot bow to Thee, hast yet left me the knees of my heart; which are bowed unto Thee evermore; as thou hast made this bed thine altar, make me thy sacrifice; and as thou makest thy Son Christ Jesus the priest, so make me his deacon, to minister to him in a cheerful surrender of my body and soul to thy pleasure, by his hands.

I come unto Thee, O God, my God, I come unto Thee, so as I can come, I come to Thee, by embracing thy coming to me, I come in the confidence, and in the application of thy servant David's promise, that thou wilt make all my bed in my sickness; all my bed; that which way soever I turn, I may turn to Thee; and as I feel thy hand upon all my body, so I may find it upon all my bed, and see all my corrections, and all my refreshings to flow from one and the same, and all from thy hand.

As thou hast made these feathers thorns, in the sharpness of this sickness, so, Lord, make these thorns feathers again, feathers of thy dove, in the peace of conscience, and in a holy recourse to thine ark, to the instruments of true comfort, in thy institutions and in the ordinances of thy church.

Forget my bed, O Lord, as it hath been a bed of sloth, and worse than sloth; take me not, O Lord, at this advantage, to terrify my soul with saying, Now I have met Thee there where thou hast so often departed from Me; but having burnt up that bed by these vehement heats, and washed that bed in these abundant sweats, make my bed again, O Lord, and enable me, according to thy command, to commune with mine own heart upon my bed, and be still; to provide a bed for all my former sins whilst I lie upon this bed, and a grave for my sins before I come to my grave; and when I have deposited them in the wounds of thy Son, to rest in that assurance, that my conscience is discharged from further anxiety, and my soul from further danger, and my memory from further calumny. Do this, O Lord, for his sake, who did and suffered so much, that thou mightest, as well in thy justice as in thy mercy, do it for me, thy Son, our Saviour, Christ Jesus.

Prayer IV

O most mighty and most merciful God, who art so the God of health and strength, as that without Thee all health is but the fuel, and all strength but the bellows of sin; behold me under the vehemence of two diseases, and under the necessity of two physicians, authorized by Thee, the bodily, and the spiritual physician.

I come to both as to Thine ordinance, and bless and glorify thy name that, in both cases, thou hast afforded help to man by the ministry of man. Even in the new Jerusalem, in heaven itself, it hath pleased Thee to discover a tree, which is a tree of life there, but the leaves thereof are for the healing of the nations. Life itself is with Thee there, for thou art life; and all kinds of health, wrought upon us here by thine instruments, descend from thence.

Thou wouldst have healed Babylon, but she is not healed. Take from me, O Lord, her perverseness, her willfulness, her refractoriness, and hear thy Spirit saying in my soul: Heal me, O Lord, for I would be healed. Ephraim saw his sickness, and Judah his wound; then went Ephraim to the Assyrian, and sent to King Jareb, yet could not he heal you, nor cure you of your wound. Keep me back, O Lord, from them who misprofess arts of healing the soul, or of the body, by means not imprinted by Thee in the church for the soul, or not in nature for the body. There is no spiritual health to be had by superstition, nor bodily by witchcraft; Thou, Lord, and only Thou, art Lord of both. Thou in Thyself art Lord of both, and Thou in thy Son art the physician, the applier of both. With his stripes we are healed, says the prophet there; there, before he was scourged, we were healed with his stripes;

how much more shall I be healed now, now when that which he hath already suffered actually is actually and effectually applied to me? Is there anything incurable, upon which that balm drops?

Any vein so empty as that that blood cannot fill it? Thou promisest to heal the earth; but it is when the inhabitants of the earth pray that Thou wouldst heal it. Thou promisest to heal their waters, but their miry places and standing waters, Thou sayest there, Thou wilt not heal. My returning to any sin, if I should return to the ability of sinning over all my sins again, Thou wouldst not pardon. Heal this earth, O my God, by repentant tears, and heal these waters, these tears, from all bitterness, from all diffidence, from all dejection, by establishing my irremovable assurance in Thee. Thy Son went about healing all manner of sickness. (No disease incurable, none difficult; he healed them in passing). Virtue went out of him, and he healed all, all the multitude (no person incurable), he healed them every whit (as himself speaks), he left no relics of the disease; and will this universal physician pass by this hospital, and not visit me? not heal me? not heal me wholly? Lord, I look not that Thou shouldst say by thy messenger to me, as to Hezekiah, "Behold, I will heal Thee, and on the third day Thou shalt go up to the house of the Lord." I look not that Thou shouldst say to me, as to Moses in Miriam's behalf, when Moses would have had her healed presently, If her father had but spit in her face, should she not have been ashamed seven days? Let her be shut up seven days, and then return; but if Thou be pleased to multiply seven days (and seven is infinite) by the number of my sins (and that is more infinite), if this day must remove me till days shall be no more, seal to me my spiritual health, in affording me the seals of thy church; and for my temporal health,

prosper thine ordinance, in their hands who shall assist in this sickness, in that manner, and in that measure, as may most glorify Thee, and most edify those who observe the issues of thy servants, to their own spiritual benefit.

Prayer V

O eternal and most gracious God, who calledst down fire from heaven upon the sinful cities but once, and openedst the earth to swallow the murmurers but once, and threwest down the tower of Siloam upon sinners but once; but for thy works of mercy repeatedst them often, and still workest by thine own patterns, as Thou broughtest man into this world, by giving him a helper fit for him here; so, whether it be thy will to continue me long thus, or to dismiss me by death, be pleased to afford me the helps fit for both conditions, either for my weak stay here, or my final transmigration from hence.

And if Thou mayest receive glory by that way (and by all ways Thou mayest receive glory), glorify Thyself in preserving this body from such infections as might withhold those who would come, or endanger them who do come; and preserve this soul in the faculties thereof from all such distempers as might shake the assurance which myself and others have had, that because Thou hast loved me Thou wouldst love me to my end, and at my end. Open none of my doors, not of my heart, not of mine ears, not of my house, to any supplanter that would enter to undermine me in my religion to Thee, in the time of my weakness, or to defame me, and magnify himself with false rumors of such a victory and surprisal of me, after I am dead. Be my salvation, and plead my salvation; work it and declare it; and as thy triumphant shall be, so let the militant church be assured that Thou wast my God, and I thy servant, to and in my consummation.

Bless Thou the learning and the labors of this man whom Thou sendest to assist me; and since Thou takest me by the hand, and puttest me into his hands (for I come to him in Thy name, who in Thy name comes to me), since I clog not my hopes in him, no, nor my prayers to Thee, with any limited conditions, but inwrap all in those two petitions, Thy kingdom come, Thy will be done, prosper him, and relieve me, in thy way, in Thy time, and in Thy measure. Amen

Prayer VI

O most mighty God, and merciful God, the God of all true sorrow, and true joy too, of all fear, and of all hope too, as Thou hast given me a repentance, not to be repented of, so give me, O Lord, a fear, of which I may not be afraid.

Give me tender and supple and conformable affections that as I joy with them that joy, and mourn with them that mourn, so I may fear with them that fear. And since Thou hast vouchsafed to discover to me, in his fear whom Thou hast admitted to be my assistance in this sickness, that there is danger therein, let me not, O Lord, go about to overcome the sense of that fear, so far as to pretermit the fitting and preparing of myself for the worst that may be feared, the passage out of this life. Many of Thy blessed martyrs have passed out of this life without any show of fear; but Thy most blessed Son himself did not so. Thy martyrs were known to be but men, and therefore it pleased Thee to fill them with Thy Spirit and Thy power, in that they did more than men; Thy Son was declared by Thee,

and by himself, to be God; and it was requisite that He should declare Himself to be man also, in the weaknesses of man. Let me not therefore, O my God, be ashamed of these fears, but let me feel them to determine where His fear did, in a present submitting of all to Thy will.

And when Thou shalt have inflamed and thawed my former coldnesses and in devotions with these heats, and quenched my former heats with these sweats and inundations, and rectified my former presumptions and negligences with these fears, be pleased, O Lord, as one made so by Thee, to think me fit for Thee; and whether it be Thy pleasure to dispose of this body, this garment, so as to put it to a farther wearing in this world, or to lay it up in the common wardrobe, the grave, for the next, glorify Thyself in thy choice now, and glorify it then, with that glory, which thy Son, our Saviour Christ Jesus, hath purchased for them whom Thou makest partakers of His resurrection. Amen.

PRAYER VII.

O eternal and most gracious God, who gavest to thy servants in the wilderness Thy manna, bread so conditioned, qualified so, as that to every man manna tasted like that which that man liked best, I humbly beseech Thee to make this correction, which I acknowledge to be part of my daily bread, to taste so to me, not as I would but as Thou wouldst have it taste, and to conform my taste, and make it agreeable to Thy will. Thou wouldst have Thy corrections taste of humiliation, but Thou wouldst have them taste of consolation too; taste of danger, but taste of assurance too. As therefore Thou hast imprinted in all thine elements of which our bodies consist two manifest qualities, so that as Thy fire dries, so it heats too; and as Thy water moists, so it cools too;

so, O Lord, in these corrections which are the elements of our regeneration, by which our souls are made thine, imprint Thy two qualities, those two operations, that, as they scourge us, they may scourge us into the way to Thee; that when they have showed us that we are nothing in ourselves, they may also show us, that Thou art all things unto us. When therefore in this particular circumstance, O Lord (but none of Thy judgments are circumstances, they are all of all substance of Thy good purpose upon us), when in this particular, that he whom Thou hast sent to assist me, desires assistants to him, Thou hast let me see in how few hours Thou canst throw me beyond the help of man, let me by the same light see that no vehemence of sickness, no temptation of Satan, no guiltiness of sin, no prison of death, not this first, this sick bed, not the other prison, the close and dark grave, can remove me from the determined and good purpose which Thou hast sealed concerning me.

Let me think no degree of this Thy correction casual, or without signification; but yet when I have read it in that language, as a correction, let me translate it into another, and read it as a mercy; and which of these is the original, and which is the translation; whether Thy mercy or Thy correction were Thy primary and original intention in this sickness, I cannot conclude, though death conclude me; for as it must necessarily appear to be a correction, so I can have no greater argument of Thy mercy, than to die in Thee and by that death to be united to him who died for me.

Prayer VIII

O eternal and most gracious God, who art of so pure eyes as that Thou canst not look upon sin, and we of so unpure constitutions as that we can present no object but sin, and therefore might justly fear that Thou wouldst turn thine eyes forever from us, as, though we cannot endure afflictions in ourselves, yet in Thee we can; so, though thou canst not endure sin in us, yet in Thy Son thou canst, and he hath taken upon himself, and presented to Thee, all those sins which might displease Thee in us.

There is an eye in nature that kills as soon as it sees, the eye of a serpent; no eye in nature that nourishes us by looking upon us; but thine eye, O Lord, does so. Look therefore upon me, O Lord, in this distress and that will recall me from the borders of this bodily death; look upon me, and that will raise me again from that spiritual death in which my parents buried me when they begot me in sin, and in which I have pierced even to the jaws of hell by multiplying such heaps of actual sins upon that foundation, that root of original sin.

Yet take me again into your consultation, O blessed and glorious Trinity; and though the Father know that I have defaced his image received in my creation; though the Son know I have neglected mine interest in the redemption; yet, O blessed Spirit, as Thou art to my conscience so be to them, a witness that, at this minute, I accept that which I have so often, so rebelliously refused, Thy blessed inspirations; be Thou my witness to them that, at more pores than this slack body sweats tears, this sad soul weeps blood; and more for the displeasure of my God, than for the stripes of his displeasure.

Take me, then, O blessed and glorious Trinity, into a reconsultation, and prescribe me any physic. If it be a long and painful holding of this soul in sickness, it is physic if I may discern Thy hand to give it; and it is physic if it be a speedy departing of this soul, if I may discern Thy hand to receive it.

PRAYER VIII.

O eternal and most gracious God, who, though thou have reserved Thy treasure of perfect joy and perfect glory to be given by thine own hands then, when, by seeing Thee as Thou art in Thyself, and knowing Thee as we are known, we shall possess in an instant, and possess forever, all that can any way conduce to our happiness, yet here also, in this world, givest us such earnests of that full payment, as by the value of the earnest we may give some estimate of the treasure, humbly and thankfully I acknowledge, that Thy blessed Spirit instructs me to make a difference of Thy blessings in this world, by that difference of the instruments by which it hath pleased Thee to derive them unto me.

As we see Thee here in a glass, so we receive from Thee here by reflection and by instruments. Even casual things come from Thee; and that which we call fortune here hath another name above. Nature reaches out her hand and gives us corn, and wine, and oil, and milk; but Thou fillest her hand before, and Thou openest her hand that she may rain down her showers upon us. Industry reaches out her hand to us and gives us fruits of our labour for ourselves and our posterity; but Thy hand guides that hand when it sows and when it waters, and the increase is from Thee. Friends reach out their hands and prefer us; but Thy hand supports that hand that supports us.

Of all these Thy instruments have I received Thy blessing, O God; but bless Thy name most for the greatest; that, as a member of the public, and as a partaker of private favors too, by Thy right hand, Thy powerful hand set over us, I have had my portion not only in the hearing, but in the preaching of Thy Gospel.

Humbly beseeching Thee, that as Thou continuest Thy wonted goodness upon the whole world by the wonted means and instruments, the same sun and moon, the same nature and industry, so to continue the same blessings upon this state and this church by the same hand, so long as that Thy Son, when he comes in the clouds, may find him, or his son, or his son's sons ready to give an account and able to stand in that judgment, for their faithful stewardship and dispensation of Thy talents so abundantly committed to them; and be to him, O God, in all distempers of his body, in all anxieties of spirit, in all holy sadnesses of soul, such a physician in Thy proportion, who are the greatest in heaven, as he hath been in soul and body to me, in his proportion, who is the greatest upon earth.

PRAYER X

O eternal and most gracious God, who as Thy Son Christ Jesus, though he knew all things, yet said he knew not the day of judgment, because he knew it not so as that he might tell us; so though Thou knowest all my sins, yet Thou knowest them not to my comfort, except Thou know them by my telling them to Thee. How shall I bring to Thy knowledge, by that way, those sins which I myself know not? If I accuse myself of original sin, wilt Thou ask me if I know what original sin is? I know not enough of it to satisfy others, but I know enough to condemn myself, and to solicit Thee.

If I confess to Thee the sins of my youth, wilt Thou ask me if I know what those sins were? I know them not so well as to name them all, nor am sure to live hours enough to name them all (for I did them then faster than I can speak them now, when everything that I did conduced to some sin), but I know them so well as to know that nothing but Thy mercy is so infinite as they. If the naming of sins of thought, word and deed, of sins of omission and of action, of sins against Thee, against my neighbor and against myself, of sins unrepented and sins relapsed into after repentance, of sins of ignorance and sins against the testimony of my conscience, of sins against Thy commandments, sins against Thy Son's Prayer, and sins against our own creed, of sins against the laws of that church, and sins against the laws of that state in which Thou hast given me my station; if the naming of these sins reach not home to all mine, I know what will. O Lord, pardon me, me, all those sins which Thy Son Christ Jesus suffered for, who suffered for all the sins of all the world; for there is no sin amongst all those which had not been my sin, if Thou hadst not been my God, and antedated me a pardon in Thy preventing grace. And since sin, in the nature of it, retains still so much of the author of it that it is a serpent, insensibly insinuating itself into my soul, let Thy brazen serpent (the contemplation of Thy Son crucified for me) be evermore present to me, for my recovery against the sting of the first serpent; that so, as I have a Lion against a lion, the Lion of the tribe of Judah against that lion that seeks whom he may devour, so I may have a serpent against a serpent, the wisdom of the serpent against the malice of the serpent, and both against that lion and serpent, forcible and subtle temptations, Thy dove with Thy olive in Thy ark, humility and peace and reconciliation to Thee, by the ordinances of Thy church. Amen.

PRAYER XI

O eternal and most gracious God, who in Thy upper house, the heavens, though there be many mansions, yet art alike and equally in every mansion; but here in Thy lower house, though Thou fillest all, yet art otherwise in some rooms thereof than in others; otherwise in Thy church than in my chamber, and otherwise in Thy sacraments than in my prayers; so though Thou be always present and always working in every room of this Thy house, my body, yet I humbly beseech Thee to manifest always a more effectual presence in my heart than in the other offices. Into the house of thine anointed, disloyal persons, traitors, will come; into Thy house, the church, hypocrites and idolaters will come; into some rooms of this Thy house, my body, temptations will come, infections will come; but be my heart Thy bedchamber, O my God, and thither let them not enter. Job made a covenant with his eyes, but not his making of that covenant, but Thy dwelling in his heart, enabled him to keep that covenant. Thy Son himself had a sadness in his soul to death, and he had a reluctation, a deprecation of death, in the approaches thereof; but he had his cordial too, Yet not my will, but thine be done. And as Thou hast not delivered us, thine adopted sons, from these infectious temptations, so neither hast Thou delivered us over to them, nor withheld Thy cordials from us. I was baptized in Thy cordial water against original sin, and I have drunk of Thy cordial blood, for my recovery from actual and habitual sin, in the other sacrament. Thou, O Lord, who hast imprinted all medicinal virtues which are in all creatures, and hast made even the flesh of vipers to assist in cordials, art able to make this present sickness, everlasting health, this weakness, everlasting strength, and this very dejection and faintness of heart, a powerful cordial.

When Thy blessed Son cried out to Thee, My God, my God, why hast Thou forsaken me? Thou didst reach out Thy hand to him; but not to deliver his sad soul, but to receive his holy soul: neither did he longer desire to hold it of Thee, but to recommend it to Thee. I see thine hand upon me now, O Lord, and I ask not why it comes, what it intends; whether Thou wilt bid it stay still in this body for some time, or bid it meet Thee this day in paradise,

I ask not, not in a wish, not in a thought. Infirmities of nature, curiosity of mind, are temptations that offer; but a silent and absolute obedience to Thy will, even before I know it, is my cordial. Preserve that to me, O my God, and that will preserve me to Thee; that, when Thou hast catechized me with affliction here, I may take a greater degree, and serve Thee in a higher place, in Thy kingdom of joy and glory. Amen.

PRAYER XII.

O eternal and most gracious God, who, though Thou have suffered us to destroy ourselves, and hast not given us the power of reparation in ourselves, hast yet afforded us such means of reparation as may easily and familiarly be compassed by us, prosper, I humbly beseech Thee, this means of bodily assistance in this Thy ordinary creature, and prosper Thy means of spiritual assistance in Thy holy ordinances. And as Thou hast carried this Thy creature, the dove, through all Thy ways through nature, and made it naturally proper to conduce medicinally to our bodily health, through the law, and made it a sacrifice for sin there, and through the gospel, and made it, and Thy Spirit in it, a witness of Thy Son's baptism there, so carry it, and the qualities of it, home to my soul, and imprint there that simplicity, that mildness, that harmlessness,

which Thou hast imprinted by nature in this creature. That so all vapours of all disobedience to Thee, being subdued under my feet, I may, in the power and triumph of Thy Son, tread victoriously upon my grave, and trample upon the lion and dragon that lie under it to devour me. Thou, O Lord, by the prophet, callest the dove the dove of the valleys, but promisest that the dove of the valleys shall be upon the mountain.

As Thou hast laid me low in this valley of sickness, so low as that I am made fit for that question asked in the field of bones, Son of man, can these bones live? So, in Thy good time, carry me up to these mountains of which even in this valley Thou affordest me a prospect, the mountain where Thou dwellest, the holy hill, unto which none can ascend but he that hath clean hands, which none can have but by that one and that strong way of making them clean, in the blood of Thy Son Christ Jesus. Amen.

PRAYER XIII.

O eternal and most gracious God, who as Thou givest all for nothing, if we consider any precedent merit in us, so givest nothing for nothing, if we consider the acknowledgment and thankfulness which Thou lookest for after, accept my humble thanks, both for Thy mercy, and for this particular mercy, that in Thy judgment I can discern Thy mercy, and find comfort in Thy corrections. I know, O Lord, the ordinary discomfort that accompanies that phrase, that the house is visited, and that Thy marks and Thy tokens are upon the patient; but what a wretched and disconsolate hermitage is that house which is not visited by Thee, and what a waif and stray is that man that hath not Thy marks upon him? These heats, O Lord, which Thou hast brought upon this body, are but Thy chafing of the wax, that Thou mightst seal me to Thee: these spots are but the letters in which Thou hast written thine own name and conveyed Thyself to me; whether for a present possession, by taking me now, or for a future reversion, by glorifying Thyself in my stay here, I limit not, I condition not, I choose not, I wish not, no more than the house or land that passeth by any civil conveyance. Only be Thou ever present to me, O my God, and this bedchamber and Thy bedchamber shall be all one room, and the closing of these bodily eyes here, and the opening of the eyes of my soul there, all one act.

PRAYER. XIV

O eternal and most gracious God, who, though Thou didst permit darkness to be before light in the creation, yet in the making of light didst so multiply that light, as that it enlightened not the day only, but the night too; though have suffered some dimness, some clouds of sadness and disconsolateness to shed themselves upon my soul, I humbly bless and thankfully glorify Thy holy name, that Thou hast afforded me the light of Thy Spirit, against which the prince of darkness cannot prevail, nor hinder his illumination of our darkest nights, of our saddest thoughts. Even the visitation of Thy most blessed Spirit upon the blessed Virgin, is called an overshadowing. There was the presence of the Holy Ghost, the fountain of all light, and yet an overshadowing; nay, except there were some light, there could be no shadow.

Let Thy merciful providence so govern all in this sickness, that I never fall into utter darkness, ignorance of Thee, or inconsideration of myself; and let those shadows which do fall upon me, faintnesses of spirit, and condemnations of myself, be overcome by the power of thine irresistible light, the God of consolation; that when those shadows have done their office upon me, to let me see, that of myself I should fall into irrecoverable darkness, Thy Spirit may do his office upon those shadows, and disperse them, and establish me in so bright a day here, as may be a critical day to me, a day wherein and whereby I may give Thy judgment upon myself, and that the words of Thy Son, spoken to his apostles, may reflect upon me, Behold I am with you always, even to the end of the world.

PRAYER XV.

O eternal and most gracious God, who art able to make, and dost make, the sick bed of Thy servants chapels of ease to them, and the dreams of Thy servants prayers and meditations upon Thee, let not this continual watchfulness of mine, this inability to sleep, which Thou hast laid upon me, be any disquiet or discomfort to me, but rather an argument, that Thou wouldst not have me sleep in Thy presence. What it may indicate or signify concerning the state of my body, let them consider to whom that consideration belongs; do Thou, who only art the Physician of my soul, tell her, that Thou wilt afford her such defensives, as that she shall wake ever towards Thee, and yet ever sleep in Thee, and that, through all this sickness, Thou wilt either preserve mine understanding from all decays and distractions which these watchings might occasion, or that Thou wilt reckon and account with me from before those violences, and not call any piece of my sickness a sin. It is a heavy and indelible sin that I brought into the world with me; it is a heavy and innumerable multitude of sins which I have heaped up since; I have sinned behind Thy back (if that can be done), by willful abstaining from Thy congregations and omitting Thy service, and I have sinned before Thy face, in my hypocrisies in prayer, in my ostentation, and the mingling a respect of myself in preaching Thy word;

I have sinned in my fasting, by repining when a penurious fortune hath kept me low; and I have sinned even in that fullness, when I have been at Thy table, by a negligent examination, by a willful prevarication, in receiving that heavenly food and physic. But as I know, O my gracious God, that for all those sins committed since, yet Thou wilt consider me, as I was in Thy purpose when Thou wrotest my name in the book of life in mine election; so into what deviations soever I stray and wander by occasion of this sickness, O God, return Thou to that minute wherein Thou wast pleased with me and consider me in that condition.

PRAYER XVI

O eternal and most gracious God, who having consecrated our living bodies to thine own Spirit, and made us temples of the Holy Ghost, dost also require a respect to be given to these temples, even when the priest is gone out of them, to these bodies when the soul is departed from them, I bless and glorify Thy name, that as Thou takest care in our life of every hair of our head, so dost Thou also of every grain of ashes after our death. Neither dost Thou only do good to us all in life and death, but also wouldst have us do good to one another, as in a holy life, so in those things which accompany our death. In that contemplation I make account that I hear this dead brother of ours, who is now carried out to his burial, to speak to me, and to preach my funeral sermon in the voice of these bells. In him, O God, Thou hast accomplished to me even the request of Dives to Abraham; Thou hast sent one from the dead to speak unto me. He speaks to me aloud from that steeple; he whispers to me at these curtains,

and he speaks Thy words: Blessed are the dead which die in the Lord from henceforth.

Let this prayer therefore, O my God, be as my last gasp, my expiring, my dying in Thee; that if this be the hour of my transmigration, I may die the death of a sinner, drowned in my sins, in the blood of Thy Son; and if I live longer, yet I may now die the death of the righteous, die to sin; which death is a resurrection to a new life. Thou killest and Thou givest life: whichsoever comes, it comes from Thee; which way soever it comes, let me come to Thee.

PRAYER XVII

O eternal and most gracious God, who hast been pleased to speak to us, not only in the voice of nature, who speaks in our hearts, and of Thy word, which speaks to our ears, but in the speech of speechless creatures, in Balaam's ass, in the speech of unbelieving men, in the confession of Pilate, in the speech of the devil himself, in the recognition and attestation of Thy Son, I humbly accept Thy voice in the sound of this sad and funeral bell. And first, I bless Thy glorious name, that in this sound and voice I can hear Thy instructions, in another man's to consider mine own condition; and to know, that this bell which tolls for another, before it come to ring out, may take me in too.

As death is the wages of sin it is due to me; as death is the end of sickness it belongs to me; and though so disobedient a servant as I may be afraid to die, yet to so merciful a master as Thou I cannot be afraid to come; and therefore into Thy hands, O my God, I commend my spirit, a surrender which I know Thou wilt accept, whether I live or die; for Thy servant David made it, when he put himself into Thy protection for his life; and Thy blessed Son made it, when he delivered up his soul at his death: declare Thou Thy will upon me, O Lord, for life or death in Thy time; receive my surrender of myself now; into Thy hands, O Lord, I commend my spirit. And being thus, O my God, prepared by Thy correction, mellowed by Thy chastisement, and conformed to Thy will by Thy Spirit, having received Thy pardon for my soul, and asking no reprieve for my body, I am bold, O Lord, to bend my prayers to Thee for his assistance, the voice of whose bell hath called me to this devotion. Lay hold upon his soul, O God, till that soul have thoroughly considered his account; and how few minutes soever it have to remain in that body, let the power of Thy Spirit recompense the shortness of time, and perfect his account before he pass away; present his sins so to him, as that he may know what Thou forgivest, and not doubt of Thy forgiveness, let him stop upon the infiniteness of those sins, but dwell upon the infiniteness of Thy mercy; let him discern his own demerits, but wrap himself up in the merits of Thy Son Christ Jesus; breathe inward comforts to his heart, and afford him the power of giving such outward testimonies thereof, as all that are about him may derive comforts from thence, and have this edification, even in this dissolution, that though the body be going the way of all flesh, yet that soul is going the way of all saints. When Thy Son cried out upon the cross, My God, my God, why hast Thou forsaken me?

He spake not so much in his own person, as in the person of the church, and of his afflicted members, who in deep distresses might fear Thy forsaking. This patient, O most blessed God, is one of them; in his behalf, and in his name, hear Thy Son crying to Thee, My God, my God, why hast Thou forsaken me?

And forsake him not; but with Thy left hand lay his body in the grave (if that be Thy determination upon him), and with Thy right hand receive his soul into Thy kingdom, and unite him and us in one communion of saints. Amen

PRAYER XVIII.

O eternal and most gracious God, I have a new occasion of thanks, and a new occasion of prayer to Thee from the ringing of this bell. Thou toldest me in the other voice that I was mortal and approaching to death; in this I may hear Thee say that I am dead in an irremediable, in an irrecoverable state for bodily health. If that be Thy language in this voice, how infinitely am I bound to Thy heavenly Majesty for speaking so plainly unto me? for even that voice, that I must die now, is not the voice of a judge that speaks by way of condemnation, but of a physician that presents health in that.

Thou presentest me death as the cure of my disease, not as the exaltation of it; if I mistake Thy voice herein, if I overrun Thy pace, and prevent Thy hand, and imagine death more instant upon me than Thou hast bid him be, yet the voice belongs to me; I am dead, I was born dead, and from the first laying of these mud walls in my conception, they have moldered away, and the whole course of life is but an active death. Whether this voice instruct me that I am a dead man now, or remember me that I have been a dead man all this while.

I humbly thank Thee for speaking in this voice to my soul; and I humbly beseech Thee also to accept my prayers in his behalf, by whose occasion this voice, this sound, is come to me. For though he be by death transplanted to Thee, and so in possession of inexpressible happiness there, yet here upon earth Thou hast given us such a portion of heaven, as that though men dispute whether Thy saints in heaven do know what we in earth in particular do stand in need of, yet, without all disputation, we upon earth do know what

Thy saints in heaven lack yet for the consummation of their happiness, and therefore Thou hast afforded us the dignity that we may pray for them. That therefore this soul, now newly departed to Thy kingdom, may quickly return to a joyful reunion to that body which it hath left, and that we with it may soon enjoy the full consummation of all in body and soul, I humbly beg at Thy hand, O our most merciful God, for Thy Son Christ Jesus' sake.

That that blessed Son of thine may have the consummation of his dignity, by entering into his last office, the office of a judge, and may have society of human bodies in heaven, as well as he hath had ever of souls; and that as Thou hatest sin itself, thy hate to sin may be expressed in the abolishing of all instruments of sin, the allurements of this world, and the world itself; and all the temporary revenges of sin, the stings of sickness and of death; and all the castles, and prisons, and monuments of sin, in the grave. That time may be swallowed up in eternity, and hope swallowed in possession, and ends swallowed in infiniteness, and all men ordained to salvation in body and soul be one entire and everlasting sacrifice to Thee, where Thou mayest receive delight from them, and they glory from Thee, for evermore. Amen.

PRAYER XIX.

O eternal and most gracious God, who though Thou passedst over infinite millions of generations, before Thou camest to a creation of this world, yet when Thou beganst, didst never intermit that work, but continuest day to day, till Thou hadst perfected all the work, and deposed it in the hands and rest of a Sabbath, though Thou have been pleased to glorify Thyself in a long exercise of my patience, with an expectation of Thy declaration of Thyself in this my sickness, yet since Thou hast now of Thy goodness afforded that which affords us some hope, if that be still the way of Thy glory, proceed in that way and perfect that work, and establish me in a Sabbath and rest in Thee, by this Thy seal of bodily restitution.

Thy priests came up to Thee by steps in the temple; Thy angels came down to Jacob by steps upon the ladder; we find no stair by which Thou Thyself camest to Adam in paradise, nor to Sodom in thine anger; for Thou, and Thou only, art able to do all at once. But O Lord, I am neither weary of Thy pace, nor weary of mine own patience. I provoke Thee not with a prayer, not with a wish, not with a hope, to more haste than consists with Thy purpose, nor look that any other thing should have entered into Thy purpose, but Thy glory. To hear Thy steps coming towards me is the same comfort as to see Thy face present with me; whether Thou do the work of a thousand years in a day, or extend the work of a day to a thousand years, as long as Thou workest, it is light and comfort. Heaven itself is but an extension of the same joy; and an extension of this mercy, to proceed at Thy leisure, in the way of restitution, is a manifestation of heaven to me here upon earth.

From that people to whom Thou appearest in signs and in types, the Jews, Thou art departed, because they trusted in them; but from Thy church, to whom Thou hast appeared in Thyself, in Thy Son, Thou wilt never depart, because we cannot trust too much in him. Though Thou have afforded me these signs of restitution, yet if I confide in them, and begin to say, all was but a natural accident, and nature begins to discharge herself, and she will perfect the whole work, my hope shall vanish because it is not in Thee. If Thou shouldst take Thy hand utterly from me, and have nothing to do with me, nature alone were able to destroy me; but if Thou withdraw Thy helping hand, alas, how frivolous are the helps of nature, how impotent the assistances of art? As therefore the morning dew is a pawn of the evening fatness, so, O Lord, let this day's comfort be the earnest of to-morrow's, so far as may conform me entirely to Thee, to what end, and by what way soever Thy mercy have appointed me.

PRAYER XX.

O eternal and most gracious God, who having married man and woman together, and made them one flesh, wouldst have them also to become one soul, so as that they might maintain a sympathy in their affections, and have a conformity to one another in the accidents of this world, good or bad; so having married this soul and this body in me, I humbly beseech Thee that my soul may look and make her use of Thy merciful proceedings towards my bodily restitution, and go the same way to a spiritual. I am come, by Thy goodness, to the use of thine ordinary means for my body, to wash away those peccant humors that endangered it.

I have, O Lord, a river in my body, but a sea in my soul, and a sea swollen into the depth of a deluge, above the sea. Thou hast raised up certain hills in me heretofore, by which I might have stood safe from these inundations of sin. Even our natural faculties are a hill, and might preserve us from some sin. Education, study, observation, example, are hills too, and might preserve us from some. Thy church, and Thy word, and Thy sacraments, and thine ordinances are hills above these; Thy spirit of remorse, and compunction, and repentance for former sin, are hills too; and to the top of all these hills Thou hast brought me heretofore; but this deluge, this inundation, is got above all my hills; and I have sinned and sinned, and multiplied sin to sin, after all these Thy assistances against sin, and where is there water enough to wash away this deluge? There is a red sea, greater than this ocean, and there is a little spring, through which this ocean may pour itself into that red sea. Let Thy spirit of true contrition and sorrow pass all my sins, through these eyes, into the wounds of Thy Son, and I shall be clean, and my soul so much better purged than my body, as it is ordained for better and a longer life.

PRAYER XXI.

O eternal and most gracious God, who hast made little things to signify great, and conveyed the infinite merits of Thy Son in the water of baptism, and in the bread and wine of Thy other sacrament, unto us, receive the sacrifice of my humble thanks, that Thou hast not only afforded me the ability to rise out of this bed of weariness and discomfort, but hast also made this bodily rising, by Thy grace, an earnest of a second resurrection from sin, and of a third, to everlasting glory.

Thy Son himself, always infinite in himself, and incapable of addition, was yet pleased to grow in the Virgin's womb, and to grow in stature in the sight of men. Thy good purposes upon me, I know, have their determination and perfection in Thy holy will upon me; there Thy grace is, and there I am altogether; but manifest them so unto me, in Thy seasons, and in Thy measures and degrees, that I may not only have that comfort of knowing Thee to be infinitely good, but that also of finding Thee to be every day better and better to me; and that as Thou gavest Saint Paul the messenger of Satan, to humble him so for my humiliation, Thou mayest give me Thyself in this knowledge, that what grace soever Thou afford me to-day, yet I should perish to-morrow if I had not had to-morrow's grace too.

Therefore I beg of Thee my daily bread; and as Thou gavest me the bread of sorrow for many days, and since the bread of hope for some, and this day the bread of possessing, in rising by that strength, which Thou the God of all strength hast infused into me, so, O Lord, continue to me the bread of life: the spiritual bread of life, in a faithful assurance in Thee; the sacramental bread of life, in a worthy receiving of Thee; and the more real bread of life in an everlasting union to Thee. I know, O Lord, that when Thou hast created angels, and they saw Thee produce fowl, and fish, and beasts, and worms, they did not importune Thee, and say, Shall we have no better creatures than these, no better companions than these? but stayed Thy leisure, and then had man delivered over to them, not much inferior in nature to themselves.

No more do I, O God, now that by Thy first mercy I am able to rise, importune Thee for present confirmation of health; nor now, that by Thy mercy I am brought to see that Thy correction hath wrought medicinally upon me, presume I upon that spiritual strength I have; but as I acknowledge that my bodily strength is subject to every puff of wind, so is my spiritual strength to every blast of vanity. Keep me therefore still, O my gracious God, in such a proportion of both strengths, as I may still have something to thank Thee for, which I have received, and still something to pray for and ask at Thy hand.

PRAYER XXII.

O eternal and most gracious God, the God of security, and the enemy of security too, who wouldst have us always sure of Thy love, and yet wouldst have us always doing something for it, let me always so apprehend Thee as present with me, and yet so follow after Thee, as though I had not apprehended Thee. Thou enlargedst Hezekiah's lease for fifteen years; Thou renewedst Lazarus's lease for a time which we know not; but Thou didst never so put out any of these fires as that Thou didst not rake up the embers, and wrap up a future mortality in that body, which Thou hadst then so reprieved. Thou proceedest no otherwise in our souls, O our good but fearful God; Thou pardonest no sin, so as that that sinner can sin no more; Thou makest no man so acceptable as that Thou makest him impeccable. Though therefore it were a diminution of the largeness, and derogatory to the fullness of Thy mercy, to look back upon the sins which in a true repentance I have buried in the wounds of Thy Son, with a jealous or suspicious eye, as though they were now my sins, when I had so transferred them upon Thy Son, as though they could now be raised to life again, to condemn me to death, when they are dead in him who is the fountain of life, yet were it an irregular anticipation, and an insolent presumption, to think that Thy present mercy extended to all my future sins, or that there were no embers, no coals, of future sins left in me. Temper therefore Thy mercy so to my soul, O my God, that I may neither decline to any faintness of spirit, in suspecting Thy mercy now to be less hearty, less sincere, than it uses to be, to those who are perfectly reconciled to Thee, nor presume so of it as either to think this present mercy an antidote against all poisons, and so expose myself to temptations, upon confidence that this Thy mercy shall preserve me, or that when I do cast myself into new sins, I may have new mercy at any time, because Thou didst so easily afford me this.

PRAYER XXIII.

O eternal and most gracious God, who, though Thou beest ever infinite, yet enlargedst Thyself by the number of our prayers, and takest our often petitions to Thee to be an addition to Thy glory and Thy greatness, as ever upon all occasions, so now, O my God, I come to Thy majesty with two prayers, two supplications.

I have meditated upon the jealousy which Thou hast of thine own honor, and considered that nothing comes nearer a violating of that honor, nearer to the nature of a scorn to Thee, than to sue out Thy pardon, and receive the seals of reconciliation to Thee, and then return to that sin for which I needed and had Thy pardon before. I know that this comes too near to a making Thy holy ordinances, Thy word, Thy sacraments, Thy seals, Thy grace, instruments of my spiritual fornications. Since therefore Thy correction hath brought me to such a participation of Thyself (Thyself, O my God, cannot be parted), to such an entire possession of Thee, as that I durst deliver myself over to Thee this minute, if this minute Thou wouldst accept my dissolution, preserve me, O my God, the God of constancy and perseverance, in this state, from all relapses into those sins which have induced Thy former judgments upon me. But because, by too lamentable experience, I know how slippery my customs of sin have made my ways of sin, I presume to add this petition too, that if my infirmity overtake me, Thou forsake me not. Say to my soul, my son, Thou hast sinned, do so no more; but say also, that though I do, Thy spirit of remorse and compunction shall never depart from me.

Thy holy apostle, St. Paul, was shipwrecked thrice, and yet still saved. Though the rocks and the sands, the heights and the shallows, the prosperity and the adversity of this world, do diversely threaten me, though mine own leaks endanger me, yet, O God, let me never put myself aboard with Hymenæus, nor make shipwreck of faith and a good conscience, and then Thy long-lived, Thy everlasting mercy, will visit me, though that which I most earnestly pray against, should fall upon me, a relapse into those sins which I have truly repented, and Thou hast fully pardoned.

Ephrem the Syrian *(ca. 306 – 373AD)He was born in Turkey to Christian parents. Little is known of his life. He is credited with writing over 400 hymns, using verse sermons to teach and introducing the early church to the benefit of music in worship. He was ordained as a deacon and a teacher in his hometown of Nisibis.*

O Lord, Heavenly King, Comforter, Spirit of Truth, have compassion and mercy on Thy sinful servant and pardon my unworthiness, and forgive me all the sins that I humanly committed today, and not only humanly but even worse than a beast - my voluntary sins, known and unknown, from my youth and from evil suggestions, and from my brazenness, and from boredom. If I have sworn by Thy Name or blasphemed it in thought, blamed or reproached anyone, or in my anger have detracted or slandered anyone, or grieved anyone, or if I have got angry about anything, or have told a lie, if I have slept unnecessarily, or if a beggar has come to me and I despised or neglected him, or if I have troubled my brother or quarreled with him, or if I have condemned anyone, or have boasted, or have been proud, or lost my temper with anyone, or if when standing in prayer my mind has been distracted by the glamour of this world, or if I have had depraved thoughts or have overeaten, or have drunk excessively, or have laughed frivolously, or have thought evil, or have seen the attraction of someone and been wounded by it in my heart, or said indecent things, or made fun of my brother's sin when my own faults are countless, or been neglectful of prayer, or have done some other wrong that I cannot remember - for I have done all this and much more.

Have mercy, my Lord and Creator, on me Thy wretched and unworthy servant, and absolve and forgive and deliver me in Thy goodness and love for men, so that, lustful, sinful and wretched as I am, I may lie down and sleep and rest in peace. And I shall worship, praise and glorify Thy most honorable Name, with the Father and His only-begotten Son, now and ever, and for all ages. Amen.

Ignatius of Loyola *(1491-July 31, 1556 AD) Ignatius was christened Inigo. He was the youngest son of a noble Spanish family from the Basque region in Castile. He was a knight until wounded by a cannon ball that crippled his legs. During his recovery he began to read the life of Christ in the gospels. He left the military and began to pursue a life of faith. He spent years in formal study eventually receiving his MA from Collège de Sainte-Barbe in Paris. He was occasionally arrested for heresy and was a part of the Catholic Reformation. It was during this time he began to formulate his work, <u>The Spiritual Exercises.</u> Later he founded the Society of Jesus, know at the Jesuits.*

Take, Lord, and receive all my liberty, my memory, my understanding and my entire will, All I have and call my own. You have given all to me. To you, Lord, I return it. Everything is yours; do with it what you will. Give me only your love and your grace. That is enough for me.

Soul of Christ, sanctify me Body of Christ, save me Blood of Christ, inebriate me Water from the side of Christ, wash me Passion of Christ, strengthen me Good Jesus, hear me Within the wounds, shelter me from turning away, keep me From the evil one, protect me At the hour of my death, call me Into your presence lead me to praise you with all your saints Forever and ever. Amen.

Lord, teach me to be generous. Teach me to serve you as you deserve; to give and not to count the cost, to fight and not to heed the wounds, to toil and not to seek for rest, to labor and not to ask for reward, save that of knowing that I do your will Honor and praise be given to Thee, O LORD God Almighty, most dear Father of heaven, for all thy mercies and loving-kindness showed unto us, in that it hath pleased thy gracious goodness freely and of thine own accord to elect and choose us to salvation before the beginning of the world. And even like continual thanks be given to Thee for creating us after thine own image; for redeeming us with the precious blood of thy dear Son, when we were utterly lost; for sanctifying us with thine Holy Spirit in the revelation and knowledge of thine holy word; for helping and succoring us in all our needs and necessities; for saving us from all dangers of body and soul; for comforting us so fatherly in all our tribulations and persecutions; for sparing us so long, and giving us so large a time of repentance.

These benefits, O most merciful Father, like as we acknowledge to have received of thine only goodness, even so we beseech Thee, for thy dear Son JESUS CHRIST's sake, to grant us always thine Holy Spirit, whereby we may continually grow in thankfulness towards Thee, and be led into all truth, and comforted in all our adversities.

O LORD, strengthen our faith; kindle it more in ferventness and love towards Thee, and our neighbors, for thy sake. Suffer us not, most dear Father, to receive thy word any more in vain; but grant us always the assistance of thy grace and Holy Spirit, that in heart, word, and deed, we may sanctify and do worship to thy name. Help to amplify and increase thy kingdom; that whatsoever thou sendest, we may be heartily well content with thy good pleasure and will. Let us not lack the thing — O Father! — without the which we cannot serve Thee; but bless thou so all the works of our hands, that we may have sufficient, and not be chargeable, but rather helpful unto others.

Be merciful, O LORD, to our offences; and seeing our debt is great, which thou hast forgiven us in JESUS CHRIST, make us to love Thee and our neighbors so much the more. Be thou our Father, our Captain and Defender in all temptations; hold thou us by thy merciful hand; that we may be delivered from all inconveniences [i.e. hardships], and end our lives in the sanctifying and honoring of thine holy name, through JESUS CHRIST our Lord and only Saviour. Amen. Let thy mighty hand and outstretched arm, O LORD, be still our defense; thy mercy and loving-kindness in JESUS CHRIST, thy dear Son, our salvation; Thy true and holy word our instruction; thy grace and Holy Spirit our comfort and consolation, unto the end and in the end. Amen.

Jerome *(c. 27 March 347 – 30 September 420 AD) His Greek name is Eusebius Sophronius Hieronymus. He was born to a wealthy Slovenian family. He is known as a translator and scholar. He is second only to Augustine in his prolific writing. He spent time as a hermit. He learned Hebrew from a converted Jew. He was not* *always in favor within the Roman Catholic Church. His greatest work is the translation of the Bible into Latin. Modern theological scholarship is indebted to Jerome for his emphasis on Ancient Hebrew as a foundational Biblical source.*

O Lord, you have given us Your word for a light to shine upon our path; grant us so to meditate on that word, and follow its teaching, that we may find in it the light that shines more and more until the perfect day. Alone with none but Thee, my God, I journey on my way. What need I fear, when Thou art near O King of night and day? More safe am I within Thy hand than if a host did round me stand. May God the Father bless us; may Christ take care of us; the Holy Ghost enlighten us all the days of our life. The Lord be our defender and keeper of body and soul, both now and forever, to the ages of ages.

Thomas a Kempis *(1380-1471) Thomas Hemerken, "little hammer", is his German name. His father was a blacksmith and his mother a school mistress. After his conversion, Thomas joined the Brethren of the Common Life at the Agnietenberg monastery where he served for 70 years writing his greatest work* <u>Imitation of Christ</u> *and instructing novices.*

Grant me, O Lord, to know what I ought to know, To love what I ought to love, To praise what delights Thee most, To value what is precious in thy sight, To hate what is offensive to Thee. Do not suffer me to judge according to the sight of my eyes, Nor to pass sentence according to the hearing of the ears of ignorant men; But to discern with a true judgment between things visible and spiritual, And above all, always to inquire what is the good pleasure of Thy will. Give us, O Lord, steadfast hearts that cannot be dragged down by false loves; give us courageous hearts that cannot be worn down by trouble; give us righteous hearts that cannot be sidetracked by unholy or unworthy goals. Give to us also, our Lord and God, understanding to know You, diligence to look for you, wisdom to recognize You, and a faithfulness that will bring us to see You face to face.

Grant me, most dear and loving Jesus, to rest in You above created things; above health and beauty, above all glory and honor; above all power and dignity, above all knowledge and skill; above all fame and praise, above all sweetness and consolation; above all hope and promise, above all merit and desire; above all gifts and favors that You can bestow and shower upon us; above all joy and jubilation that the mind can conceive and know; above angels and archangels and all the hosts of Heaven; above all things visible and invisible; and above everything that is not Yourself, O my God.

O Lord, my God, You transcend all things. You alone are most high, most mighty, most sufficient and complete, most sweet and comforting. You alone are most full of beauty and glory, in whom all good things in their perfection exist, both now and ever have been, and ever will be. All, therefore, is too small and unsatisfying that You can give me beside yourself, or that You can reveal and promise me of yourself unless I can see and fully possess You. For my heart cannot rest nor be wholly content until it rests in You, rising above all Your gifts and creatures.

O Lord Jesus Christ, spouse of the soul, lover of purity, and Lord of creation, who will give me wings of perfect liberty, that I may fly to You, and be at rest? When shall I be set free, and taste Your sweetness, O Lord, my God? When shall I become recollected in You, that for love of You alone in a manner not known to all men, and above all perception and measure?

But now I mourn and bear my unhappy lot with grief, for many evils happen in this vale of sorrows, which often disturb, sadden, and darken my path. They often hinder and distract, entice, and entangle me, so that I cannot approach You freely, nor yet enjoy the sweet embrace which You prepare for the souls of the blessed.

O Jesus, brightness of eternal glory and comfort of the pilgrim soul, hear my cry, and regard my utter desolation. Words fail me in Your presence; let my silence speak for me. How long will my Lord delay His coming? Come to me, Lord, poor and little as I am, and bring me joy. Stretch out Your hand, and deliver me from all my misery and pain. Come, Lord, come, for without You no day or hour is happy; without You my table is without its guest, for You alone are my joy. Sadness is my lot, and I am like a man imprisoned and loaded with chains, until You refresh me with the light of Your presence, and show me Your face as my friend. Let others seek whom they will besides you, but nothing ever can or will give me joy but Yourself alone, my God, my hope, and my eternal salvation. I will not keep silent, nor cease from urgent prayer till Your grace returns and my heart leaps at the sound of Your voice. Amen.

O Lord, my God, You are my all and every good. And what am I, that I should presume to address You? I am the poorest of Your servants and a wretched worm, far more poor and worthless than I can ever realize or express. Yet, Lord, remember that I am nothing: I have nothing, and can do nothing. You alone are good, just and holy; You can do all things, fill all things, bestow all things, leaving only the wicked empty-handed.

Remember Your mercies, Lord, and fill my heart with Your grace, since it is Your will that none of Your works should be worthless. How can I endure this life of sorrows, unless You strengthen me with Your mercy and grace?

Do not turn Your face from me; do not delay Your coming, nor withdraw Your consolation form me, lest my soul become like a waterless desert. Teach me, O Lord, to do Your will; teach me to live worthily and humbly in Your sight; for You are my wisdom, who know me truly, and who knew me before the world was made, and before I had my being. Amen.

Deepen your love in me, O Lord, that I may learn in my inmost heart how sweet it is to love, to be dissolved, and to plunge myself into Your love. Let Your love possess and raise me above myself, with a fervor and wonder beyond imagination. Let me sing the song of love. Let me follow you, my beloved, into the heights. Let my soul spend itself in Your praise, rejoicing for love. Let me love you more than myself, and myself only for Your own sake. Let me love all men who truly love you, as the law of love commands, which shines out from you.

Love is swift, pure, tender, joyful, and pleasant. Love is strong, patient, faithful, prudent, long-suffering, vigorous, and never self-seeking. For when a man is self-seeking he abandons love. Love is watchful, humble, and upright; love is not fickle and sentimental, nor is it intent on vanities. It is sober, pure, steadfast, quiet, and guarded in all the senses. Love is submissive and obedient to superiors, mean and contemptible in its own sight, devoted and thankful to God, trusting and hoping in him even when not enjoying his sweetness; for none can live in love without suffering.

Whoever is not prepared to endure everything, and to stand firmly by the will of the beloved, is not worthy to be called a lover. A lover must willingly accept every hardship and bitterness for the sake of his beloved, and must never desert him because of adversity. Amen.

Thérèse of Lisieux *(2 January 1873 – 30 September 1897) Marie Francoise-Therese Martin lived a hidden life and "wanted to be unknown." She died at the age of 24 of tuberculosis. Her last days were filled with physical suffering. She left a spiritual memoir* L'histoire d'une ame The Story of a Soul. *During her life she was relatively obscure, but her devotion to Jesus Christ during her life and suffering has been an encouragement to many.*

Greetings to you, living God. You are mine before all things. I am endlessly glad that I can speak to you without guile. When my enemies pursue me, I flee to Your arms where I can complain about my suffering while you incline Yourself to me. You well know how you can pluck the strings of my soul. Ah, begin at once that you may be ever blessed. I am a low-born bride; and yet you are my lawful husband. I shall ever rejoice about this. remember how well you can caress the pure soul on Your lap and do it, Lord, to me now, even though I am not worthy of you.

Ah, Lord, draw me up to you. Then I shall be pure and radiant. If you abandon me to myself, I shall remain dark and sluggish. Thus does God answer: I respond to Your greeting with such a heavenly flood: were I to give myself to you in all my power, You would not preserve Your human life. You well know I must hold back my might and hide my splendor to let you remain in earthly misery until all my sweetness rises up to the heights of eternal glory, and my strings shall play sweetly for you in tune with the true value of Your patient love.

Still, before I begin, I want to tune my heavenly strings in Your soul, so that you might persevere even longer. For well-born brides and noble knights must undergo a long and intensive preparation at great cost. "O Lord, if it could ever happen to me that I might gaze upon you as my heart desires and hold you in my arms, then the divine pleasures of Your love would needs permeate my soul to the degree possible for people on earth. What I would be willing to suffer thereafter has never been seen by human eyes. Indeed, a thousand deaths were too little. Such, Lord, is my painful longing for you!

O eternal Word! O my Savior! Thou art the divine Eagle whom I love and who allurest me. Thou who, descending to this land of exile, didst will to suffer and to die, in order to bear away each single soul and plunge it into the very heart of the Blessed Trinity—Love's eternal home! Thou who, returning to Thy realm of light, dost still remain hidden here in our vale of tears under the semblance of the white Host.... O eternal Eagle, it is Thy wish to nourish me with Thy divine substance, a poor little being who would fall into nothingness if Thy divine glance did not give me life at every moment .... Forgive me, O Jesus, if I tell Thee that Thy love reacheth even unto folly, and at the sight of such folly, what wilt Thou but that my heart should leap up to Thee? How could my trust know any bounds? I know well that for Thy sake the saints have made themselves foolish—being "eagles" they have done great things. Too little for such mighty deeds, my folly lies in the hope that Thy love wilt accept me as a victim …. O my divine Eagle! As long as Thou willest, I shall remain with my gaze fixed upon Thee, for I long to be fascinated by Thy divine eyes, I long to become Love's prey.

I am filled with the hope that one day Thou wilt swoop down upon me, and bearing me away to the source of Love, wilt plunge me at last into its glowing abyss, that I may become forever its happy victim. Amen.

Martin Luther (Luder) *(10 November 1483 – 18 February 1546) Luther's father wanted him to become a lawyer. Luther gave himself to the church after fearing for his life during a thunderstorm. He went on for his education to receive a doctor's degree in Theology. Martin Luther was a reformer, a translator, an author, a hymn writer, a husband, and a father of six children.*

Morning Prayer

My Heavenly Father, I thank you, through Jesus Christ, Your beloved Son, that you kept me safe from all evil and danger last night. Save me, I pray, today as well, from every evil and sin, so that all I do and the way that I live will please you. I put myself in Your care, body and soul and all that I have. Let Your holy angels be with me, so that the evil enemy will not gain power over me. Amen.

Evening Prayer

My heavenly Father, I thank You, through Jesus Christ, Your beloved Son, that you have protected me, by Your grace. Forgive, I pray, all my sins and the evil I have done. Protect me, by Your grace, tonight. I put myself in Your care, body and soul and all that I have. Let Your holy angels be with me, so that the evil enemy will not gain power over me. Amen.

Sacristy Prayer

Lord God, you have appointed me as a bishop and pastor in Your Church, but you see how unsuited I am to meet so great and difficult a task. If I had lacked Your help, I would have ruined everything long ago. Therefore, I call upon you: I wish to devote my mouth and my heart to you; I shall teach the people. I myself will learn and ponder diligently upon Your Word. Use me as Your instrument - but do not forsake me, for if ever I should be on my own, I would easily wreck it all. Amen.

Lord God, heavenly Father, I ask and would be assured that my petitions shall and must be nothing less than yea and amen. Otherwise I will not pray nor have intercession made for me. Not that I am righteous or worthy, for I know very well and confess that I am unworthy. I have earned Thine eternal wrath and hell fire with my great and many sins. But in this that Thou dost command and constrain me to pray in the Name of Thy dear Son, our Lord Jesus Christ, I am still somewhat obedient. Upon this challenge and consolation of Thine infinite goodness, not on account of my own righteousness, do I kneel or stand before Thee, and pray what is upon my heart concerning those who are in need of Thy help. If Thou dost not help us, O Lord, Thou wilt offend and dishonor Thy Name. Thou wilt surely spare Thyself, lest the world would say Thou wert an ungracious and dreadful God. Preserve us from such a misfortune.

Remember, dear heavenly Father, how Thou hast at all times supported and helped Thy people. I will not cease to knock but will continue to cry aloud and to plead to the end of my life. Amen.

Macarius of Egypt *(295-392 A.D) Macarius was married and widowed before he entered the priesthood. He is known as one of the Desert Fathers. Little is known of his life. He became a priest after age 40. He founded a monastery and fifty homilies have been traditionally ascribed to him.*

O Eternal God and King of all creation, Who hast granted me to arrive at this hour, forgive me the sins that I have committed today in thought, word and deed, and cleanse, O Lord, my humble soul from all defilement of flesh and spirit. And grant me, O Lord, to pass the sleep of this night in peace, that when I rise from my bed I may please Thy most holy Name all the days of my life and conquer my flesh and the fleshless foes that war with me. And deliver me, O Lord, from vain and frivolous thoughts, and from evil desires which defile me. For Thine is the kingdom, the power and the glory of the Father, Son and Holy Spirit, now and ever, and to the ages of ages. Amen.

George MacDonald *(10 December 1824 – 18 September 1905) MacDonald was a Scottish author, pastor and poet. He was a friend of Lewis Carroll, Mark Twain, and a contemporary of Charles Dickens. He is widely known for his fantasy writing which began as a way to pay the bills when his congregation tried to starve him out of the ministry. His novels were foundational in the communication of Theology through fictional characters.*

O Lord, my God, how long Shall my poor heart pant for a boundless joy? How long, O mighty

Spirit, shall I hear The murmur of Truth's crystal waters slide From the deep caverns of their endless being, But my lips taste not, and the grosser air choke each pure inspiration of Thy will?

I am a denseness 'twixt me and the light; I cannot round myself; my purest thought, ere it is thought, hath caught the taint of earth, And mocked me with hard thoughts beyond my will. I would be a wind Whose smallest atom is a viewless wing, All busy with the pulsing life that throbs to do Thy bidding; yea, or the meanest thing That has relation to a changeless truth, Could I but be instinct with Thee-each thought The lightning of a pure intelligence, And every act as the loud thunder-clap Of currents warring for a vacuum.

Lord, clothe me with Thy truth as with a robe; Purge me with sorrow; I will bend my head And let the nations of Thy waves pass over, Bathing me in Thy consecrated strength; And let Thy many-voiced and silver winds Pass through my frame with their clear influence, O save me; I am blind; lo, thwarting shapes Wall up the void before, and thrusting out Lean arms of unshaped expectation, beckon Down to the night of all unholy thoughts.

Oh, when at midnight one of Thy strong angels Stems back the waves of earthly influence that shape unsteady continents around me, and they draw off with the devouring gush of exile billows that have found a home, leaving me islanded on unseen points, Hanging 'twixt Thee and chaos-I have seen Unholy shapes lop off my shining thoughts, And they have lent me leathern wings of fear, of baffled pride and harrowing distrusta; and Godhead, with its crown of many stars, its pinnacles of flaming holiness, and voice of leaves in the green summer-time, has seemed the shadowed image of a self! Then my soul blackened; and I rose to find and grasp my doom, and cleave the arching deeps of desolation.

O Lord, my soul is a forgotten well clad round with its own rank luxuriance; A fountain a kind sunbeam searches for, sinking the lustre of its arrowy finger through the long grass its own strange virtue hath blinded up its crystal eye withal: Make me a broad strong river coming down with shouts from its high hills, whose rocky hearts throb forth the joy of their stability in watery pulses from their inmost deeps; and I shall be a vein upon Thy world, circling perpetual from the parent deep.

Most mighty One, confirm and multiply my thoughts of good; help me to wall each sacred treasure round with the firm battlements of special action. Alas, my holy happy thoughts of Thee make not perpetual nest within my soul, but like strange birds of dazzling colors stoop the trailing glories of their sunward speed for one glad moment, filling my blasted boughs with the sunshine of their wings. Make me a forest of gladdest life wherein perpetual spring lifts up her leafy tresses in the wind. Lo, now I see Thy trembling starlight sit among my pines, and Thy young moon slide down my arching boughs with a soft sound of restless eloquence! And I can feel a joy as when Thy hosts of trampling winds, gathering in maddened bands, roar upward through the blue and flashing day round my still depths of uncleft solitude.

Hear me, O Lord, when the black night draws down upon my soul, and voices of temptation darken down the misty wind, slamming Thy starry doors with bitter jests:-'Thou fool!' they seem to say, 'thou hast no seed of goodness in thee; all thy nature hath been stung right through and through; thy sin hath blasted thee and made thee old; thou hadst a will, but thou hast killed it dead, and with the fulsome garniture of life built out the loathsome corpse; thou art a child of night and death, even lower than a worm; gather the skirts up of thy shadowy self, and with what resolution thou hast left fall on the damned spikes of doom!' Oh, take me like a child, if Thou hast made me for Thyself, my God, and lead me up Thy hills. I shall not fear, so Thou wilt make me pure, and beat back sin with the terrors of Thine eye: it fears me not as once it might have feared Thine own good image, but lays bold siege at my heart's doors.

Oh, I have seen a thing of beauty stand in the young moonlight of its upward thoughts, and the old earth came round it with its gifts of gladness, whispering leaves, and odorous plants, until its large and spiritual eye burned with intensest love: my God, I could have watched it evermore with Argus-eyes, lest when the noontide of the summer's sun let down the tented sunlight on the plain, his flaming beams should scorch my darling flower; and through the fruitless nights of leaden gloom, of plashing rains, and knotted winds of cold, yea, when Thy lightnings ran across the sky, and the loud stumbling blasts fell from the hills upon the mounds of death, I could have watched guarding such beauty like another life! But, O my God, it changed!-Yet methinks I know not if it was not I! Its beauty turned to ghastly loathsomeness! Then a hand spurned me backwards from the clouds, and with the gather of a mighty whirlwind, drew in the glittering gifts of life. How long, O Lord, how long? I am a man lost in a rocky place! Lo, all Thy echoes smite me with confusion of varied speech,-the cry of vanished Life rolled upon nations' sighs-of hearts uplifted against despair-the stifled sounds of Woe sitting perpetual by its grey cold well- or wasted toil climbing its endless hills with quickening gasps-or the thin winds of Joy that beat about the voices of the crowd!

Lord, hast thou sent Thy moons to mock us with perpetual hope? Lighted within our breasts the love of love to make us ripen for despair, my God? Oh, dost thou hold each individual soul strung clear upon Thy flaming rods of purpose? Or does Thine inextinguishable will stand on the steeps of night with lifted hand filling the yawning wells of monstrous space with mixing thought-drinking up single life as in a cup? and from the rending folds of glimmering purpose, do all Thy navied stars slide through the gloom with mystic melody, like wishes on a brow? Oh, is my soul, hung like a dewdrop in Thy grassy ways, drawn up again into the rack of change even through the lustre which created it? O mighty one, Thou wilt not smite me through with scorching wrath, because my spirit stands bewildered in Thy circling mysteries! Oh lift the burdened gloom that chokes my soul with dews of darkness; smite the lean winds of death that run with howls around the ruined temples, blowing the souls of men about like leaves.

Lo, the broad life-lands widen overhead, star-galaxies arise like drifting snow, and happy life goes whitening down the stream of boundless action, whilst my fettered soul sits, as a captive in a noisome dungeon watches the pulses of his withered heart lave out the sparkling minutes of his life on the idle flags! Come in the glory of Thine excellence, rive the dense gloom with wedges of clear light, and let the shimmer of Thy chariot wheels burn through the cracks of night! So slowly, Lord, to lift myself to Thee with hands of toil, climbing the slippery cliffs of unheard prayer! Lift up a hand among my idle days- One beckoning finger:

I will cast aside the clogs of earthly circumstance and run up the broad highways where the countless worlds sit ripening in the summer of Thy love. Send a clear meaning sparkling through the years; burst all the prison-doors, and make men's hearts bush up like fountains with Thy melody; brighten the hollow eyes; fill with life's fruits the hands that grope and scramble down the wastes; and let the ghastly troops of withered ones come shining o'er the mountains of Thy love.

Lord, Thy strange mysteries come thickening down upon my head like snowflakes, shutting out the happy upper fields with chilly vapor. Shall I content my soul with a weak sense of safety? Or feed my ravenous hunger with sore purged hopes, that are not hopes but fears clad in white raiment? The creeds lie in the hollow of men's hearts like festering pools glassing their own corruption; the slimy eyes stare up with dull approval, and answer not when Thy bright starry feet move on the watery floors: oh, shake men's souls together like the gathering of all oceans rent from their hidden chambers, till the waves lift up their million voices of high joy along the echoing cliffs!

Come thus, O Lord, with nightly gifts of stars, and lay a hand of mighty peace upon the quivering flood. O wilt thou hear me when I cry to Thee? I am a child lost in a mighty forest; the air is thick with voices, and strange hands reach through the dusk, and pluck me by the skirts. There is a voice which sounds like words from home, but, as I stumble on to reach it, seems to leap from rock to rock: oh, if it is willing obliquity of sense, descend, heal all my wanderings, take me by the hand, and lead me homeward through the shadows.

Let me not by my willful acts of pride block up the windows of Thy truth, and grow a wasted, withered thing, that stumbles on down to the grave with folded hands of sloth and leaden confidence. Amen.

Mechthild of Magdeburg *(c.1207-c. 1294) Mechthild was born in Saxony. She was a part of Bequine movement, a Christian lay order who did not take formal vows, in the middle ages. She wrote extensively often criticizing church leaders for their profligate lives. Her work is Das fließende Licht der Gottheit (The Flowing Light of Divinity), comprised of seven books written between 1250 and 1280. Eventually she was ostracized for her critical treatment of the clergy. Her works were translated into Latin, but she was one of the first to write theological works in her native German.*

I cannot dance, O Lord, unless you lead me. If you will that I leap joyfully then you must be the first to dance and to sing! Then, and only then, will I leap for love. Then will I soar from love to knowledge, from knowledge to fruition, from fruition to beyond all human sense. And there I will remain and circle for evermore. Amen.

Andrew Murray *(9 May 1828 – 18 January 1917) Andrew Murray was a South African Dutch Reformed pastor. Murray was born in South Africa, but was educated in Scotland, the Netherlands and Germany. He wrote extensively about prayer, authoring 240 books. One of his best known works is* <u>With Christ in the School of</u>

Prayer. *His first parish was over 50,000 square miles which he covered several times a year in a wagon drawn by oxen.*

Blessed Lord! Whoever livest to pray, Thou canst teach me too to pray, me too to live ever to pray. In this Thou lovest to make me share Thy glory in heaven, that I should pray without ceasing, and ever stand as a priest in the presence of my God.

Lord Jesus! I ask Thee this day to enroll my name among those who confess that they know not how to pray as they ought, and specially ask Thee for a course of teaching in prayer. Lord! Teach me to tarry with Thee in the school, and give Thee time to train me. May a deep sense of my ignorance, of the wonderful privilege and power of prayer, of the need of the Holy Spirit as the Spirit of prayer, lead me to cast away my thoughts of what I think I know, and make me kneel before Thee in true teachableness and poverty of spirit. And fill me, Lord, with the confidence that with such a teacher as Thou art I shall learn to pray.

In the assurance that I have as my teacher, Jesus who is ever praying to the Father, and by His prayer rules the destinies of His Church and the world, I will not be afraid. As much as I need to know of the mysteries of the prayer-world, Thou wilt unfold for me. And when I may not know, Thou wilt teach me to be strong in faith, giving glory to God. Blessed Lord! Thou wilt not put to shame Thy scholar who trusts Thee, nor, by Thy grace, would he Thee either. Amen.

Blessed Lord! I adore the love with which Thou didst teach a woman, who had refused Thee a cup of water, what the worship of God must be. I rejoice in the assurance that Thou wilt no less now instruct Thy disciple, who comes to Thee with a heart that longs to pray in spirit and in truth. O my Holy Master! Do teach me this blessed secret. Teach me that the worship in spirit and truth is not of man, but only comes from Thee; that it is not only a thing of times and seasons, but the outflowing of a life in Thee.

Teach me to draw near to God in prayer under the deep impression of my ignorance and my having nothing in myself to offer Him, and at the same time of the provision Thou, my Savior, makest for the Spirit's breathing in my childlike stammerings. I do bless Thee that in Thee I am a child, and have a child's liberty of access; that in Thee I have the spirit of Sonship and of worship in truth. Teach me, above all, Blessed Son of the Father, how it is the revelation of the Father that gives confidence in prayer; and let the infinite Fatherliness of God's Heart be my joy and strength for a life of prayer and of worship. Amen.

Blessed Savior! with my whole heart I do bless You for the appointment of the inner chamber, as the school where You meet each of Your pupils alone, and reveal to him the Father. O my Lord! Strengthen my faith so in the Father's tender love and kindness, that as often as I feel sinful or troubled, the first instinctive thought may be to go where I know the Father waits me, and where prayer never can go unblessed. Let the thought that He knows my need before I ask, bring me, in great restfulness of faith, to trust that He will give what His child requires. O let the place of secret prayer become to me the most beloved spot of earth. And, Lord! hear me as I pray that You would everywhere bless the closets of Your believing people. Let Your wonderful revelation of a Father's tenderness free all young Christians from every thought of secret prayer as a duty or a burden, and lead them to regard it as the highest privilege of their life, a joy and a blessing. Bring back all who are discouraged, because they cannot find ought to bring You in prayer. O give them to understand that they have only to come with their emptiness to Him who has all to give, and delights to do it.

Not, what they have to bring the Father, but what the Father waits to give them, be their one thought. And bless especially the inner chamber of all Your servants who are working for You, as the place where God's truth and God's grace is revealed to them, where they are daily anointed with fresh oil, where their strength is renewed, and the blessings are received in faith, with which they are to bless their fellow-men. Lord, draw us all in the closet nearer to Yourself and the Father. Amen.

OUR FATHER.' We thank You, Lord, for these Living Blessed Words which You has given us. We thank You for the millions who in them have learnt to know and worship the Father, and for what they have been to us. Lord! it is as if we needed days and weeks in Your school with each separate petition; so deep and full are they. But we look to You to lead us deeper into their meaning: do it, we pray You, for Your Name's sake; Your name is Son of the Father. Lord! You didst once say: No man knows the Father save the Son, and he to whom the Son wills to reveal Him.' And again: I made known unto them Your name, and will make it known, that the love wherewith You have loved Me may be in them.' Lord Jesus! reveal to us the Father. Let His name, His infinite Father-love, the love with which He loved You, according to Your prayer, BE IN US. Then shall we say aright, OUR FATHER!' Then shall we apprehend Your teaching, and the first spontaneous breathing of our heart will be: Our Father, Your Name, Your Kingdom, Your Will.' And we shall bring our needs and our sins and our temptations to Him in the confidence that the love of such a Father care for all. Blessed Lord! we are Your scholars, we trust You; do teach us to pray, OUR FATHER.' Amen.

Oh, Lord Jesus! Teach me to understand and believe what You have now promised me. It is not hid from You, O my Lord, with what reasonings my heart seeks to satisfy itself, when no answer comes. There is the thought that my prayer is not in harmony with the Father's secret counsel; that there is perhaps something better You would give me; or that prayer as fellowship with God is blessing enough without an answer.

And yet, my blessed Lord, I find in Your teaching on prayer that You didst not speak of these things, but didst say so plainly, that prayer may and must expect an answer. You dost assure us that this is the fellowship of a child with the Father: the child asks and the Father gives. Blessed Lord! Your words are faithful and true. It must be, because I pray amiss, that my experience of answered prayer is not clearer. It must be, because I live too little in the Spirit, that my prayer is too little in the Spirit, and that the power for the prayer of faith is wanting. Lord! teach me to pray. Lord Jesus! I trust You for it; teach me to pray in faith. Lord! teach me this lesson of today: Every one that asks receives. Amen.

Blessed Lord! You know that this, though it be one of the first and simplest and most glorious lessons in Your school, is to our hearts one of the hardest to learn: we know so little of the love of the Father. Lord!

teach us so to live with the Father that His love may be to us nearer, clearer, dearer, than the love of any earthly father. And let the assurance of His hearing our prayer be as much greater than the confidence in an earthly parent, as the heavens are higher than earth, as God is infinitely greater than man. Lord! show us that it is only our unchildlike distance from the Father that hinders the answer to prayer, and lead us on to the true life of God's children. Lord Jesus! it is father-like love that wakens childlike trust. O reveal to us the Father, and His tender, pitying love, that we may become childlike, and experience how in the child-life lies the power of prayer. Blessed Son of God! the Father loves You and hath given You all things.

And You love the Father, and have done all things He commanded You, and therefore have the power to ask all things. Lord! Give us Your own Spirit, the Spirit of the Son. Make us childlike, as You wert on earth. And let every prayer be breathed in the faith that as the heaven is higher than the earth, so God's Father-love, and His readiness to give us what we ask, surpasses all we can think or conceive. Amen.

Father in heaven! You didst send Your Son to reveal Yourself to us, Your Father-love, and all that that love has for us. And He has taught us, that the gift above all gifts which You wouldst bestow in answer to prayer is, the Holy Spirit. O my Father! I come to You with this prayer; there is nothing I would--may I not say, I do--desire so much as to be filled with the Spirit, the Holy Spirit. The blessings He brings are so unspeakable, and just what I need. He sheds abroad Your love in the heart, and fills it with Yourself. I long for this. He breathes the mind and life of Christ in me, so that I live as He did, in and for the Father's love. I long for this. He endues with power from on high for all my walk and work. I long for this. O Father! I beseech You, give me this day the fullness of Your Spirit. Father! I ask this, resting on the words of my Lord: HOW MUCH MORE THE HOLY SPIRIT.' I do believe that You hear my prayer; I receive now what I ask; Father! I claim and I take it: the fullness of Your Spirit is mine. I receive the gift this day again as a faith gift; in faith I reckon my Father works through the Spirit all He has promised.

The Father delights to breathe His Spirit into His waiting child as He tarries in fellowship with Himself. Amen.

O my Blessed Lord and Teacher! I must come to You in prayer. Your teaching is so glorious, and yet too high for me to grasp. I must confess that my heart is too little to take in these thoughts of the wonderful boldness I may use with Your Father as my Friend. Lord Jesus! I trust You to give me Your Spirit with Your Word, and to make the Word quick and powerful in my heart. I desire to keep Your Word of this day: Because of his importunity he will give him as many as he needs.' Lord! teach me more to know the power of persevering prayer. I know that in it the Father suits Himself to our need of time for the inner life to attain its growth and ripeness, so that His grace may indeed be assimilated and made our very own. I know that He would fain thus train us to the exercise of that strong faith that does not let Him go even in the face of seeming disappointment. I know He wants to lift us to that wonderful liberty, in which we understand how really He has made the dispensing of His gift dependent on our prayer. Lord! I know this: O teach me to see it in spirit and truth. And may it now be the joy of my life to become the almoner of my Rich Friend in heaven, to care for all the hungry and perishing, even at midnight, because I know MY FRIEND, who always gives to him who perseveres, because of his importunity, as many as he needs. Amen.

Blessed Lord! You have this day again given us another of Your wondrous lessons to learn. We humbly ask You, O give us to see aright the spiritual realities of which You have been speaking.

There is the harvest which is so large, and perishing, as it waits for sleepy disciples to give the signal for labourers to come. Lord, teach us to look out upon it with a heart moved with compassion and pity.

There are the labourers, so few. Lord, show us how terrible the sin of the want of prayer and faith, of which this is the token. And there is the Lord of the harvest, so able and ready to send them forth. Lord, show us how He does indeed wait for the prayer to which He has bound His answer. And there are the disciples, to whom the commission to pray has been given: Lord, show us how You canst pour down Your Spirit and breathe upon them, so that Your compassion and the faith in Your promise shall rouse them to unceasing, prevailing prayer. O our Lord! we cannot understand how You canst entrust such work and give such power to men so slothful and unfaithful. We thank You for all whom You art teaching to cry day and night for labourers to be sent forth. Lord, breathe Your own Spirit on all Your children, that they may learn to live for this one thing alone--the Kingdom and glory of their Lord--and become fully awake to the faith of what their prayer can accomplish. And let all our hearts in this, as in every petition, be filled with the assurance that prayer, offered in loving faith in the living God, will bring certain and abundant answer. Amen.

Lord Jesus! teach me to pray with all my heart and strength, that there may be no doubt with You or with me as to what I have asked. May I so know what I desire that, even as my petitions are recorded in heaven, I can record them on earth too, and note each answer as it comes. And may my faith in what Your Word has promised be so clear that the Spirit may indeed work in me the liberty to will that it shall come.

Lord! Renew, strengthen, sanctify wholly my will for the work of effectual prayer. Blessed Saviour!

I do beseech You to reveal to me the wonderful condescension You show us, thus asking us to say what we will that You should do, and promising to do whatever we will. Son of God! I cannot understand it; I can only believe that You have indeed redeemed us wholly for Yourself, and dost seek to make the will, as our noblest part, Your most efficient servant. Lord! I do most unreservedly yield my will to You, as the power through which Your Spirit is to rule my whole being. Let Him take possession of it, lead it into the truth of Your promises, and make it so strong in prayer that I may ever hear Your voice saying: Great is your faith: be it unto you even as you will.' Amen.

Blessed Lord! You didst come from the Father to show us all His love, and all the treasures of blessing that love is waiting to bestow. Lord! You have this day again flung the gates so wide open, and given us such promises as to our liberty in prayer, that we must blush that our poor hearts have so little taken it in. It has been too large for us to believe. Lord! We now look up to You to teach us to take and keep and use this precious word of Your: All things whatsoever you ask, believe that you have received.' Blessed Jesus! it is Yourself in whom our faith must be rooted if it is to grow strong. Your work has freed us wholly from the power of sin, and opened the way to the Father;

Your Love is ever longing to bring us into the full fellowship of Your glory and power; Your Spirit is ever drawing us upward into a life of perfect faith and confidence; we are assured that in Your teaching we shall learn to pray the prayer of faith. You will train us to pray so that we believe that we receive, to believe that we really have what we ask.

Lord! Teach me so to know and trust and love You, so to live and abide in You, that all my prayers rise up and come before God in You, and that my soul may have in You the assurance that I am heard. Amen.

O my God! I do believe in You. I believe in You as the Father, Infinite in Your Love and Power. And as the Son, my Redeemer and my Life. And as the Holy Spirit, Comforter and Guide and Strength. Three-One God, I have faith in You. I know and am sure that all that You art You art to me, that all You have promised You will perform. Lord Jesus! increase this faith. Teach me to take time, and wait and worship in the Holy Presence until my faith takes in all there is in my God for me. Let it see Him as the Fountain of all Life, working with Almighty Strength to accomplish His will on the world and in me. Let it see Him in His love longing to meet and fulfill my desires. Let it so take possession of my heart and life that through faith

God alone may dwell there. Lord Jesus, help me! with my whole heart would I believe in God. Let faith in God each moment fill me. O my Blessed Saviour! How can Your Church glorify You, how can it fulfill that work of intercession through which Your kingdom must come, unless our whole life be FAITH IN GOD. Blessed Lord! speak Your Word, HAVE FAITH IN GOD,' unto the depths of our souls. Amen.

O Lord Jesus! how continually You have to reprove us for our unbelief! How strange it must appear to You, this terrible incapacity of trusting our Father and His promises. Lord! Let Your reproof, with its searching, Because of your unbelief,' sink into the very depths of our hearts, and reveal to us how much of the sin and suffering around us is our blame. And then teach us, Blessed Lord, that there is a place where faith can be learned and gained,--even in the prayer and fasting that brings into living and abiding fellowship with Yourself and the Father.

O Saviour! You Yourself art the Author and the Perfecter of our faith; teach us what it is to let You live in us by Your Holy Spirit. Lord! our efforts and prayers for grace to believe have been so unavailing. We know why it was: we sought for strength in ourselves to be given from You. Holy Jesus! do at length teach us the mystery of Your life in us, and how You, by Your Spirit, dost undertake to live in us the life of faith, to see to it that our faith shall not fail. O let us see that our faith will just be a part of that wonderful prayer-life which You give in them who expect their training for the ministry of intercession, not in word and thought only, but in the Holy Unction You give, the inflowing of the Spirit of Your own life. And teach us how, in fasting and prayer, we may grow up to the faith to which nothing shall be impossible. Amen.

Blessed Father! You art Love, and only he that abides in love abides in You and in fellowship with You. The Blessed Son hath this day again taught me how deeply true this is of my fellowship with You in prayer.

O my God! let Your love, shed abroad in my heart by the Holy Spirit, be in me a fountain of love to all around me, that out of a life in love may spring the power of believing prayer. O my Father! grant by the Holy Spirit that this may be my experience, that a life in love to all around me is the gate to a life in the love of my God. And give me especially to find in the joy with which I forgive day by day whoever might offend me, the proof that Your forgiveness to me is a power and a life.

Lord Jesus! my Blessed Teacher! teach You me to forgive and to love. Let the power of Your blood make the pardon of my sins such a reality, that forgiveness, as shown by You to me, and by me to others, may be the very joy of heaven. Show me whatever in my intercourse with fellowmen might hinder my fellowship with God, so that my daily life in my own home and in society may be the school in which strength and confidence are gathered for the prayer of faith. Amen.

Blessed Lord! who didst in Your high-priestly prayer ask so earnestly for the unity of Your people, teach us how You dost invite and urge us to this unity by Your precious promise given to united prayer. It is when we are one in love and desire that our faith has Your presence and the Father's answer. O Father! we pray for Your people, and for every smaller circle of those who meet together, that they may be one. Remove, we pray, all selfishness and self-interest, all narrowness of heart and estrangement, by which that unity is hindered. Cast out the spirit of the world and the flesh, through which Your promise loses all its power. O let the thought of Your presence and the Father's favour draw us all nearer to each other.

Grant especially Blessed Lord, that Your Church may believe that it is by the power of united prayer that she can bind and loose in heaven; that Satan can be cast out; that souls can be saved; that mountains can be removed; that the kingdom can be havened. And grant, good Lord! that in the circle with which I pray, the prayer of the Church may indeed be the power through which Your Name and Word are glorified. Amen.

O Lord my God! teach me now to know Your way, and in faith to apprehend what Your Beloved Son has taught: He will avenge them speedily.' Let Your tender love, and the delight You have in hearing and blessing Your children, lead me implicitly to accept Your promise, that we receive what we believe, that we have the petitions we ask, and that the answer will in due time be seen. Lord! we understand the seasons in nature, and know to wait with patience for the fruit we long for--O fill us with the assurance that not one moment longer than is needed will You delay, and that faith will have the answer. Blessed Master! You have said that it is a sign of God's elect that they cry day and night. O teach us to understand this. You know how speedily we grow faint and weary. It is as if the Divine Majesty is so much beyond the need or the reach of continued supplication, that it does not become us to be too importunate. O Lord! Do teach me how real the labour of prayer is. I know how here on earth, when I have failed in an undertaking, I can often succeed by renewed and more continuing effort, by giving more time and thought: show me how, by giving myself more entirely to prayer, to live in prayer, I shall obtain what I ask. And above all, O my blessed Teacher!

Author and perfecter of faith, let by Your grace my whole life be one of faith in the Son of God who loved me and gave Himself for me--in whom my prayer gains acceptance, in whom I have the assurance of the answer, in whom the answer will be mine. Lord Jesus! in this faith I will pray always and not faint. Amen.

Everlasting God! The Three-One and Thrice Holy! in deep reverence would I with veiled face worship before the holy mystery of Your Divine Being. And if it please You, O most glorious God, to unveil aught of that mystery, I would bow with fear and trembling, lest I sin against You, as I meditate on Your glory. Father! I thank You that You bear this name not only as the Father of Your children here on earth, but as having from eternity subsisted as the Father with Your only-begotten Son. I thank You that as Father You canst hear our prayer, because You have from eternity given a place in Your counsels to the asking of Your Son. I thank You that we have seen in Him on earth, what the blessed intercourse was He had with You in heaven; and how from eternity in all Your counsels and decrees there had been room left for His prayer and their answers. And I thank You above all that through His true human nature on Your throne above, and through Your Holy Spirit in our human nature here below, a way has been opened up by which every human cry of need can be taken up into and touch the Life and the

Love of God, and receive in answer whatsoever it shall ask. Blessed Jesus! in whom as the Son the path of prayer has been opened up, and who gives us assurance of the answer, we beseech You, teach Your people to pray. O let this each day be the sign of our sonship, that, like You, we know that the Father hears us always. Amen.

Lord! what is man, that You are mindful of him? and the son of man, that You visit him? for You has made him a little lower than the angels, and have crowned him with glory and honour. You madest him to have dominion over the work of Your hands: You have put all things under his feet. O Lord our Lord, how excellent is Your name in all the earth! Lord God!

How low has sin made man to sink. And how terribly has it darkened his mind, that he does not even know his Divine destiny, to be Your servant and representative.

Alas! that even Your people, when their eyes are opened, are so little ready to accept their calling and to seek to have power with God, that they may have power with men too to bless them. Lord Jesus! it is in You the Father hath again crowned man with glory and honour, and opened the way for us to be what He would have us. O Lord, have mercy on Your people, and visit Your heritage! Work mightily in Your Church, and teach Your believing disciples to go for their royal priesthood, and in the power of prayer, to which You have given such wonderful promises, to serve Your kingdom, to have rule over the nations, and make the name of God glorious in the earth. Amen.

O my Lord! I have this day again heard words from You which pass my comprehension. And yet I cannot do aught but in simple childlike faith take and keep them as Your gift to me too. You have said that in virtue of Your going to the Father, he that believeth on You will do the works which You have done, and greater works. Lord! I worship You as the Glorified One, and look for the fulfillment of Your promise. May my whole life just be one of continued believing in You. So purify and sanctify my heart, make it so tenderly susceptible of Yourself and Your love, that believing on You may be the very life it breathes. And You have said that in virtue of Your going to the Father, whatsoever we ask, You will do. From Your throne of power You would make Your people share the power given You, and work through them as the members of Your body, in response to their believing prayers in Your Name.

Power in prayer with You, and power in work with men, is what You has promised Your people and me too. Blessed Lord! Forgive us all that we have so little believed You and Your promise, and so little proved Your faithfulness in fulfilling it. O forgive us that we have so little honoured Your all-prevailing Name in heaven or upon earth. Lord! Teach me to pray so that I may prove that Your Name is indeed all-prevailing with God and men and devils. Yea, teach me so to work and so to pray that You canst glorify Yourself in me as the Omnipotent One, and do Your great work through me too. Amen.

Blessed Lord Jesus! I come again to You. Every lesson You give me convinces me more deeply how little I know to pray aright. But every lesson also inspires me with hope that You are going to teach me, that You art teaching me not only to know what prayer should be, but actually to pray as I ought. O my Lord! I look with courage to You, the Great Intercessor, who didst pray and dost hear prayer, only that the Father may be glorified, to teach me too to live and to pray to the glory of God. Saviour! To this end I yield myself to You again. I would be nothing. I have given self, as already crucified with You, to the death. Through the Spirit its workings are mortified and made dead; Your life and Your love of the Father are taking possession of me.

A new longing begins to fill my soul, that every day, every hour, that in every prayer the glory of the Father may be everything to me. O my Lord! I am in Your school to learn this: teach You in me. Do You, the God of glory, the Father of glory, my God and my Father, accept the desire of a child who has seen that Your glory is indeed alone worth living for. O Lord!

Show me Your glory. Let it overshadow me. Let it fill the temple of my heart. Let me dwell in it as revealed in Christ. And do You Yourself fulfill in me Your own good pleasure, that Your child should find his glory in seeking the glory of his Father. Amen.

Beloved Lord! do teach me to take this promise anew in all its simplicity, and to be sure that the only measure of Your holy giving is our holy willing. Lord! Let each word of this Your promise be anew made quick and powerful in my soul. You say: Abide in me! O my Master, my Life, my All, I do abide in You. Give You me to grow up into all Your fullness. It is not the effort of faith, seeking to cling to You, nor even the rest of faith, trusting You to keep me; it is not the obedience of the will, nor the keeping the commandments; but it is Yourself living in me and in the Father, that alone can satisfy me. It is Yourself, my Lord, no longer before me and above me, but one with me, and abiding in me; it is this I need, it is this I seek. It is this I trust You for. You say: Ask whatsoever you will! Lord! I know that the life of full, deep abiding will so renew and sanctify and strengthen the will that I shall have the light and the liberty to ask great things. Lord! let my will, dead in Your death, living in Your life, be bold and large in its petitions. You say: It shall be done.

O You who art the Amen, the Faithful and True Witness, give me in Yourself the joys confidence that You will make this word yet more wonderfully true to me than ever, because it hath not entered into the heart of man to conceive what God hath prepared for them that love Him. Amen.

Blessed Lord! Your lesson this day has again discovered to me my folly. I see how it is that my prayer has not been more believing and prevailing. I was more occupied with my speaking to You than Your speaking to me. I did not understand that the secret of faith is this: there can be only so much faith as there is of the Living Word dwelling in the soul. And Your word had taught me so clearly: Let every man be swift to hear, slow to speak; let not your heart be hurry to utter anything before God. Lord, teach me that it is only with Your word taken up into my life that my words can be taken into Your heart; that Your word, if it be a living power within me, will be a living power with You; what Your mouth hath spoken Your hand will perform. Lord! Deliver me from the uncircumcised ear. Give me the opened ear of the learner, wakened morning by morning to hear the Father's voice. Even as You didst only speak what You didst hear, may my speaking be the echo of Your speaking to me. When Moses went into the tabernacle to speak with Him, he heard the voice of One speaking unto him from off the mercy-seat.'

Lord, may it be so with me too. Let a life and character bearing the one mark, that Your words abide and are seen in it, be the preparation for the full blessing: Ask whatsoever you will, and it shall be done unto you.' Amen.

Blessed Master! Teach me to apprehend fully what I only partly realize, that it is only through the will of God, accepted and acted out in obedience to His commands, that we obtain the power to grasp His will in His promises and fully to appropriate them in our prayers. And teach me that it is in the path of fruit-bearing that the deeper growth of the branch into the Vine can be perfected, and we attain to the perfect oneness with Yourself in which we ask whatsoever we will.

O Lord! Reveal to us, we pray You, how with all the hosts of heaven, and with Yourself the Son on earth, and with all the men of faith who have glorified You on earth, obedience to God is our highest privilege, because it gives access to oneness with Himself in that which is His highest glory--His all perfect will. And reveal to us, we pray You, how in keeping Your commandments and bearing fruit according to Your will, our spiritual nature will grow up to the full stature of the perfect man, with power to ask and to receive whatsoever we will. O Lord Jesus! Reveal Yourself to us, and the reality of Your purpose and Your power to make these Your wonderful promises the daily experience of all who utterly yield themselves to You and Your words. Amen.

Blessed Lord! It is as if each lesson You give me has such fullness and depths of meaning, that if I can only learn that one, I shall know how to pray aright. This day I feel again as if I needed but one prayer every day: Lord! Teach me what it is to pray in Your Name.

Teach me so to live and act, to walk and speak, so to do all in the Name of Jesus, that my prayer cannot be anything else but in that blessed Name too.

And teach me, Lord! to hold fast the precious promise that WHATSOEVER we ask in Your Name, You will do, the Father will give. Though I do not yet fully understand, and still less have fully attained, the wondrous union You meanest when You say, IN MY NAME, I would yet hold fast the promise until it fills my heart with the undoubting assurance: Anything in the Name of Jesus.

O my Lord! let Your Holy Spirit teach me this. You didst say of Him, The Comforter, whom the Father shall send IN MY NAME.' He knows what it is to be sent from heaven in Your Name, to reveal and to honour the power of that Name in Your servants, to use that Name alone, and so to glorify You. Lord Jesus! let Your Spirit dwell in me, and fill me. I would, I do yield my whole being to His rule and leading. Your Name and Your Spirit are one; through Him Your Name will be the strength of my life and my prayer. Then I shall be able for Your Name's sake to forsake all, in Your Name to speak to men and to God, and to prove that this is indeed the Name above every name. Lord Jesus! O teach me by Your Holy Spirit to pray in Your Name. Amen.

O my God! in holy awe I bow before You, the Three in One. Again I have seen how the mystery of prayer is the mystery of the Holy Trinity. I adore the Father who ever hears, and the Son who ever lives to pray, and the Holy Spirit, proceeding from the Father and the Son, to lift us up into the fellowship of that ever-blessed, never-ceasing asking and receiving. I bow, my God, in adoring worship, before the infinite condescension that thus, through the Holy Spirit, takes us and our prayers into the Divine Life, and its fellowship of love.

O my Blessed Lord Jesus! Teach me to understand Your lesson, that it is the indwelling Spirit, streaming from You, uniting to You, who is the Spirit of prayer. Teach me what it is as an empty, wholly consecrated vessel, to yield myself to His being my life. Teach me to honour and trust Him, as a living Person, to lead my life and my prayer. Teach me specially in prayer to wait in holy silence, and give Him place to breathe within me His unutterable intercession. And teach me that through Him it is possible to pray without ceasing, and to pray without failing, because He makes me partaker of the never-ceasing and never-failing intercession in which You, the Son, dost appear before the Father. Yea, Lord, fulfill in me Your promise, At that day you shall ask in my Name. Verily, verily, I say unto you, Whatsoever you shall ask the Father in my Name, that will He give.' Amen.

Blessed Lord! In lowly adoration I would again bow before You. Your whole redemption work has now passed into prayer; all that now occupies You in maintaining and dispensing what You didst purchase with Your blood is only prayer. You ever live to pray.

And because we are and abide in You, the direct access to the Father is always open, our life can be one of unceasing prayer, and the answer to our prayer is sure. Blessed Lord! You have invited Your people to be Your fellow-workers in a life of prayer. You have united Yourself with Your people and make them as Your body share with You in that ministry of intercession through which alone the world can be filled with the fruit of Your redemption and the glory of the Father. With more liberty than ever I come to You, my

Lord, and beseech You: Teach me to pray. Your life is prayer, Your life is mine. Lord! teach me to pray, in You, like You.

And, O my Lord! Give me specially to know, as You didst promise Your disciples, that You art in the Father, and I in You, and You in me. Let the uniting power of the Holy Spirit make my whole life an abiding in You and Your intercession, so that my prayer may be its echo, and the Father hear me in You and You in me. Lord Jesus! let Your mind in everything be in me, and my life in everything by in You. So shall I be prepared to be the channel through which Your intercession pours its blessing on the world. Amen.

O my Blessed High Priest! who am I that You should thus invite me to share with You in Your power of prevailing intercession! And why, O my Lord! Am I so slow of heart to understand and believe and exercise this wonderful privilege to which You have redeemed Your people. O Lord! Give Your grace that this may increasingly be my unceasing life-work--in praying without ceasing to draw down the blessing of heaven on all my surroundings on earth. Blessed Lord! I come now to accept this my calling. For this I would forsake all and follow You. Into Your hands I would believingly yield my whole being: form, train, inspire me to be one of Your prayer-legion, wrestlers who watch and strive in prayer, Israels, God's princes, who have power and prevail. Take possession of my heart, and fill it with the one desire for the glory of God in the ingathering, and sanctification, and union of those whom the Father hath given You. Take my mind and let this be my study and my wisdom, to know when prayer can bring a blessing. Take me wholly and fit me as a priest ever to stand before God and to bless in His Name. Blessed Lord! Be it here, as through all the spiritual life:

You all, I nothing. And be it here my experience too that he that has and seeks nothing for himself, receives all, even to the wonderful grace of sharing with You in Your everlasting ministry of intercession. Amen.

Blessed Lord Jesus! Gethsemane was Your school, where You didst learn to pray and to obey. It is still Your school, where You lead all Your disciples who would fain learn to obey and to pray even as You. Lord! teach me there to pray, in the faith that You has atoned for and conquered our self-will, and canst indeed give us grace to pray like You. O Lamb of God! I would follow You to Gethsemane, there to become one with You, and to abide in You as You dost unto the very death yield Your will unto the Father. With You, through You, in You, I do yield my will in absolute and entire surrender to the will of the Father. Conscious of my own weakness, and the secret power with which self-will would assert itself and again take its place on the throne, I claim in faith the power of Your victory. You didst triumph over it and deliver me from it. In Your death I would daily live; in Your life I would daily die. Abiding in You, let my will, through the power of Your eternal Spirit, only be the tuned instrument which yields to every touch of the will of my God. With my whole soul do I say with You and in You, Father! Not as I will, but as You will.' And then, Blessed Lord! Open my heart and that of all Your people, to take in fully the glory of the truth, that a will given up to God is a will accepted of God to be used in his service, to desire, and purpose, and determine, and will what is according to God's will. A will which, in the power of the Holy Spirit the indwelling God, is to exercise its royal prerogative in prayer, to loose and to bind in heaven and upon earth, to ask whatsoever it will, and to say it shall be done. O Lord Jesus! teach me to pray. Amen.

Blessed Master! With my whole heart I thank You for this blessed lesson, that the path to a life full of answers to prayer is through the will of God. Lord! Teach me to know this blessed will by living it, loving it, and always doing it. So shall I learn to offer prayers according to that will, and to find in their harmony with God's blessed will, my boldness in prayer and my confidence in accepting the answer. Father! it is Your will that Your child should enjoy Your presence and blessing. It is Your will that everything in the life of Your child should be in accordance with Your will, and that the Holy Spirit should work this in Him. It is Your will that Your child should live in the daily experience of distinct answers to prayer, so as to enjoy living and direct fellowship with Yourself. It is Your will that Your Name should be glorified in and through Your children, and that it will be in those who trust You. O my Father! let this Your will be my confidence in all I ask.

Blessed Saviour! Teach me to believe in the glory of this will. That will is the eternal love, which with Divine power works out its purpose in each human will that yields itself to it. Lord! Teach me this. You canst make me see how every promise and every command of the word is indeed the will of God, and that its fulfillment is secured to me by God Himself. Let thus the will of God become to me the sure rock on which my prayer and my assurance of an answer ever rest. Amen.

O You my blessed High Priest, accept the consecration in which my soul now would respond to Your message. I believe in the HOLY PRIESTHOOD OF YOUR SAINTS, and that I too am a priest, with power to appear before the Father, and in the prayer that avails much bring down blessing on the perishing around me. I believe in the POWER OF YOUR PRECIOUS BLOOD to cleanse from all sin, to give me perfect confidence toward God, and bring me near in the full assurance of faith that my intercession will be heard.

I believe in the ANOINTING OF THE SPIRIT, coming down daily from You, my Great High Priest, to sanctify me, to fill me with the consciousness of my priestly calling, and with love to souls, to teach me what is according to God's will, and how to pray the prayer of faith. I believe that, as You my Lord Jesus art Yourself in all things my life, so You, too, art THE SURETY FOR MY PRAYER-LIFE, and will Yourself draw me up into the fellowship of Your wondrous work of intercession.

In this faith I yield myself this day to my God, as one of His anointed priests, to stand before His face to intercede in behalf of sinners, and to come out and bless in His Name. Holy Lord Jesus! accept and seal my consecration. Youa, Lord, do You lay Your hands on me, and Yourself consecrate me to this Your holy work. And let me walk among men with the consciousness and the character of a priest of the Most High God.

Unto Him that loved us, and washed us from our sins IN HIS OWN BLOOD, AND HATH MADE US kings and priests unto God and His Father; TO HIM be glory and dominion forever and ever. Amen.

O my Father, with my whole heart do I praise You for this wondrous life of never-ceasing prayer, never-ceasing fellowship, never-ceasing answers, and never-ceasing experience of my oneness with Him who ever lives to pray. O my God! keep me ever so dwelling and walking in the presence of Your glory, that prayer may be the spontaneous expression of my life with You.

Blessed Saviour! with my whole heart I praise You that You didst come from heaven to share with me in my needs and cries, that I might share with You in Your all-prevailing intercession. And I thank You that You have taken me into the school of prayer, to teach the blessedness and the power of a life that is all prayer. And most of all, that You have taken me up into the fellowship of Your life of intercession, that through me too Your blessings may be dispensed to those around me.

Holy Spirit! With deep reverence I thank You for Your work in me. It is through You I am lifted up into a share in the intercourse between the Son and the Father, and enter so into the fellowship of the life and love of the Holy Trinity Spirit of God! perfect Your work in me; bring me into perfect union with Christ my Intercessor. Let Your unceasing indwelling make my life one of unceasing intercession. And let so my life become one that is unceasingly to the glory of the Father and to the blessing of those around me. Amen.

Origen *(c. 185–254 AD) Origen was the son of Christian parents. His father, Leonidas, was martyred for his faith. Origen supported his mother and 8 siblings by teaching. He is credited with founding two schools, one in Alexandria and another in Caesarea.*

He was a scholar and perhaps the first to establish what is today called Systematic Theology. When in his sixties he was tortured for his faith and even though he was released, he later died of his injuries from the torture. He saw the primacy of Scripture as the foundation of faith and practice.

O Educator, be gracious to Thy children, O Educator, Father, Guide of Israel, Son and Father, both one, Lord. Give to us, who follow Thy command, to fulfill the likeness of Thy image, and to see, according to our strength, the God who is both a good God and a Judge who is not harsh. Do thou Thyself bestow all things on us who dwell in Thy peace, who have been placed in Thy city, who sail the sea of sin unruffled, that we may be made tranquil and supported by the Holy Spirit, the unutterable Wisdom, by night and day, unto the perfect day, to sing eternal thanksgiving to the one only Father and Son, Son and Father, Educator and Teacher with the Holy Spirit.

Patrick *(c389-461AD) Patrick was the son of Christian parents. His father was a deacon and his grandfather a priest. Patrick was taken captive in England at the age of sixteen by an Irish chieftain. After six years as a shepherd Patrick escaped, walked to the coast and found passage on a ship. He returned to his home for a time before training for the priesthood. Patrick returned to Ireland with followers and began to spread the gospel. His greatest written work is his <u>Confessions</u>. Little is known about the actual dates and events of his life.*

Lord, because you have made me, I owe you the whole of my love; because you have redeemed me, I owe you the whole of myself; because you have promised so much, I owe you my whole being. Moreover, I owe you as much more love than myself as you are greater than I, for whom you gave yourself and to whom you promised yourself. I pray you, Lord, make me taste by love what I taste by knowledge; let me know by love what I know by understanding. I owe you more than my whole self, but I have no more, and by myself I cannot render the whole of it to you. Draw me to you, Lord, in the fullness of your love. I am wholly yours by creation; make me all yours, too, in love. I rise today Through the strength of heaven -Light of sun, Radiance of moon, Splendor of fire, Speed of lightning, Swiftness of wind, Depth of sea, Stability of earth, Firmness of rock. Amen.

Francis de Sales *(21 August 1567 – 28 December 1622) François de Sales; He was born into a noble French family, the oldest of six sons. He was educated as a gentleman and eventually received doctorates in law and Theology. François possessed a deep faith and a gentle spirit. He wrote of God's Theology of love that should guide the life of every believer. Eventually he became the Roman Catholic Bishop of Geneva but because of the strong influence of John Calvin he was not able to live in Switzerland. He wrote <u>Introduction for a Divine Life</u> for laypeople and "Treatise on the Love of God."*

O my God, I thank you and I praise you for accomplishing your holy and all-lovable will without any regard for mine. With my whole heart, in spite of my heart, do I receive this cross I feared so much! It is the cross of Your choice, the cross of Your love.

I venerate it; nor for anything in the world would I wish that it had not come, since You willed it. I keep it with gratitude and with joy, as I do everything that comes from

Your hand; and I shall strive to carry it without letting it drag, with all the respect and all the affection which Your works deserve. Amen.

Yet, O Lord, though I have no feeling of confidence in You, nevertheless, I know that You are my God, that I am all Yours, and that I have no hope but in Your goodness; so, I abandon myself entirely into Your Hands." It is always in our power to make these acts; although we have difficulty in performing them, still there is no impossibility. Thus we testify faithfulness to our Lord. My God, I give you this day. I offer you, now, all of the good that I shall do and I promise to accept, for love of you, all of the difficulty that I shall meet. Help me to conduct myself during this day in a manner pleasing to you. Amen.

Lord, I am Yours, and I must belong to no one but You. My soul is Yours, and must live only by You. My will is Yours, and must love only for You. I must love You as my first cause, since I am from You. I must love You as my end and rest, since I am for You. I must love You more than my own being, since my being subsists by You. I must love You more than myself, since I am all Yours and all in You. Amen.

May Thy heart dwell always in our hearts! May Thy blood ever flow in the veins of our souls! O sun of our hearts, thou givest life to all things by the rays of Thy goodness I will not go until Thy heart has strengthened me, O Lord Jesus! May the heart of Jesus be the king of my heart! Blessed be God. Amen

(A Syriac Christmas liturgy - late third or early fourth century)

We ask you, Master, be our helper and defender. Rescue those of our number in distress; raise up the fallen; assist the needy; heal the sick; turn back those of your people who stray; feed the hungry; release our captives; revive the weak; encourage those who lose heart. Let all the nations realize that you are the only God, that Jesus Christ is your Child, and that we are your people and the sheep of your pasture.

Charles Haddon Spurgeon *(June 19,1834-January 31,1892) Called the "Prince of Preachers" Pastor of the Metropolitan Tabernacle in London, England. Author, preacher, founder of the Baptist Union in England. The sun never set on his ministry.*

Help from on High O THOU who art King of kings and Lord of lords, we worship Thee. "Before Jehovah's awful throne We bow with sacred joy." We can truly say that we delight in God. There was a time when we feared Thee, O God, with the fear of bondage. Now we reverence, but we love as much as we reverence. The thought of Thine Omnipresence was once horrible to us. We said ; "Whither shall we flee from His presence ? " and it seemed to make hell itself more dreadful, because we heard a voice, " If I make my bed in hell, behold, Thou art there."

But now, O Lord, we desire to find Thee. Our longing is to feel Thy presence, and it is the heaven of heavens that Thou art there. The sick bed is soft when Thou art there.

The furnace of affliction grows cool when Thou art there, and the house of prayer when Thou art present is none other than the house of God, and it is the very gate of heaven. Come near, our Father, come very near to Thy children. Some of us are very weak in body and faint in heart. Soon, O God, lay Thy right hand upon us and say unto us, "Fear not." Peradventure, some of us are alike, and the world is attracting us. Come near to kill the influence of the world with Thy superior power. Even to worship may not seem easy to some. The dragon seems to pursue them, and floods out of his mouth wash away their devotion. Give to them great wings as of an eagle, that each one may fly away into the place prepared for him, and rest in the presence of God to-day. Amen.

Our Father, come and rest Thy children now. Take the helmet from our brow, remove from us the weight of our heavy armor for a while, and may we just have peace, perfect peace, and be at rest. Oh ! help us, we pray Thee, now. As Thou hast already washed Thy people in the fountain filled with blood and they are clean, now this morning wash us from defilement in the water. With the basin and with the ewer, O Master, wash our feet again. It will greatly refresh; it will prepare us for innermost fellowship with Thyself. So did the priests wash ere they went into the holy place. Lord Jesus, take from us now everything that would hinder the closest communion with God. Any wish or desire that might hamper us in prayer remove, we pray Thee.

Any memory of either sorrow or care that might hinder the fixing of our affection wholly on our God, take it away now. What have we to do with idols anymore? Thou hast seen and observed us. Thou knowest where the difficulty lies. Help us against it, and may we now come boldly, not into the Holy place alone, but into the Holiest of all, where we should not dare to come if our great Lord had not rent the veil, sprinkled the mercy seat with His own blood, and bidden us enter.

Now, we have come close up to Thyself, to the light that shineth between the wings of the Cherubim, and we speak with Thee now as a man speaketh with his friends. Our God, we are Thine. Thou art ours. We are now concerned in one business, we are leagued together for one battle. Thy battle is our battle, and our fight is Thine, Help us, we pray Thee.

Thou who didst strengthen Michael and his angels to cast out the dragon and his angels, help poor flesh and blood that to us also the word may be fulfilled : "The Lord shall bruise Satan under your feet, shortly." Our Father, we are very weak. Worst of all we are very wicked if left to ourselves, and we soon fall a prey to the enemy. Therefore help us, We confess that sometimes in prayer when we are nearest to Thee at that very time some evil thought comes in, some wicked desire. Oh ! what poor simpletons we are. Lord help us. We feel as if we would now come closer to Thee still, and hide under the shadow of Thy wings. We wish to be lost in God. We pray that Thou mayest live in us, and not we live, but Christ live in us and show Himself in us and through us. Lord sanctify us. Oh! that Thy spirit might come and saturate every faculty, subdue every passion, and use every power of our nature for obedience to God. Come, Holy Spirit, we do know Thee ; Thou hast often overshadowed us. Come, more fully take possession of us.

Standing now as we feel we are right up at the mercy seat our very highest prayer is for perfect holiness, complete consecration, entire cleansing from every evil. Take our heart, our head, our hands, our feet, and use us all for

Thee. Lord take our substance, let us not hoard it for ourselves, nor spend it for ourselves.

Take our talent, let us not try to educate ourselves that we may have the repute of being wise, but let every gain of mental attainment be still that we may serve Thee better. May every breath be for Thee; may every minute be spent for Thee.

Help us to live while we live and while we are busy in the world as we must be, for we are called to it, may we sanctify the world for Thy service. May we be lumps of salt in the midst of society. May our spirit and temper as well as our conversation be heavenly; may there be an influence about us that shall make the world the better before we leave it Lord hear us in this thing. And now that we have Thine ear we would pray for this poor world in which we live. We are often horrified by it. O, Lord, we could wish that we did not know anything about it for our own comfort. We have said, " Oh ! for a lodge in some vast wilderness." We hear of oppression and robbery and murder, and men seem let loose against each other. Lord, have mercy upon this great and wicked world. What is to be done with these millions ? What can we do ? At least help every child of Thine to do his utmost. May none of us contribute to the evil directly or indirectly, but may we contribute to the good that is in it. We feel we may speak with Thee now about this, for when Thy servant Abraham stood before Thee and spake with such wonderful familiarity to Thee, he pleaded for Sodom; and we plead for London.

We would follow the example of the Father of the Faithful and pray for all great cities, and indeed for all the nations. Lord let Thy kingdom come. Send forth Thy light and Thy truth. Chase the old dragon from his throne, with all his hellish crew.

Oh ! that the day might come when even upon earth the Son of the woman, the Man-child, should rule the nations, not with a broken staff of wood, but with an enduring scepter of iron, full of mercy, but full of power, full of grace, but yet irresistible. Oh! that that might soon come, the personal advent of our Lord ! We long for the millennial triumph of His Word.

Until then, O Lord, gird us for the fight, and make us to be among those who overcome through the blood of the Lamb and through the word of our testimony, because we " love not our lives unto the death." We lift our voice to Thee in prayer ; also, for all our dear ones. Lord bless the sick and make them well as soon as it is right they should be. Sanctify to them all they have to bear. There are also dear friends who are very weak ; some that are very trembling. God bless them. While the tent is being taken down may the inhabitant within look on with calm joy, for we shall by-and-by "be clothed upon with our house that is from heaven." Lord help us to sit very loose by all these things here below. May we live here like strangers and make the world not a house but an inn, in which we sup and lodge, expecting to be on our journey tomorrow.

Lord save the unconverted, and bring out, we pray Thee, from among them those who are converted, but who have not confessed Christ. May the Church be built up by many who, having believed, are baptized unto the sacred name. We pray Thee go on and multiply the faithful in the land.

Oh! That Thou wouldst turn the hearts of men to the gospel once more. Thy servant is often very heavy in heart because of the departures from the faith. Oh! bring them back; let not Satan take away any more of the stars with his tail, but may the lamps of God shine bright.

Oh! Thou that walkest amongst the seven-golden candlesticks trim the flame, pour forth the oil, and let the light shine brightly and steadily. Now, Lord, we cannot pray any longer, though we have a thousand things to ask for. Thy servant cannot, so he begs to leave a broken prayer at the mercy seat with this at the foot of it : We ask in the name of Jesus Christ Thy Son. Amen.

Thanks be unto God O LORD God, help us now really to worship Thee. We would thank Thee for this occasion. We bless Thy name for setting- apart this hallowed season. Lord, wilt Thou shut the door upon the world for us ? Help us to forget our cares. Enable us to rise clean out of this world. May we get rid of all its down-dragging tendencies. May the attractions of these grosser things be gone, and do Thou catch us away to Thyself. We do not ask to be entranced nor to see an angel in shining-apparel, but we do ask that by faith we may see Jesus, and may His presence be so evidently realized among us that we may rejoice as well as if our eyes beheld Him, and love Him and trust Him and worship Him as earnestly as we should do if we could now put our fingers into the print of the nails. O, Thou precious Lord Jesus Christ, we do adore Thee with all our hearts. Thou art Lord of all. We bless Thee for becoming man that Thou mightest be our next of kin, and being next of kin we bless Thee for taking us into marriage union with Thyself and for redeeming us and our inheritance from the captivity into which we were sold.

Thou hast paid Thy life for Thy people; Thou hast ransomed Thy folk with Thy heart's blood. Be Thou, therefore, forever beloved and adored. And now Thou art not here for Thou art risen. Our souls would track the shining way by which Thou hast ascended through the gate of pearl up to Thy Father's throne.

We seem to see Thee sitting there, man, yet God, reigning over all things for Thy people, and our ears almost catch the accents of the everlasting song which rolls up at Thy feet:

"Worthy is the Lamb that was slain to receive honour, and power, and glory, and dominion, and might for ever and ever." Lord, we say, "Amen." From the outskirts of the crowd that surround Thy throne we lift up our feeble voices in earnest "Amens," for Thou wast slain and hast redeemed us to God by Thy blood and hast made us kings and priests unto God, and we shall reign with Thee, for though far off by space, we know that we are very near to Thy heart. Thou lookest over the heads of the angelic squadrons to behold us, and Thou dost hear the praises — aye, and the groans of Thy well-beloved, for are not we most near Thee, Thy flesh and Thy bones? We know we are. We feel the ties of kinship within us.

We our best Beloved's are, and He is ours, and we are longing to get through the crowd that surround Him, and to get to the forefront, and there to bow prostrate at the dear feet that were nailed to the tree for us, and worship the Lamb who liveth for ever and ever, Who has pre- vailed to take the book and loose the seven seals thereof, to Whom be glory, world without end. Hallelujah!

O, Saviour, accept these our poor praises. They come from those Thou lovest, and as we prize any little things that come from those we love, so do we feel that Thou wilt accept the thanksgiving, the reverential homage of Thy people, redeemed ones who are a people near unto Thee, whose names are graven on the palms of Thy hands, of whom Thou art the active head and for whom Thy heart beats true and full of love e'en now.

Oh, we can say we love Thee ; we wish we loved Thee more; but Thou art very dear to us. There is naught on earth like Thee. For the love of Thy name we would live and die. If we think we love Thee more than we do, we pray that we may yet love Thee more than we think. Oh, take these hearts right away and unite them with Thine own, and be Thou heart and soul and life and everything to us ; for whom have we in heaven but Thee, and there is none upon earth we desire beside Thee. We worship the Father, we worship the Son, we worship the Holy Ghost with all the powers of our being. We fall prostrate before the awful yet glorious throne of the Infinite Majesty of heaven. The Lord accept us since we offer these praises in the name of Jesus. And now most blessed Lord, look down upon those who do not love Thee. O Redeemer, look upon them with those eyes of Thine which are as flames of fire. Let them see how ill they treat Thee.

May they consider within themselves how dire is the ingratitude which can be negligent of a Savior's blood, indifferent from a Savior's heart. Oh, bring the careless and the godless to seek for mercy. Let those that are postponing serious things begin to see that the very thought of postponement of the claims of Christ is treason against His Majesty. O Saviour, dart Thine arrows abroad and let them wound many that they may fall down before Thee and cry out for mercy. But there are some who are wounded ; broken hearts that seek peace — men and women, like Cornelius, that want to hear the words which God commands. Amen.

Oh, come Divine Physician, and bind up every broken bone. Come with Thy sacred nard which Thou hast compounded of Thine own heart's blood, and lay it home to the wounded conscience, and let it feel its power. Oh ! give peace to those whose conscience is like the troubled sea which cannot rest.

O God, our God, let not the teaching of the Sunday-school, the preaching of the Evangelists, he personal visitations of individual minds, let not any of these efforts be in vain. Do give conversions. We groan out this prayer from our very heart, yet can we also sing it, for Thou hast heard us plenteously already, and our heart doth rejoice in God the Saviour who worketh so graciously among the children of men. We have been astonished as the Holy Ghost has fallen even upon the chief of sinners, and men afar off from God have been brought in. But, Lord, do more of this among us. Let us see greater things than these. Where we have had one saved, let us have an hundred to the praise of the glorious name and the Well-beloved.

Lord keep us all from sin; teach us how to walk circumspectly; enable us to guard our minds against error of doctrine, our hearts against wrong feelings, and our lives against evil actions. Oh, may we never speak unadvisedly with our lips, nor give way to anger. Above all, keep us from covetousness which is idolatry, and from malice which is of the devil. Grant unto us to be full of sweetness and light. May love dwell in us and reign in us.

May we look not every man on his own things, but every man on the things of others. Give us to live for Jesus. There is no life like it. Help us to be Christly men, Christ's men, and may we in all things reflect the light which we receive from Him.

Bless our beloved Church and all its organizations. O God, take care of it. Oh! do thou make every member of the Church a pastor over others. Let all strive together for the good of all, and so may Thy kingdom come among us. And do Thou prosper all the churches of Jesus Christ. What we ask for ourselves we seek for them. Let missionaries especially be helped by Thy Spirit, and may there come a day in which the minds of men may be better prepared to receive the Gospel, and may Messiah's Kingdom come to the overthrow of her that sitteth on the Seven Hills and to the eternal waning of Mohammed's moon, to the overthrow of every idol, that Christ alone may reign. Our whole heart comes out in this. Reign, Immanuel, reign; sit on the high throne; ride on Thy White Horse ; and let the armies of heaven follow Thee, conquering and to conquer. Come, Lord Jesus; even so, come quickly. Amen and amen.

The Love Without Measure or End LORD, we would come to Thee, but do Thou come to us. Draw us and we will run after Thee. Blessed Spirit, help our infirmities, for we know not what we should pray for as we ought. Come, Holy Spirit, and give right thoughts and right utterance that we may all be able to pray in the common prayer, the whole company feeling that for each one there is a portion.

We are grateful as we remember that if the minister in the sanctuary should not be able to pray for any one of us there is One who bears the names of all His redeemed upon His breast, and upon His shoulder, who will take care with the love of His heart and the power of His arm to maintain the cause of all His own.

Dear Saviour, we put ourselves under Thy sacred patronage. Advocate with the Father, plead for us this day, yea, make intercession for the transgressors. We desire to praise the name of the Lord with our whole heart, so many of us as have tasted that the Lord is gracious. Truly Thou hast delivered us from the gulf of dark despair, wherein we wretched sinners lay. Thou hast brought us up also out of the horrible pit and out of the miry clay, Thou hast set our feet upon a rock, and the new song which Thou hast put into our mouths we would not stifle, but we would bless the Lord whose mercy endureth forever.

We thank Thee, Lord, for the love without beginning which chose us or ever the earth was, for the love without measure which entered into covenant for our redemption, for the love without failure which in due time appeared in the person of Christ and wrought out our redemption, for that love which has never changed, though we have wandered ; that love which abideth faithful even when we are unfaithful.

O God, we praise Thee for keeping us till this day, and for the full assurance that Thou wilt never let us go. Some can say, "He restoreth my soul," they had wandered, wandered sadly, but Thou hast brought them back again. Lord keep us from wandering, then will we sing, "Unto^ Him that is able to keep us from stumbling and to present us faultless before His presence with exceeding joy."

Bless the Lord, our inmost soul blesses the Lord. Blessed be the Father, the Son, and the Holy Spirit, the Triune ; blessed be the Lord for every office sustained by each divine person, and for the divine blessing which has come streaming down to us through each one of those condescending titles worn by the Father, Son, and the Holy Spirit.

We feel like singing all the time ; we would take down our harp from the willows, if we had hung it there, and we would waken every string to the sweetest melody of praise unto the Lord our God. Yet, Lord, we cannot close with praise, for we are obliged to come before Thee with humble confession of sin. We are not worthy of the least of all these favours ; we cannot say, " He is worthy for whom Thou shouldst do this thing," nay, but we are altogether unworthy, and Thy gifts are according to the riches of Thy grace, for which again we praise Thee.

Lord, forgive us all our sin. May Thy pardoned ones have a renewed sense of their acceptance in the Beloved. If any cloud has arisen to hide Thee from any believing eye, take that cloud away. If in our march through this world, so full of mire as it is, we have any spot on us, dear Saviour, wash our feet with that blessed foot-bath, and then say to- us, "Ye are clean every whit."

May we know it so, that there is no condemnation, no separation ; sin is removed as to its separating as well as its destroying power, and may we enter into full fellowship with God May we walk in the light as God is in the light, and have fellowship with Him, while the blood of Jesus Christ, His Son, cleanseth us from all sin.

Let no child of Thine have any dead work upon his conscience, and may our conscience be purged from dead works to serve the living and true God. And oh! if there are any that after having made the profession of religion have gone astray by any form of sin. Lord, restore them. If they have fallen by strong drink, if they have fallen by unchastity, if they have fallen by dishonesty, if, in any way, they have stained their garments, Oh ! that Thy mighty grace might bring them back and put them yet among the children.

But give them not up, set them not as Adam, make them not as Jeroboam, but let Thy repentings be kindled and Thy bowels of compassion be moved for them, and let them also be moved, and may they return with weeping and with supplication, and find Thee a God ready to pardon.

Furthermore, we ask of Thee, our Father, this day to perfect Thy work within our hearts. We are saved, but we would be saved from sin of every form and degree; from sins that lie within, and we are scarcely aware that they are there. If we have any pride of which we are not conscious, any un- belief of which we are not aware, if there is a clinging to the creature, a form of idolatry which we have not yet perceived, we pray Thee, Lord, to search us as with candles till Thou dost spy out the evil and then put it away.

We are not satisfied with pardoned sin, "We pray, create in me a clean heart, O God, and renew a right spirit within me." Help us in our daily life, in our families, in our relations as husbands or wives, parents or children, masters or servants, in our business transactions with our fellow men, in our dealings with the Church of God, may we be true, upright, pure; kept from the great transgression because we are kept from the minor ones.

Oh! that we may be such as glorify Christ. Save us, we pray Thee, from the common religion; give us the peculiar grace of a peculiar people. May we abide in Christ, may we live near to God. Let not the frivolities of the world have any power over us whatever. May we be too full grown in grace to be bewitched with the toys which are only becoming in children.

Oh! give us to serve Thee, and especially, and this prayer we have already prayed but we pray it again, make us useful in the salvation of our fellow man. O Lord, have we lived so long in the world and yet are our children unconverted? May we never rest until they are truly saved. Have we been going up and down in business, and are those round about us as yet un-aware of our Christian character? Have we never spoken to them the Word of Life? Lord, arouse us to a deep concern for all with whom we come in contact from day to day. Make us all missionaries at home or in the street, or in our workshop, wherever Providence has cast our lot, may we there shine as lights in the world.

Lord, keep us right, true in doctrine, true in experience, true in life, true in word, true in deed. Let us have an intense agony of spirit concerning the many who are going down to the everlasting fire of which our Master spoke. Lord save them! LORD, SAVE THEM! Stay, we pray Thee, the torrents of sin that run down the streets of London; purge the dead sea of sin, in which so many of the heathen are lying a soak. Oh! That the day were come when the name of Jesus shall be a household word, when everybody knew of His love, and of His death, and of His blood, and of its cleansing power. Lord, save men, gather out the company of the redeemed people; let those whom the Father gave to Christ be brought out from among the ruins of the fall to be His joy and crown.

"Let the people praise Thee, O God, yea, let all the people praise Thee." Let the ends of the earth fear Him who died to save them. Let the whole earth be filled with the glory of God. This is our great prayer, and we crown it with this: Come, Lord Jesus, come Lord and tarry not!

Come in the fullness of Thy power and the splendor of Thy glory! Come quickly, even so come quickly. Lord Jesus. Amen.

O LORD God! the Fountain of all Fullness, we, who are nothing but emptiness, come unto Thee for all supplies, nor shall we come in vain, since we bear with us a plea which is all pre- valent. Since we come commanded by Thy Word, encouraged by Thy promise, and preceded by Christ Jesus, our great High Priest, we know that whatsoever we shall ask in prayer, believing, we shall receive. Only do Thou help us now to ask right things, and may the utterances of our mouth be acceptable in Thy sight, O God our Strength and our Redeemer.

We would first adore Thy blessed and ever-to-be-beloved Name. "All the earth doth worship Thee, the Father everlasting." Heaven is full of Thy glory. Oh! that men's hearts were filled therewith, that the noblest creatures Thou hast made, whom Thou didst set in the Paradise of God, for whom the Saviour shed His blood, loved Thee with all their hearts. The faithful, chosen, called, and separated, join in the everlasting song. All Thy redeemed praise Thee, O God! As the God of our election we extol Thee for Thine everlasting and immutable love. As the God and Father of our Lord Jesus Christ, we bless Thee for that unspeakable gift, the offering of Thine Only-begotten.

Words are but air, and tongues but clay, and Thy compassion is divine, therefore it is not possible that any words of ours should "reach the height of this great argument," or sound forth Thy worthy praise for this superlative deed of grace.

We bless Thee, also. Divine Son of God, co-equal and co-eternal with the Father, that Thou didst not disdain to be born of the Virgin, and that, being found in fashion like a man^ thou didst not refuse to be obedient unto death, even the death of the cross. Let Thy brows be girt with something better than thorns; let the eternal diadem for ever glitter there. Thou wast slain, and hast redeemed us to God by Thy blood; unto Thee be glory, and honour, and power, and majesty, and dominion, and might, for ever and ever ! And equally, most blessed Spirit, Thou who didst brood over chaos and bring it into order, Thou who didst beget the Son of God's body of flesh. Thou who didst quicken us to spiritual life, by whose divine energy we are sanctified, and hope to be made meet to be partakers of the inheritance of the saints in light, unto Thee, also, be hallelujahs, world without end! O Lord! Our soul longeth for words of fire, but we cannot reach them! Oh! When shall we drop this clay which now is so uncongenial to our song? When shall we be able with wings to mount upward to Thy throne, and having learned some flaming sonnets that have once been sung by cherubim above, we shall praise Thee forever? Yet even these are not rich enough for Thy glory. We would sing unto Thee a new song. We will, when we reach the heavenly shore, become leaders of the eternal music. " Day without night " will we "circle God's throne rejoicing," and count it the fullness of our glory, our bliss, our heaven, to wave the palm and cast our crowns with our songs at Thy feet for ever and ever!

Our Father, which art in heaven ; next to this we would offer prayer for those who never think of Thee; who, though created by Thee, are strangers to Thee ; who are fed by Thy bounty, and yet never lift their voices to Thee, but live for self, for the world, for Satan, for sin. Father, these cannot pray for themselves for they are dead; Thy quickened children pray for them.

These will not come to Thee, for, like sheep, they are lost; but do Thou seek them, Father, and bring them back. Oh! our glorious Lord, Thou hast taught us to pray for others, for the grace which could have met with such undeserving sinners as we are must be able to meet with the vilest of the vile. Oh! we cannot boast of what we are ; we cannot boast of what we have been by nature. Had we our doom we had now been in hell.

Had we this day our proper, natural, and deserved position, we should still have been in the gall of bitterness and in the bond of iniquity. 'Tis Thy rich, free, sovereign, distinguishing grace which has brought us up out of the miry clay, and set our feet upon a rock. And shall we even refuse to pray for others ? Shall we leave a stone unturned for their conversion ? Shall we not weep for those who have no tears and cry for those who have no prayers ? Father, we must and we will. " Fain our pity would reclaim And snatch the fire-brands from the flame." There are those who are utterly careless about Divine Things. Wilt Thou impress them ! May some stray shot reach their conscience ! Oh ! that they may be led solemnly to consider their position and their latter end ! May thoughts of death and of eternity dash like some mighty waves, irresistibly against their souls ! Oh ! may heaven's light shine into their conscience ! May they begin to ask themselves where they are, and what they are, and may they be turned unto the Lord with full purpose of heart.

There are others who are concerned, but they are halting between two opinions. There are some that we love in the flesh who have not yet decided for God. Behold it trembles in the balance ! Cast in Thy cross, O Jesus, and turn the scale ! Oh ! Love irresistible, come forth, and carry by blessed storm the hearts which have not yet yielded to all the attacks of the law ! Oh ! that some who never could be melted, even by the furnace of Sinai, may be dissolved by the beams of love from the tearful eyes of Jesus !

Lord, Lord, if there be a heart that is saying, "Now, behold I yield; lo! at Thy feet rebellion's weapons I lay down, and cease to be Thy foe, Thou King of kings " — if there be one who is saying, "I am willing to be espoused unto Christ, to be washed in His blood, to be called in His righteousness " — bring that willing sinner in now !

May there be no longer delay, but may this be the time when, once for all, the great transaction shall be done, and they shall be their Lord's, and He shall be theirs. Oh ! that we could pour out our soul in prayer for the unconverted! Thou knowest where they will all be in a few years ! Oh ! by Thy wrath, we pray Thee, let them not endure it ! By the flames of hell be pleased to ransom them from going down into the pit ! By everything that is dreadful in the wrath to come we do argue with Thee to have mercy upon these sons of men, even upon those who have no mercy upon themselves. Father, hast Thou not promised Thy Son to see of His soul's travail? We point Thee to the ransom paid; we point Thee once again to the groans of Thy Son, to His agony, and bloody sweat ! Turn, turn Thy glorious eyes thither, and then look on sinners, and speak the word, and bid them live.

Righteous Father, refresh every corner of the vineyard, and on every branch of the vine let the dew of heaven rest. Oh! that Thou wouldest bless Thy church throughout the world ! Let visible union be established, or if not that, yet let the invisible union which has always existed be better recognized by believers. Wilt Thou repair our schisms; wilt Thou repair the breaches which have been made in the walls of Zion?

Oh! that Thou wouldest purge us of everything unscriptural, till all Christians shall come to the law and to the testimony, and still keep the ordinances and the doctrines as they were committed to the apostles by Christ!

Remember our land in this time of need. Do Thou be pleased by some means to relieve the distress prevalent. Quicken the wheels of commerce that the many who are out of employment in this city may no longer be crying for work and bread. Oh ! that Thou wouldest make wars to cease, to the ends of the earth, or, when they break out break Thou the slave's fetters thereby, and though desperate be the evil, yet grant that Satan may cast out Satan, and may his kingdom be divided, and so fall.

Above all. Thou long-expected Messiah, do Thou come! Thine ancient people who despised Thee once are waiting for Thee in Thy second coming, and we, the Gentiles, who knew Thee not, neither regarded Thee, we, too, are watching for Thine advent. Make no tarrying, O Jesus! May Thy feet soon stand again on Olivet! Thou shalt not have this time there to sweat great drops of blood, but Thou shalt come to proclaim the year of vengeance for Thy foes, and the year of acceptance for Thy people.

"When wilt thou the heavens rend, In majesty come down?" Earth travails for Thy coming. The whole creation groaneth in pain together until now. Thine own expect Thee; we are longing till we are weary for Thy coming. Come quickly. Lord Jesus, come quickly. Amen and Amen.

OUR God and Father, draw us to Thyself by Thy Spirit, and may the few minutes that we spend in prayer be full of the true spirit of supplication. Grant that none of us with closed eyes may yet be looking abroad over the fields of vanity, but may our eyes be really shut to every- thing else now but that which is spiritual and Divine. May we have communion with God in the secret of our hearts, and find Him to be to us as a little sanctuary.

O Lord, we do not find it easy to get rid of distracting thoughts, but we pray Thee help us to draw the sword against them and drive them away, and as when the birds came down upon his sacrifice Abraham drove them away, so may we chase away all cares, all thoughts of pleasure, everything else, whether it be pleasing or painful, that would keep us away from real fellowship with the Father and with His Son Jesus Christ. We would begin with adoration. We worship from our hearts the Three in One^ the infinitely glorious Jehovah, the only living and true God We adore the Father, the Son, and the Holy Ghost, the God of Abraham, of Isaac, and of Jacob. We are not yet ascended to the place where pure spirits behold the face of God, but we shall soon be there, perhaps much sooner than we think, and we would be there in spirit now, casting our crowns upon the glassy sea before the throne of the Infinite Majesty, and ascribing glory and honor, and power and praise, and dominion and might to Him that sitteth upon the throne, and unto the Lamb forever and ever.

All the Church doth worship Thee, O God, every heart renewed by grace takes a delight in adoring Thee, and we, among the rest, though least and meanest of them all, yet would bow as heartily as any worshipping, loving, praising, in our soul, being silent unto God because our joy in Him is altogether inexpressible.

Lord help us to worship Thee in life as well as lip. May our whole being be taken up with Thee. As when the fire fell down on Elijah's sacrifice of old and licked up even the water that was in the trenches, so may the consuming fire of the Divine Spirit use up all our nature, and even that which might seem to hinder, even out of that may God get glory by the removal of it. Thus would we adore.

But, oh ! Dear Saviour, we come to Thee, and we remember what our state is, and the condition we are in encourages us to come to Thee now as beggars, as dependents upon Thy heavenly charity. Thou art a Saviour, and as such Thou art on the outlook for those that need saving, and here we are, here we come. We are the men and women Thou art looking for, needing a Saviour.

Great Physician, we bring Thee our wounds and bruises and putrefying sores, and the more diseased we are and the more conscious we are to-day of the depravity of our nature, of the deep-seated corruption of our hearts, the more we feel that we are the sort of beings that Thou art seeking for, for the whole have no need of a physician but they that are sick. Glorious Benefactor, we can meet Thee on good terms, for we are full of poverty, we are just as empty as we can be. We could not be more abjectly dependent than we are. Since Thou wouldest display Thy mercy here is our sin; since Thou wouldest show Thy strength here is our weakness; since Thou wouldest manifest Thy lovingkindness here are our needs ; since Thou wouldest glorify Thy grace here are we, such persons as can never have a shadow of a hope except through Thy grace, for we are undeserving, ill-deserving, hell-deserving, and if Thou do not magnify Thy grace in us we must perish forever. And somehow we feel it sweet to come to Thee in this way. If we had to tell Thee that we had some good thing in us which Thou didst require of us, we should be questioning whether we were not flattering ourselves and presumptuously thinking that we were better than we are.

Lord Jesus, we come just as we are ; this is how we came at first, and this is how we come still, with all our failures, with all our transgressions, with all and everything that is what it ought not to be we come to Thee. We do bless Thee that Thou dost receive us and our wounds, and by Thy stripes we are healed ; Thou dost receive us and our sins, and by Thy sin- bearing we are set clear and free from sin. Thou dost receive us and our death, even our death, for Thou art He that liveth and was dead, and art alive for evermore. We just come and lie at Thy feet, obedient to that call of Thine, "Come unto Me all ye that labour and I will give you rest." Let us feel sweet rest, since we do come at Thy call. May some come that have never come till this day, and may others who have been coming- these many years consciously come again, coming unto Thee as unto a living stone, chosen of God and precious, to build our everlasting hopes upon.

But, Lord, now that we are come so near Thee, and on right terms with Thee, we venture to ask Thee this, that we that love Thee may love Thee very much more. Oh! since Thou hast been precious, Thy very name has music in it to our ears, and there are times when Thy love is so inexpressibly strong upon us that we are carried away with it. We have felt that we would gladly die to in- crease Thine honour. We have been willing to lose our name and our repute if so be Thou mightest be glorified, and truly we often feel that if the crushing of us would lift Thee one inch the higher, we would gladly suffer it.

For oh! Thou blessed King, we would set the crown on Thy head, even if the sword should smite our arm off at the shoulder blade. Thou must be King whatever becomes of us; Thou must be glorified whatever becomes of us.

But yet we have to mourn that we cannot get always to feel as we should this rapture and ardour of love. Oh! At times Thou dost manifest Thyself to us so charmingly that heaven itself could scarce be happier than the world becomes when Thou art with us in it. But when Thou art gone and we are in the dark, oh! give us the love that loves in the dark, that loves when there is no comfortable sense of Thy presence. Let us not be dependent upon feeling-, but may we ever love Thee, so that if Thou didst turn Thy back on us by the year together we would think none the less of Thee, for Thou art unspeakably to be beloved whatsoever Thou doest, and if Thou dost give us rough words, yet still we would cling to Thee, and if the rod be used till we tingle again, yet still will we love Thee, for

Thou art infinitely to be beloved of all men and angels, and Thy Father loved Thee. Make our hearts to love Thee evermore the same.

With all the capacity for love that there is in us, and with all the more that Thou canst give us, may we love our Lord in spirit and in truth. Help us, Lord, to conquer sin out of love to Thee. Help some dear strugglers that have been mastered by sin sometimes, and they are struggling against it; give them the victory, Lord, and when the battle gets very sharp, and they are tempted to give way a little, help them to be very firm and very strong, never giving up hope in the Lord Jesus, and resolving that if they perish they will perish at His feet and nowhere else but there.

Lord raise up in our churches many men and women that are all on fire with love to Christ and His Divine Gospel.

Oh! give us back again men like Antipas, Thy faithful martyr, men like Paul, Thy earnest servant who proclaimed Thy truth so boldly. Give us Johns, men to whom the Spirit may speak, who shall bid us hear what the Spirit saith unto the churches. Lord revive us! Lord revive us; revive Thy work in the midst of the years in all the churches. Return unto the Church of God in this country, return unto her. Thine adversaries think to have it all their own way, but they will not, for the Lord liveth, and blessed be our Rock.

Because of truth and righteousness, we beseech Thee lay bare Thine arm in these last days. O Shepherd of Israel, deal a heavy blow at the wolves and keep Thy sheep in their own true pastures, free from the poisonous pastures of error. O God we would stir Thee up. We know Thou sleepest not, and yet sometimes it seems as if Thou didst sleep awhile and leave things to go on in their own way.

We beseech Thee awake. Plead Thine own cause. We know Thine answer, "Awake! awake! Put on thy strength, O Zion." This we would do, Lord, but we cannot do it unless Thou dost put forth Thy strength to turn our weakness into might. Great God, save this nation! O God of heaven and earth, stay the floods of infidelity and of filthiness that roll over this land. Would God we might see better days! Men seem entirely indifferent now. They will not come to hear the Word as once they did. God of our fathers let Thy Spirit work again among the masses. Turn the hearts of the people to the hearing of the Word, and convert them when they hear it. May it be preached with the Holy Ghost sent down from heaven. Our hearts are weary for Thee, thou King, Thou King forgotten in thine own land. Thou King despised among Thine own people, when wilt Thou yet be glorious before the eyes of all mankind?

Come, we beseech Thee, come quickly, or if Thou comest not personally, send forth the Holy Spirit with a greater power than ever that our hearts may leap within us as they see miracles of mercy repeated in our midst. Father glorify Thy Son. Somehow our prayer always comes to this before we have done. "Father glorify Thy Son that Thy Son also may glorify Thee," and let the days come when He shall see of the travail of His soul and shall be satisfied. Bless all work done for Thee, whether it be in the barn or in the cathedral, silently and quietly at the street door, or in the Sunday-school or in the classes, O Lord bless Thy work. Hear also prayers that have been put up by wives for their husbands, children for their parents, parents for their children. Let the holy service of prayer never cease, and let the intercession be accepted of God, for Jesus Christ's sake. Amen.

GREAT God, there was a time when we dreaded the thought of coming near to Thee, for we were guilty and Thou wast angry with us, but now we will praise Thee because Thine anger is turned away, and Thou comfortest us. Ay, and the very throne which once was a place of dread has now become the place of shelter. I flee unto Thee to hide me. We long now to get right away from the world, even from the remembrance of it, and have fellowship with the world to come by speaking with Him that was, and is, and is to come, the Almighty. Lord we have been worried and wearied oftentimes with care, but with Thee care comes to an end, all things are with Thee, and when we live in Thee we live in wealth, in sure repose, in constant joy. We have to battle with the sons of men against a thousand errors and unrighteousnesses, but when we flee to Thee, there all is truth and purity and holiness, and our heart finds peace.

Above all, we have to battle with ourselves, and we are very much ashamed of ourselves. After many years of great mercy, after tasting of the powers of the world to come, we still are so weak, so foolish ; but, oh ! when we get away from self to God there all is truth and purity and holiness, and our heart finds peace, wisdom, completeness, delight, joy, victory. Oh! Bring us, then, we pray Thee, now near to Thyself. Let us bathe ourselves in communion with our God. Blessed be the love which chose us before the world began. We can never sufficiently adore Thee for Thy sovereignty, the sovereignty of love which saw us in the ruins of the Fall, yet loved us notwithstanding all. We praise the God of the Eternal Council Chamber and of the Everlasting Covenant, but where shall we find sufficiently fit words with which to praise Him who gave us grace in Christ His Son, before He spread the starry sky.

We also bless Thee, O God, as the God of our redemption, for Thou hast so loved us as to give even Thy dear Son for us. He gave Himself, His very life for us that He might redeem us from all iniquity and separate us unto Himself to be His peculiar people, zealous for good works. Never can we sufficiently adore free grace and dying love. The wonders of Calvary never cease to be wonders, they are growingly marvelous in our esteem as we think of Him who washed 'US from our sins in His own blood. Nor can we cease to praise the God of our regeneration who found us dead and made us live, found us at enmity and reconciled us, found us loving the things of . this world and lifted us out of the slough and mire of selfishness and worldliness into the love of divine everlasting things.

O Spirit of God we love Thee this day, especially for dwelling in us. How canst Thou abide in so rude a habitation. How canst Thou make these bodies to be Thy temples, and yet Thou dost so, for which let Thy name be had in reverence so long as we live. O Lord we would delight ourselves in Thee this day. Give us faith and love and hope that with these three graces we may draw very near to the Triune God. Thou wilt keep us, Thou wilt preserve us, Thou wilt feed us, Thou wilt lead us, and Thou wilt bring us to the mind of God, and there wilt Thou show us Thy love, and in the glory everlasting and boundless, there wilt Thou make us know and taste and feel the joys that cannot be expressed. But a little longer waiting and we shall come to the golden shore ; but a little longer fighting and we shall receive the crown of life that fadeth not away. Lord get us up above the world. Come, Holy Spirit, heavenly Dove, and mount and bear us on Thy wings, far from these inferior sorrows and inferior joys, up where eternal ages roll.

May we ascend in joyful contemplation, and may our spirit come back again, strong for all its service, armed for all its battles, armoured for all its dangers, and made ready to live heaven on earth, until by-and- bye we shall live heaven in heaven. Great Father, be with Thy waiting people, any in great trouble do Thou greatly help ; any that are despondent do Thou sweetly comfort and cheer ; any that have erred, and are smarting under their own sin, do Thou bring them back and heal their wounds ; any that this day are panting after holiness do Thou give them the desire of their hearts ; any that are longing for usefulness do Thou lead them into ways of usefulness.

Lord, we want to live while we live. We do pray that we may not merely groan out an existence here below, nor live as earthworms crawling back into our holes and dragging now and then a seed leaves with us ; but oh! give us to live as we ought to live, with a new life that Thou hast put into us, with the divine quickening which has lifted us as much above common men as men are lifted above the beasts that perish. Do not let us always be hampered like poor half-hatched birds within the egg ; may we chip the shell today and get out into the glorious liberty of the children of God. Grant us this, we pray Thee. Lord visit our church. We have heard Thy message to the churches at Ephesus; it is a message to us also.

Oh! Do not let any of us lose our first love. Let not our church grow cold and dead. We are not, we fear, what once we were. Lord revive us! All our help must come from Thee. Give back to the church its love, its confidence, its holy daring, its consecration, its liberality, its holiness. Give back all it ever had and give it much more.

Take every member and wash his feet, Sweet Lord, most tenderly, and set us with clean feet in a clean road, with a clean heart to guide them, and do Thou bless us as Thou art wont to do after a divine fashion. Bless us, our Father, and let all the churches of Jesus Christ partake of like care and tenderness. Walking among the golden candlesticks trim every lamp and make every light, even though it burneth but feebly now, to shine out gloriously through Thy care. Now bless the sinners. Lord convert them. O God, save men, save this great city, this wicked city, this slumbering dead city. Lord, arouse it, arouse it by any means, that it may turn unto its God.

Lord save sinners all the world over, and let Thy precious Word be fulfilled. "Behold He cometh with clouds." Why dost Thou tarry?

Make no tarrying, O, our Lord. And now unto Father, Son, and Holy Ghost be glory for ever and ever. Amen.

OUR Father, when we read Thy description of human nature we are sure it is true, for Thou hast seen man ever since his fall, and Thou hast been grieved at heart concerning- him. More- over, Thou hast such a love towards him that Thou didst not judge him harshly; and every word that Thou hast spoken must be according to truth. Thou hast measured and computed the iniquity of man, for Thou hast laid it on the Well-Beloved; and we know Thou hast not laid upon Him more than is meet. O God, we are distressed, we are bowed down greatly when we see what is the condition to which we and all our race have fallen. "Where is boasting then? " And yet we grieve to say that we do boast, and have boasted; and that our 'fellow-men are great at boasting; whereas they ought rather to lay their hands upon their mouths before Thee. It has become a wonder to us that Thou shouldst look upon man at all ; the most hateful object in creation must be a man, because he slew Thy Son, because he has multiplied rebellions against a just and holy law. And yet truly there is no sight that gives Thee more pleasure than man, for Jesus was a man ; and the brightness of His glory covers all our shame ; and the pureness and perfectness of His obedience shines like the sun in the midst of the thick darkness. For His sake Thou art well pleased, and Thou dost dwell with us.

Lord, we once thought that those descriptions of our heart were somewhat strained, but we think not so now, for verily we perceive that had it not been for restraint which held us like fetters we, in our unregenerate state, were capable of anything; for, even now, when we are regenerate,

the old sin that abideth in us is capable of reaching to a high degree of infamy; and did not the new life restrain the old death we know not what we might yet become. We thought once we were humble; but we soon found that our pride will feed on any current flattery that is laid at our door. We thought we were believers, but sometimes we are so doubting, so unbelieving, so vexed with skepticism that we should not certainly choose to follow: that is Thy work in us.

By nature we are such liars that we think Thee a liar too; the surest token of our untruthfulness, that we think that Thou canst be untrue. Oh, this base heart of ours! hath it not enough tinder in it to set on fire the course of nature ?

If a spark do but fall into it, any one of our members left to itself would dishonour Christ, deny the Lord that bought us, and turn back into perdition.

We are altogether ashamed. Truly in us is fulfilled Thine own Word : " Thou shalt be a shame, and never open thy mouth anymore." For Thy love to us hath silenced us, that great love hath hidden boasting from us ; Thy great love, wherewith Thou lovedst us even when we were dead in trespasses and sins; Thy great love wherewith Thou hast loved us still, despite our ill manners, our wanderings, our shortcomings, and our excesses.

Oh, the matchless love of God ! Truly if there be any glory it must be all the Lord's ; if there be any virtue it is the result of grace ; if there be any- thing whatsoever that lifts us above the devil himself it is the work of the Divine Spirit, to whom be glory! And now at the remembrance of all this, and being in Thy presence, we do yet rejoice that covered is our unrighteousness; from condemnation we are free, and we are the favoured of the Lord.

Thou hast given us, O Lord, to taste of that love which is not merely laid up for us, but we have enjoyed it, and do enjoy it still. Our heart knows the Father's love, for we have received the spirit of adoption, whereby we cry, "Abba Father." And we joy and rejoice in the redemption of our spirits, and we expect the redemption of our bodies, when, at the coming of the Lord they too shall be raised incorruptible, and we shall be changed.

O Jesus, Thou wilt bring Thy Israel out of Egypt, and not a hoof shall be left behind; no, not a bone, nor a piece of Thine elect shall be left in the hands of the adversary. We shall come out clean, delivered by Him Who doeth nothing by halves, but Who on the cross said, "It is finished." Who much more will say it on His throne: Glory be unto Father, Son and Holy Ghost, Who hath lifted us up from our ruin and condemnation, and made us new creatures, and justified us, and guaranteed us eternal life, which eternal life shall be manifested at the coming of the Lord. All glory be unto His ever blessed name for ever and ever ! And now, Lord, during the few days that remain to us here below, be it all our business to cry, "Behold the Lamb!" Oh! teach these hearts to be always conscious of Thy love; and then these lips, that they may set out as best they can by Thy divine help the matchless story of the Cross.

Oh I do give us to win many to Jesus let us not be barren, but may we have to cry that we are the beloved of the Lord, and our offspring with us. May we have many spiritual offspring that shall go with us to the throne, that we may say before Him, I and the children that Thou hast given me." Lord bless the work of the Church and all its branches ; and let Thy kingdom come into the hearts of multitudes by its means. Remember all churches that are really at work for Jesus, and all private individuals, workers alone, workers by themselves. Let the Lord's own name be made known by tens of thousands. Give the Word, and great may be the multitude of them that publish it. Let all this, our beloved country, know Christ, and come to His feet ; let the dark places of this huge city be enlightened with the sweet name of Jesus. And then let the heathen know Thee, and the utter- most parts of the earth hear of Thee.

Oh! from the tree declare Thou Thy salvation, and from the throne let it be published in proclamations of a king. "Let the people praise Thee, O God; yea, let all the people praise Thee." Our heart seems as if it had not anything else to ask for when it reaches to this; yet would we go back a moment and say: Lord, forgive us our sins; Lord, sanctify our persons; Lord, guide us in difficulty; Lord, supply our needs. The Lord teach us; the Lord perfect us ; the Lord comfort us ; the Lord make us meet for the appearing of His Son from heaven !

And now we come back to a theme that still seems to engross our desires. Oh ! that Christ might come. Oh ! that His word might be made known to the uttermost ends of the earth! Lord, they die, they perish, they pass away by multitudes! Every time the sun rises and sets they pass away! Make no tarrying, we beseech Thee. Give wings to the feet of Thy messengers, and fire to their mouths, that they may proclaim the Word with Pentecostal swiftness and might. Oh ! that Thy kingdom might come, and Thy will be done on earth as it is in heaven, for Thine is the kingdom, the power and the glory, for ever and ever. Amen.

OUR Father, we worship and love Thee ; and it is one point of our worship that Thou art holy. Time was when we loved Thee for Thy mercy ; we knew no more ; but now Thou hast changed our hearts and made us in love with goodness, purity, justice, true holiness ; and we understand now why "the cherubim and seraphim continually do cry. Holy, Holy, Lord God of hosts."

We adore Thee because Thou art holy, and we love Thee for Thine infinite perfection. For now we sigh and cry after holiness ourselves. Sanctify us wholly, spirit, soul and body. Lord, we mourn over the sins of our past life and our present shortcomings. We bless Thee Thou hast forgiven us; we are reconciled to Thee by the death of Thy Son. There are many who know that they have been washed, and that He that beareth away sin has borne their sin away.

These are they who now cry to Thee to be delivered from the power of sin, to be delivered from the power of temptation without, but especially from indwelling sin within. Lord purify us in head, heart and hand ; and if it be needful that we should be put into the fire to be refined as silver is refined, we would even welcome the fire if we may be rid of the dross. Lord save us from constitutional sin, from sins of temperament, from sins of our surroundings.

Save us from ourselves in every shape, and grant us especially to have the light of love strong within us. May we love God; may we love Thee, O Saviour; may we love the people of God as being members of one body in connection with Thee. May we love the guilty world with that love which desires its salvation and conversion ; and may we love not in word only, but in deed and in truth. May we help the helpless, comfort the mourner, sympathize with the widow and fatherless,

and may we be always ready to put up with wrong, to be long suffering, to be very patient, full of forgiveness, counting it a small thing that we should forgive our fellow-men since we have been for- given of God. Lord tune our hearts to love, and then give us an inward peace, a restfulness about everything.

May we have no burden to carry, because, though we have a burden, we have rolled it upon the Lord May we take up our cross, and because Christ has once died on the cross may our cross become a comfort to us. May we count it all joy when we fall into divers trials, knowing that in all this God will be glorified. His image will be stamped upon us, and the eternal purpose will be fulfilled, where- in He has predestinated us to be conformed unto the image of His Son.

Lord look upon Thy people. We might pray about our troubles. We will not ; we will only pray against our sins. We might come to Thee about our weariness, about our sickness, about our disappointment, about our poverty; but we will leave all that, we will only come about sin. Lord make us holy, and then do what Thou wilt with us. We pray Thee help us to adorn the doctrine of God our Saviour in all things.

If we are fighting- against sin — "the sin which doth so easily beset us " — Lord lend us heavenly weapons and heavenly strength that we may cut the giants down, these men of Anak that come against us. We feel very feeble. Oh! make us strong in the Lord, in the power of His might. May we never let sin have any rest in us, may we chase it, drive it out, slay it, hang it on a tree, abhor it, and may we "cleave to that which is good."

Some of us are trying, striving after some excellent virtue. Lord help strugglers; enable those that contend against great difficulties only to greater grace, more faith, and so to bring them nearer to God. Lord we will be holy; by Thy grace we will never rest until we are. Thou hast begun a good work in us and Thou wilt carry it on. Thou wilt work in us to will and to do of Thine own good pleasure.

Lord help the converted child to be correct in his relation to his parents; help the Christian father or mother to be right in dealing with children, " may they not provoke their children to anger lest they may discourage." Take away willfulness from the young; take away impatience from the old. Lord help Christian men of business.

May they act uprightly; may Christian masters never be hard to their servants, to their workpeople; and may Christian workpeople give to their masters that which is just and equal in the way of work in return for wage. May we as Christian men be always standing upon our rights, but always be willing each one to minister to the help of others. And, oh that as Christians we might be humble! Lord take away that stiff-necked, that proud look; take away from us the spirit of " stand by, for I am holier than Thou; " make us condescend to men of low estate; ay, and even to men of low morals, low character. May we seek them out, seek their good.

Oh! Give to the Church of Christ an intense love for the souls of men. May it make our hearts break to think that they will perish in their sin. May we grieve every day because of the sin of this City. Set a mark upon our forehead and let us be known to Thyself as men that sigh and cry for all the abominations that are done in the midst of the City.

O God save us from a hard heart, an unkind spirit, that is insensible to the woes of others. Lord preserve Thy people also from worldliness, from rioting, from drunkenness, from chambering and wantonness, from strife and envy, from everything that would dishonor the name of Christ that we bear. Lord make us holy. Our prayer comes back to this. Make us holy; cleanse the inside and let the outside be clean too. Make us holy, O God: do this for Christ's sake. Not that we hope to be saved by our own holiness, but that holiness is salvation. Then we are saved from sin. Lord help Thy poor children to be holy. Oh! keep us so if we are so; keep us even from stumbling, and present us faultless before Thy presence at last. We pray for friends that are ill, for many that are troubled because of the illness of others. We bring before. Thee every case of trouble and trial known to us, and ask for Thy gracious intervention. We pray for Thy ministers everywhere; for Thy missionary servants.

Remember brethren that are making great sacrifice out in the hot sun or in the cold and frozen north. Everywhere preserve those who for Christ's sake carry their lives in their hands. And our brethren at home, in poverty many of them, working for Christ, Lord accept them and help us to help them. Sunday-school teachers, do Thou remember them; and the tract visitors from door to door, and the City missionaries, and the Bible women, all who in any way endeavor to bring Christ under the notice of men. O, help them all. We will offer but one more prayer, and it is this. Lord look in pity upon any who are not in Christ. May they be converted. May they pass from death to life, and they will never forget it; may they see the eternal light for the first time, and they will remember it even in Eternity. Father help us ; bless us now for Jesu's sake. Amen.

OUR Father, we bless Thy name that we can say from the bottom of our hearts, "Abba, Father." It is the chief joy of our lives that we have become the children of God by faith which is in Christ Jesus, and we can in the deep calm of our spirit say, "Our Father, which art in heaven, hallowed be Thy name; Thy kingdom come; Thy will be done in earth as in heaven." Lord, we thank Thee for the liberty which comes to our emancipated spirit through the adoption which Thou hast made us to enjoy.

When we were in servitude the chains were heavy, for we could not keep Thy law; there was an inward spirit of rebellion; when the commandment came it irritated our corrupt nature and sin revived, and we died even when we had some strivings after better things, yet the power that was in us lusted into evil, and the spirit of the Hagarene was upon us; we wanted to fly from the Father's house; we were wild men, men of the wilderness, and we loved not living in the Father's house.

O God, we thank Thee that we have not been cast out. Indeed, if Thou hadst then cast out the child of the bondwoman Thou hadst cast us out, but now through sovereign grace all is altered with us. Blessed by Thy name. It is a work of divine power and love over human nature, for now we are the children of the promise, certainly not born according to the strength of the human will, or of blood, or of birth, but born by the Holy Ghost through the power of the Word, begotten again unto a lively hope by the resurrection of Jesus Christ from the dead, children of the Great Father who is in heaven, having His life within us. Now, like Isaac, we are heirs according to promise and heirs of the promise, and we dwell at home in the Father's house, and our soul is satisfied as with marrow and fatness, and our mouth shall praise Thee as with joyful lips.

O God, we would not change places with angels, much less with kings of the earth. To be indeed Thy sons and daughters — the thought of it doth bring to our soul a present heaven, and the fruition of it shall be our heaven, to dwell forever in the house of the Lord, and go no more out, but to be His sons and His heirs for ever and ever.

Our first prayer is for others who as yet are in bondage. We thank Thee, Lord, that Thou hast given them the spirit of bondage and made them to fear. We are glad that they should be brought to feel the evil of sin, to feel the perfection of Thy law, to know something of the fiery nature of Thy justice, and so to be shut up unto salvation by grace through faith.

But, Lord, let them not tarry long under the pedagogue, but may the schoolmaster with his rod bring them to Christ. Lord, cure any of Thy chosen of self-righteousness; deliver them from any hope in their own abilities, but keep them low. Bring them out of any hope of salvation by their own prayers or their own repentance. Bring them to cast themselves upon Thy grace to be saved by trusting in Christ. Emancipate them from all observance of days, weeks, months, years, and things of human institution, and bring them into the glorious liberty of the children of God that Thy law may become their delight, Thyself become their strength, their all, Thy Son become their joy and their crown. We do pray this with all our hearts. Lord, deliver any of Thy children from quarrelling with Thee. Help us to be always at one with our God. "It is the Lord; let Him do what seemeth Him good," and blessed be His name for ever and ever.

God bless our country, and the sister country across the flood, and all lands where Thy name is known and reverenced, and heathen lands where it is unknown. God bless the outposts, the first heralds of mercy, and everywhere may the Lord's kingdom come and His name be glorified. Glory be unto the Father, and to the Son, and to the Holy Ghost ; as it was in the beginning, is now, and ever shall be, world without end. Amen.

O THOU blessed God, we must be helped of Thy Spirit or we cannot worship Thee aright. Behold the holy angels adore Thee, and the hosts redeemed by blood bring everlasting Hallelujahs to Thy feet. What are we, the creatures of a day, polluted with sin, that we should think that we can praise Thee?

And yet the music of praise were not complete if Thy children did not join in it, even those of them who are still in this world below. Help us, then; enable us to tune our harps and to fetch forth music from our spirit. Verily, Lord, if there are any creatures in the world that can praise Thee we ought to do so. Each one among us feels that he has some special reason for gratitude. Lord, it is an unspeakable mercy to know Thee to know Thee as our reconciled God, to know Thee as our Father in Christ

Jesus, who has forgiven us all our trespasses. Oh! it is unspeakably sweet to come and rest in Thee, and to know that there is now no cause of quarrel between us and Thee; on the contrary, that we are bound to one another by a covenant which in infinite tenderness and mercy Thou hast made, that Thy people might have strong consolation, and might boldly take hold on Thee.

Oh! the joy of knowing that we are Thine forever, thine in the trials of life, and thine in the last dread trial of death and then Thine in resurrection, thine throughout eternity. We do therefore worship Thee, O God, not as a constraining- nor under terror or pressure, but cheerfully and gladly, ascribing unto Thee praise, and power, and dominion, and glory, and honour, world without end. We wish we knew how to do something for Thee.

We pray that we may be helped to do so ere we die; yea, that every flying hour may confess that we have brought Thy Gospel some renown; that we may so live as to extend the Redeemer's kingdom at least in some little measure; that ours may not be a fruitless, wasted life ; that no faculty of ours may lay by and rust; but to the utmost of our capacity may we be helped of the Divine Spirit to spend our whole life in real adoration.

We know that he prays that serves, he praises that gives, he adores that obeys, and the life is the best music. Oh! set it to good music, we pray Thee, and help us all through to keep to each note, and may there be no false note in all the singing of our life, but all be according to that sacred score which is written out so fully in the life music of our Lord.

We beseech Thee to look down upon Thy children, and cheer us. Lord, hold us up. Come, Holy Spirit, like a fresh, bracing wind, and let our spirit, through Thy Spirit, rise upward toward God. We would with much shamefacedness acknowledge our transgressions and sins. There are some that never felt the burden of sin at all. Lord, lay it on them; press them with it. Almighty God, vex their souls; let them find no rest till they find rest in Thee. May they never be content to live and die in sin, but of Thine infinite mercy come to them, and make them sorry for their sin.

As for Thy people we are grieved to think that we do not live better than we do. Blessed be Thy name for every fruit of holiness, for every work of faith, but oh! for more. Thou hast changed the tree; it is no longer a bramble ; it can bring forth figs, but now we want to bring forth more of these sweet fruits. The Lord make us to love Christ intensely, to love the souls of men most heartily, to love Thy truth with earnestness, to love the name of Jesus above everything. May we be ravished with the sound of it. The Lord give us to have every grace, not only love, but faith, and hope, and holy gentleness, meekness, patience, brotherly love. Build us up, we pray Thee, Lord, in all knowledge, and in all experience, and give us with this submission to Thy will, holy resignation, great watchfulness, much carefulness in our speech, that we may rule the tongue, and so rule the whole body.

The Lord pour out His Spirit upon us that every chamber of our nature may be sweetened and perfumed with the indwelling of God, till our imagination shall only delight in things chaste and pure ; till our memory shall cast out the vile stuff from the dark chambers ; till we shall expect and long for heavenly things, and our treasure shall all be in heaven and our heart be there. Take our highest manhood, Lord, and saturate it in Thy love, till like Gideon's fleece it is filled with dew, every lock and every single fleck of it, not a single portion of it left unmoistened by the dew from heaven. How we do bless Thee for many that are striving to walk as Christ walked, and who are also trying to bring others to Christ. O Lord help us in this struggle after holiness and usefulness; and as Thou hast given to many the desire of their hearts in this respect up to a certain measure; now enlarge their hearts, and give them more both of holiness and usefulness.

Oh! Give us to be like trees planted by the rivers of water, that we ourselves may be vigorous, and then give us to bring forth abundant fruit according to our season, to the praise and glory of God. Our desire is that we may be quickened in our progress toward the celestial life. Visit us with Thy salvation. Lord, let us not only have life, but let us have it more abundantly. May we every one of us quicken

His pace, and may we run more earnestly than ever toward the mark that is set before us. Remember all Thy Church throughout the whole world. Prosper missionary operations. Be with any ministers or missionaries that are depressed for lack of success. Be with any that are rejoicing because of success. May each heart be kept in a right state, so that Thou mayest use Thy servants to the utmost of possibility.

O God, send us better days than these, we pray Thee. We thank Thee for all the light there is, but send us more light. We thank Thee for what life there is among Christians, but send more of it. Bind the churches together in unity, and then give them such speed, such force, such power that they shall break into the ranks of the adversary, and the victory shall be unto Christ and to His people. Remember our dear country. Bless the Sovereign. Remember all those that lead our legislature. Be gracious unto all ranks and conditions of men. Have mercy upon all that are poor and needy, all that are sick and sorrowing, and that are tossed upon the sea. Remember the prisoners and such as have no helper. Be gracious to such as are in the article of death; and, finally, let the day come when the Sun shall shine forth in all His brightness, even Christ Jesus shall be manifested, to be admired in them that believe, and to make glad the whole creation. Make no tarrying, O Thou Sun of Righteousness, but come forth speedily. We ask it for Thy name's sake. Amen.

JEHOVAH our God, we thank Thee for leaving on record the story of Thine ancient people. It is full of instruction to ourselves. Help us to take its warning to avoid the faults into which they fell! Thou art a covenant God, and Thou keepest Thy promises and Thy Word never faileth. We have proved this so hitherto : " Thus far we find that promise good, Which Jesus ratified with blood."

But as for ourselves we are like Israel of old, a fickle people, and, we confess it was great shame, there are days when we take the timbrel and we sing with Miriam "unto the Lord who triumphed gloriously," and yet, we grieve to say it, not many hours after, we are thirsty, and we cry for water, and we murmur in our tents ; the brackish Marah turns our heart and we are grieved with our God. Sometimes we bow before Thee with reverence and awe when we behold Thy Sinai altogether on a smoke ; but there have been times when we have set up the golden calf and we have said of some earthly things, "These be Thy gods, O Israel." We believe with intensity of faith and then doubt with a horribleness of doubt. Lord, Thou hast been very patient with us. Many have been our provocations, many have been Thy chastisements, but : " Thy strokes are fewer than our crimes. And lighter than our guilt." "Thou hast not dealt with us after our sins, nor rewarded us according to our iniquities." Blessed be Thy name !

And now fulfil that part of the covenant wherein Thou hast said, " A new heart also will I give Thee and a right spirit will I put within Thee. I will put My fear in their hearts and they shall not depart from Me." Hold us fast and then we shall hold fast to Thee.

Turn us and we shall be turned; keep us and we shall keep Thy statutes. We cry to Thee that we may no more provoke Thee. We beg Thee rather to send the serpents among us than to let sin come among us. Oh! That we might have our eye always on the brazen serpent that healeth all the bites of evil, but may we not look to sin nor love it. Let not the devices of Balaam and of Balak prevail against us, to lead Thy people away from their purity.

Let us not be defiled with false doctrine or with unholy living, but may we walk as the separated people of God and keep ourselves unspotted from the world. Lord, we would not grieve Thy Spirit. Oh! may we never vex Thee so as to lead Thee in Thy wrath to say, " They shall not enter into my rest." Bear with us still for His dear sake whose blood is upon us. Bear with us still and send not the destroying angel as Thou didst to Egypt, but again fulfil that promise of Thine, "When I see the blood I will pass over you." Just now may we be consciously passed over by the Spirit of condemnation ; may we know in our hearts that "there is therefore now no condemnation to them that are in Christ Jesus." May we feel the peace giving power of the Divine absolution. May we come into Thy holy presence with our feet washed in the brazen laver, hearing our great High Priest say to us, "Ye are clean every whit." Thus made clean may we draw near to God through Jesus Christ our Lord. Further, our heavenly Father, we come before Thee now washed in the blood, wearing the snow white robe of Christ's righteousness, and we ask Thee to remember Thy people. Some are sore burdened; lighten the burden or strengthen the shoulder. Some are bowed down with fear ; peradventure they mistrust ; forgive the mistrust and give a great increase of faith that they may trust Thee where they cannot trace Thee.

The Lord remember any who bear the burden of others. Some cry to Thee day and night about the sins of the times, about the wanderings of Thy Church. Lord hear our prayers ! We would bear this yoke for Thee, but help us to bear it without fearing so as to distrust Thee. May we know that Thou wilt take care of Thine own case and preserve Thine own truth, and may we therefore be restful about it all. Some are crying to Thee for the conversion of relatives and friends ; this burden they have taken up to follow after Jesus in the cross bearing. Grant them to see the desire of their heart fulfilled. God save our children and children's children, and if we have unconverted relatives of any kind, the Lord have mercy upon them for Christ's sake. Give us joy in them — as much joy in them as Christians as we have had sorrow about them as unbelievers.

Further, be pleased to visit Thy Church with the Holy Spirit. Renew the day of Pentecost in our midst, and in the midst of all gatherings of Thy people may there come the downfall of the holy fire, the uprising of the heavenly wind. May matters that are now slow and dead become quick and full of life, and may the Lord Jesus Christ be exalted in the midst of His Church which is His fullness, "the fullness of Him that filleth all in all." May multitudes be converted ; may they come flocking to Christ with holy eagerness to find in Him a refuge as the doves fly to their dovecotes. Oh! For salvation work throughout these islands and across the sea and in every part of the world, especially in heathen lands. Bring many to Christ's feet, we pray Thee, everywhere where men are ready to lay down their lives that they may impart the heavenly life of Christ. Work, Lord, work mightily! Thy Church cries to Thee. Oh, leave us not! We can do nothing without Thee!

Our strength is wholly Thine ! Come to us with great power, and let Thy Word have free course and be glorified. Remember every one that calls Thee Father. May a Father's love look on all the children. May the special need of each one be supplied, the special sorrow of each one be assuaged. May we be growing Christians, may we be working Christians, may we be perfected Christians, may we come to the fullness of the stature of men in Christ Jesus. Lord Jesus Thou art a great pillar ; in Thee doth all fullness dwell. Thou didst begin Thy life with filling the water pots ·to the full ; Thou didst fill Simon Peter's boat until it began to sink; Thou didst fill the house where Thy people were met together with the presence of the Holy Ghost ; Thou dost fill heaven ; Thou wilt surely fill all things; fill us, oh! Fill us today with all the fullness of God, and make Thy people thus joyful and strong, and gracious and heavenly! But we cannot leave off our prayer when we have prayed for Thy people, though we have asked large things ; we want Thee to look among the thousands and millions round about us who know Thee not. Lord, look on the masses who go nowhere to worship. Have pity upon them ; Father forgive them, for they know not what they do. Give a desire to hear Thy Word. Send upon the people some desire after their God. O Lord take sinners in hand Thyself. Oh! Come and reach obstinate, obdurate minds ; let the careless and the frivolous begin to think upon eternal things. May there be an uneasiness of heart, a sticking of the arrows of God in their loins, and may they seek too the great Physician and find healing this very day. Ah! Lord, Thou sayest "To-day, if ye will hear His voice," and we take up the echo. Save men today, even to-day. Bring them Thy Spirit in power that they may be willing to rest in Christ. Lord hear, forgive, accept and bless, for Jesu's sake. Amen

Our Father, which art in heaven, hallowed be Thy name. Thy kingdom come, Thy will be done on earth as it is in heaven." We fear that we often begin our prayer with petitions for ourselves, and put our daily bread before Thy kingdom, and the pardoning of our sins before the hallowing of Thy name. We would not do so to-day, but guided by our Lord's model of prayer, we would first pray for Thy glory ; and here, great God, we would adore Thee. Thou hast made us and not we ourselves. We are Thy people, and the sheep of Thy pasture. All glory be unto Thee, Jehovah, the only living and true God.

With heart and mind, and memory and fear, and hope and joy, we worship the Most High. It well becomes us to put our shoes from off our feet when we draw near to God, for the place whereon we stand is holy ground. If God in the bush demanded the unsandalled foot of the prophet, how much more shall God in Christ Jesus? With lowliest reverence, with truest love, we worship God in Christ Jesus, uniting therein with all the redeemed host above, with angels and principalities and powers. We cannot cast crowns at His feet, for we have none as yet, but if there be any virtue, if there be any praise. if there be about us anything of grace and good repute, we ascribe it all to God. We cannot veil our faces with our wings, for we have none, but we veil them with something better than angelic wings, the blood and righteousness of Jesus Christ.

With these we cover our faces, with these we cover our feet, and with these we fly up to God in holiest fellowship of God Glory, and honour, and power, and dominion be unto Him that sitteth upon the throne, and unto the Lamb forever and forever.

Great God, we long that Thou mayest be known unto the ends of the earth, that the idols may be utterly abolished. We long that false doctrine may fly like birds of darkness before the light and Thy coming. Reign Thou in the hearts of our fellow men. Lord, subdue sin, and under Thy feet let drunkenness, and unchastity, and oppression, and every form of wickedness be put away by the Gospel of Jesus Christ and His Holy Spirit. Oh! That today, even today, many hearts might be won to God. Convince men of the wrong of being alienated from God, put into their hearts sorrow for sin and dread of wrath to come, and lead and drive men to Christ. Oh ! how we pray for this, the salvation of our fellow-men, not so much for their sakes as for the sake of the glory of God and the rewarding of Christ for His pain.

We do with all our hearts pray "Thy kingdom come, Thy will be done on earth, as it is in heaven." Lord, help us to do Thy will. Take the crippled kingdom of our manhood and reign Thou over it. Let spirit and body be consecrated to God. May there be no reserves ; may everything be given up to Thee. Reign forever! Pierced King, despised and nailed to a tree, sit Thou on the glorious high throne in our hearts, and may our lives prove that Thou art Lord over us; by our every thought and desire, and imagination, and word, and act, in every respect being under Thy divine control.

Thy people breathe to Thee out of their very hearts the prayer that Thou mayest reign over us without a rival. O Saviour, use for Thyself what Thou hast bought with blood, and drive out the enemy, and let no power have any dominion over us except the power of Thy good Spirit which worketh righteousness and peace.

We pray today also that Thy truth may prevail against the many anti-Christs that have gone forth against it. Our Father, restore a pure language to Thy Zion once again.

Take away, we pray Thee, the itching for new doctrine, the longing for that which is thought to be scientific and wise above what is written, and may Thy Church come to her moorings, may she cast anchor in the truth of God and there abide ; and if it be Thy will may we live to see brighter and better times.

If it might be so we would pray for the coming of our Lord very speedily to end these sluggish years, these long delaying days. But, if He come not, yet put power into Thy truth and quicken Thy Church that she may become energetic for the spread of it, that so Thy kingdom may come. This do we seek first and above everything, the glory of God. We ask for grace that we may live with this end in view. May we lay ourselves out to it. May this be our morning thought, the thought that we have in our minds when we lay awake at nights. What shall I do, my Saviour, to praise? How can I make Him illustrious and win another heart to His throne? Now bless us; forgive us our trespasses wherein we have sinned against Thee. Seal our pardon upon our consciences, and make us feel that as we truly forgive them that trespass against us, so hast Thou forgiven us all our iniquities. We pray Thee lead us not into temptation. Do not try us. Lord, nor suffer the devil to try us. If we must be tried then deliver us from evil, and especially from the evil one, that he may get no dominion over us. Oh! Keep us. Lord. This life is full of trial There are many that are perplexed about temporary things. Let not the enemy lead them to do or think aught that is amiss, because of the straitness of supply. Others are blessed with prosperity. Lord, let it not be a curse to them. Let them know how to abound as well as to suffer loss.

In all things may they be instructed to glorify God, not only with all they are, but with all they have, and even with all they have not, by a holy contentment to do without that which it doth not please Thee to bestow.

And then. Lord, give us day by day our daily bread ; provide for Thy poor people ; let them not think that the provision for themselves rests fully on themselves ; but may they cry to Thee, for Thou hast said, "Thy bread shall be given Thee. Thy waters shall be sure." If we follow Thee, if Thou lead us into a desert, Thou wilt strew our path with manna. May Thy people believe this, and let them have no care, but like the birds of the air which neither sow nor gather into barns, and yet are fed, so may Thy people be. But, above all, give us spiritual help. Give us wisdom, which is profitable to get. Give us the absence of all self-seeking, and a complete yielding up of our desires to the will of God. Help us to be as Christ was, who was not His own, but gave Himself to His Father for our sins; so may we for His sake give ourselves up to do or suffer the will of our Father who is in heaven.

Remember Thy people in their families and convert their children ; give us help and strength; spare precious lives that are in danger ; be gracious to any that are dying ; may the life of God swallow up the death of the body. Prepare us all for Thy glorious advent ; keep us waiting and watching, and do Thou come quickly to our heart's desire, for we pray "Thy kingdom come, Thy will be done on earth, as it is in heaven, for Thine is the kingdom, and the power and the glory, forever and ever." Amen

OUR Father, Thy children who know Thee delight themselves in Thy presence. We are never happier than when we are near Thee.

We have found a little heaven in prayer. It has eased our load to tell Thee of its weight; it has relieved our wound to tell Thee of its smart; it has restored our spirit to confess to Thee its wanderings. No place like the mercy seat for us. We thank Thee, Lord, that we have not only found benefit in prayer, but in the answers to it we have been greatly enriched. Thou hast opened Thy hid treasures to the voice of prayer; Thou hast supplied our necessities as soon as ever we have cried unto Thee; yea, we have found it true: "Before they call I will answer, and while they are yet speaking I will hear."

We do bless Thee, Lord, for instituting the blessed ordinance of prayer. What could we do without it, and we take great shame to ourselves that we should use it so little. We pray that we may be men of prayer, taken up with it, that it may take us up and bear us as on its wings towards heaven. And now at this hour wilt Thou hear the voice of our supplication. First, we ask at Thy hands, great Father, complete forgiveness for all our trespasses and shortcomings. We hope we can say with truthfulness that we do from our heart forgive all those who have in any way trespassed against us. There lies not in our heart, we hope, a thought of enmity towards any man. However we have been slandered or wronged, we would, with our inmost heart, forgive and forget it all.

We come to Thee and pray that, for Jesu's sake, and through the virtue of the blood once shed for many for the remission of sins. Thou wouldest give us perfect pardon of every transgression of the past. Blot out, O God, all our sins like a cloud, and let them never be seen again. Grant us also the peace-speaking word of promise applied by the

Holy Spirit, that being justified by faith we may have peace with God through Jesus Christ our Lord.

Let us be forgiven and know it, and may there remain no lingering question in our heart about our reconciliation with God, but by a firm, full assurance based upon faith in the finished work of Christ, may we stand as forgiven men and women against whom transgression shall be mentioned never again for ever. And then. Lord, we have another mercy to ask which shall be the burden of our prayer. It is that Thou wouldest help us to live such lives as pardoned men should live.

We have but a little time to tarry here, for our life is but a vapour; soon it vanishes away ; but we are most anxious that we may spend the time of our sojourning here in holy fear, that grace may be upon us from the commencement of our Christian life even to the earthly close of it. Lord, Thou knowest there are some that have not yet begun to have for Thee, and the prayer is now offered that they may to-day be born again. Others have been long in Thy ways, and are not weary of them. We sometimes wonder that Thou art not weary of us, but assuredly we delight ourselves in the ways of holiness more than ever we did. Oh that our ways were directed to keep Thy statutes without slip or flaw. We wish we were perfectly obedient in thought, and word, and deed, entirely sanctified.

We shall never be satisfied till we wake up in Christ's likeness, the likeness of perfection itself. Oh! work us to this self-same thing, we beseech Thee. May experience teach us more and more how to avoid occasions of sin. May we grow more watchful ; may we have a greater supremacy over our own spirit ; may we be able to control ourselves under all circumstances, and so act that if the

Master were to come at any moment we should not be ashamed to give our account into His hands.

Lord, we are not what we want to be. This is our sorrow. Oh! that Thou wouldest, by Thy Spirit, help us in the walks of life to adorn the doctrine of God our Saviour in all things. As men of business, as work-people, as parents, as children, as servants, as masters, whatever we may be, may we be such that Christ may look upon us with pleasure. May His joy be in us, for then only can our joy be full.

Dear Saviour, we are Thy disciples, and Thou art teaching us the art of living ; but we are very dull and very slow, and besides, there is such a bias in our corrupt nature, and there are such examples in the world, and the influence of an ungodly generation tells even upon those that know Thee. O, dear Saviour, be not impatient with us, but still school us at Thy feet, till at last we shall have learned some of the sublime lessons of self-sacrifice, of meekness, humility, fervor, boldness, and love which Thy life is fit to teach us.

O Lord, we beseech Thee mold us into Thine own image. Let us live in Thee and live like Thee. Let us gaze upon Thy glory till we are trans- formed by the sight, and become Christ-like among the sons of men. Lord, hear the confessions of any that have back-slidden, who are rather marring Thine image than perfecting it. Hear the prayers of any that are conscious of great defects during the past. Give them peace of mind by pardon, but give them strength of mind also to keep clear of such mischief in the future. O Lord, we are sighing and crying more and more after Thyself. The more we have of Thee the more we want Thee ; the more we grow like Thee ; the more we perceive our defects, and the more we pine after a higher standard, to reach even unto perfection's self. Oh help us. Spirit of the living God, continue still to travail in us. Let the groanings that cannot be uttered be still within our Spirit, for these are growing pains, and we shall grow while we can sigh and cry, while we can confess and mourn; yet this is not without a blessed hopefulness that He that hath begun a good work in us will perfect it in the day of Christ. Bless, we pray Thee, at this time, the entire Church of God in every part of the earth.

Prosper the work and service of Christian people, however they endeavour to spread the kingdom of Christ. Convert the heathen ; enlighten those that are in any form of error. Bring the entire Church back to the original form of Christianity. Make her first pure, and then she shall be united. O, Saviour, let Thy kingdom come. Oh! that Thou wouldest reign, and Thy will be done in earth, as it is in heaven. We pray Thee use every one of us according as we have ability to be used. Take us, and let no talent lie to canker in the treasure house, but may every pound of Thine be put out in trading for Thee in the blessed market of soul-winning. Oh give us success. Increase the gifts and graces of those that are saved. Bind us in closer unity to one another than ever. Let peace reign ; let holiness adorn us. Hear us as we pray for all countries, and then for all sorts of men, from the Sovereign on the throne to the peasant in the cottage. Let the benediction of heaven descend on men, through Jesus Christ our Lord. Amen.

LORD, we are longing to draw near ; may Thy Spirit draw us near. We come by the way of Christ our Mediator. We could not approach Thee, O our God, if it were not for Him, but in Him we come boldly to the throne of heavenly grace. Nor can we come without thanksgiving — thanksgiving from the heart, such as the ongue can never express. Thou hast chosen us from before the foundation of the world, and this well-head of mercy sends forth streams of loving- kindness never ceasing. Because we were chosen we have been redeemed with precious blood. Bless the Lord ! And we have been called by the Holy Spirit out of the world, and we have been led to obey that wondrous call which hath quickened us and renewed us, and made us the people of God, given us adoption into the Divine Family. Bless the Lord!

Our hearts would pause as we remember the greatness of each one of Thy favours, and we would say, "Bless the Lord, O my soul, and all that is within me, bless His holy name." When we consider our utter unworthiness before con- version, and our great faultiness since, we can but admire the riches of abounding grace which God has manifested to us unworthy ones. Bless the Lord ! And when we think of all that Thou hast promised to give, which our faith embraces as being really ours, since the covenant makes it sure, we know not how abundantly enough to utter the memory of Thy great goodness. We would make our praises equal to our expectations, and our expectations equal to Thy promises. We can never rise so high. We give to Thee, however, the praise of our entire being ; unto Jehovah, the God of Abraham, the God of Isaac, and the God of Jacob, the Creator of the world, the redeemed of men, unto Jehovah be glory for ever and ever, and let all His people praise Him.

Let the redeemed of the Lord say so, whom He hath redeemed from the hand of the enemy. O Lord, Thy works praise Thee, but Thy saints bless Thee; and this shall be our heaven ; yea, our heaven of heavens eternally, to praise and magnify the great and ever blessed God. May many a maiden this day, may many a man break forth and say, with the virgin of old, "My soul doth magnify the Lord and my spirit doth rejoice in God my Saviour."

May there be going up this day sweet incense of praise laid by holy hands, privately upon the altar of God. May the place be filled with the smoke thereof, not perhaps to the consciousness of every one, but to the acceptance of God who shall smell a sweet savour of rest in Christ, and then in the praises of His people in Him.

But, Lord, when we have praised Thee we have to foil the woe; yea, we have to cover the face and cover the feet and stand before Thee to worship in another fashion, for we confess that we are evil, evil in our original, and though renewed by sovereign grace Thy people cannot speak of being clean, rid of sin. There is sin which dwelleth in us which is our daily plague. O God, we humble ourselves before Thee. We ask that our faith may clearly perceive the blood of the atonement and the covering of the perfect righteousness of Christ; and may we come afresh, depending alone on Jesus. "I, the chief of sinners am, but Jesus died for me." May this be our one hope, that Jesus died and rose again, and that for His sake we are accepted in the Beloved. May every child of Thine have his conscience purged from dead works to serve the true and living God May there be no cloud between us and our Heavenly Father; nay, not even a mist, not even the morning mist that soon is gone. May we walk in the light as God is in the light.

May our fellowship with the Father and with His Son, Jesus Christ, be unquestionable ; may it be fuel; may it fill us with joy ; may it be a most real fact this day; may we enjoy it to the full, knowing whom we have believed, knowing who is our Father, knowing who it is that dwells in us, even the Holy Spirit.

Take away from us everything which now might hinder our delighting ourselves in God. May we come to God this day with a supreme joy ; may we speak of Him as "God my exceeding joy; yea, mine own God is He." O God give us a sense of property in Thyself. May we come near to Thee, having no doubt and nothing whatsoever that shall spoil the beautiful simplicity of a child- like faith which looks up into the great face of God and saith, "Our Father, which art in heaven." There are those who never repented of sin and never believed in Christ, and consequently the wrath of God abideth on them. They are living without God, they are living in darkness. O God in Thy great mercy look upon them. They do not look at Thee, but do Thou look at them. May the sinner see his sin and mourn it; see His Saviour and accept Him; see himself saved, and go on his way rejoicing. Father, do grant us this.

Once more we pray Thee bless Thy Church. Lord quicken the spiritual life of believers. Thou hast given to Thy Church great activity, for which we thank Thee. May that activity be supported by a corresponding inner life. Let us not get to be busy here and there with Martha, and forget to sit at Thy feet with Mary. Lord, restore to Thy Church the love of strong doctrine. May Thy truth yet prevail. Purge out from among Thy Church these who would lead others away from the truth as it is in Jesus, and give back the old power and something more.

Give us Pentecost; yea, many Pentecosts in one, and may we live to see Thy Church shine forth clear as the sun and fair as the moon, and terrible as an army with banners. God grant that we may live to see better days. But if perilous times should come in these last days make us faithful.

Raise up in England, raise up in Scotland, men that shall hold the truth firmly as their fathers did. Raise up in every country where there has been a faithful church men that will not let the vessel drift upon the rocks. O God of the Judges, Thou who didst raise up first one and then another when the people went astray from God; raise up for us still (our Joshuas are dead) our Deborahs, our Baraks, our Gideons and Jephthahs, and Samuels, that shall maintain for God His truth, and worst the enemies of Israel. Lord look upon Thy Church in these days. Lord revive us. Lord restore us. Lord give power to Thy Word again that Thy name may be glorified.

Remember the Church of God in this land in all its various phases and portions, and pour out Thy Spirit upon it. Remember the multitude of Thy people across the sea in America, prosper them, bless them with the increase of God. And wherever Thou hast a people may Jesus dwell with them and reveal Himself to His own, for Christ's sake, to whom be glory with the Father and with the Holy Ghost, for ever and ever. Amen.

OUR God, we stand not afar off as Israel did in Sinai, nor does a veil hang dark between Thy face and ours ; but the veil is rent by the death of our Divine Lord and Mediator, Jesus Christ, and in His name we come up to the mercy seat all blood besprinkled, and here we present our prayers and our praises accepted in Him.

We do confess that we are guilty; we bow our heads and confess that we have broken Thy law and the covenant of which it is a part. Didst Thou deal with us under the covenant of works none of us could stand. We must confess that we deserve Thy wrath and to be banished forever from Thy presence.

But Thou hast made a new covenant, and we come under its divine shadow; we come in the name of Jesus. He is our High Priest; He is our righteousness; He is the well-beloved in whom Thou art well pleased. Holy Spirit teach us how to pray. Let us know what we should pray for as we ought. Our first prayer is: Be Thou adored; reign Thou over the whole earth; hallowed be Thy name. We desire to see all men submit themselves to Thy gracious government.

We wish especially that in the hearts of Thine own there may be an intense love for Thee and a perfect obedience to Thee. Grant this to each one of us. We would each one pray, " Lord, sanctify me; make me obedient; write Thy law upon my heart and upon my mind." Make our nature so clean that temptation cannot defile it. "Lead us not into temptation, but deliver us from the Evil One." May our course be very clean, our path be very straight; may we keep our garments unspotted from the world; and in thought and desire and imagination, in will and in purpose, may we be holy as God is holy. O God, we pray again fulfil that covenant promise, "I will take away the heart of stone out of your flesh, and I will give you a heart of flesh." May we be very tender towards Thee; may we feel Thy faintest monition; may even the gentlest breath of Thy Spirit suffice to move us; may we not be "as the horse or as the mule which have no understanding; whose mouth must be held in with bit and bridle, lest they come near unto us."

May we be as children obedient to a father; may we yield our members cheerfully to the instruments of righteousness; may we have a natural desire wrought in the new nature towards everything that is pure and honest, unselfish and Christly. O, Spirit of God dwell in us. Is not this also a covenant promise,

"I will put My Spirit within Thee, and I will make Thee to walk in My ways." Dwell with us Holy Spirit; rule over us Holy Spirit ; transform us to Thy own likeness, O Holy Spirit! Then shall we be clean; then shall we keep the law. We would offer a prayer to Thee for those who are quite strange to the work of the Spirit of God, who have never owned their God, who have behaved as if there were no God.

Open their eyes that they may see God even though that sight should make them tremble and wish to die. O ! let none of us live without our God and Father. Take away the heart of stone, take away the frivolities, the levity, the giddiness of our youth, and give us in downright earnest to seek true happiness where alone it can be found, in reconciliation to God, and in conformity to His will.

Lord save the careless, save the sinful, the drunkard, take away from him his cups. The unholy and unjust men, deliver these from their filthiness; the dishonest and false, renew them in their lives; and any that are lovers of pleasure, dead while they live, and any that are lovers of self, whose life is bounded by the narrowness of their own being, the Lord renew them, regenerate them, make them new creatures in Christ Jesus. For this we do fervently pray.

Lord God the Holy Ghost, may faith grow in men ; may they believe in Christ to the saving of their souls. May their little faith brighten into strong faith, and may their strong faith ripen into the full assurance of faith.

May we all have this last blessing ; may we believe God fully; may we never waver. Resting in the Great Surety and High Priest of the New Covenant may we feel "the peace of God which passeth all understanding," and may we enter into rest.

Bless Thy people that are at rest, and deepen that rest. May the rest that Thou givest be further enhanced by the rest which they find when they take Thy yoke upon them and learn of Thee. May Thy Word be very sweet to them. May there come over our spirits a deep calm, as when Christ hushed both winds and waves. May we feel not only resignation to Thy will, but delight in it, feeling pleased with all the Lord provides. May we rest in our God and be quite happy in the thought that our sins and our iniquities He will remember no more. He has brought us into covenant with Him by a covenant which can never fail, so like David we may say this morning: "Although my house be not so with God, yet He hath made with me an everlasting covenant, ordered in all things and sure."

Lord, bless Thy Word throughout the world. Prosper all missions amongst the heathen, all work among the Mohammedans; and, Oh ! Send Thy grace to the churches at home. Turn the current of thought which sets so strong in the wrong direction, and bring men to love the simplicities of the Gospel. Remember our country in great mercy, and in all ranks and conditions of men do Thou give the blessing. May there be multitudes come to Christ from among the poorest of the poor, and let the wealthy be led away from their sin, and brought to Jesus' feet. Be gracious to the Sovereign and Royal Family, and to all that are in authority over us. May peace and order be maintained, and let not the peace of the world be broken.

But what of all this? Our heart goes far beyond all this : " Thy will be done on earth, as it is in heaven; for Thine is the kingdom, and the power and the glory, for ever and ever." "Come, Lord Jesus, come quickly." All things are in Thy hand, come quickly ; the cries of Thy people persuade Thee, "the Spirit and the bride say, come," make no tarrying, O, our Redeemer, and unto the Father, to the Son, and to the Holy Ghost, the God of Abraham, and God of our Lord Jesus Christ be glory for ever and ever. Amen.

OUR God, we come to Thee by Jesus Christ who has gone within the veil on our behalf and ever liveth to make intercession for us. Our poor prayers could never reach Thee were it not for Him, but His hands are full of sweet perfume which makes our pleading sweet with Thee. His blood is sprinkled on the mercy seat, and now we know that Thou dost always hear those who approach Thee through that ever blessed name. We have deeply felt our entire unworthiness even to lift up our eyes to the place where Thine honour dwelleth. Thou hast made us to die to our self-righteousness. We pray now because we have been quickened ; we have received a new life, and the breath of that life is prayer. We have risen from the dead, and we also make intercession through the life which Christ has given us. We plead with the living God with living hearts be- cause He has made us to live. Our first prayer shall be for those who do not pray. There is an ancient promise of Thine, "I am found of them that sought Me not ; I said, Behold Me, behold Me, to a people that were not a people." Prove the sovereignty of Thy grace, the priority of Thy power, which runs before the will of man, by making many willing in this the day of Thy power, and calling the things that are not as though they were.

May the day come in which they that are in their graves shall hear the voice of God, and they that hear shall live. How very often Thou shewest Thy mighty power. O Lord, we bless Thee that the voice of God has called many to Christ.

Those that are. hardened have felt a softness stealing over their spirits; those who were careless have been compelled to sit down and think ; those that were wrapped up in earthly things have been compelled to think of eternal things ; and thinking, have been disturbed, and driven to despair, but afterwards led to Thee, even to Thee, dear Saviour, who wast lifted high upon the cross that by Thy death sinners might live.

But, Lord, we next would pray that Thine own people should know somewhat of the quickening of the Spirit of God. Lord, we thank Thee for the very least life to God, for the feeblest ray of faith and glimmering of hope. We are glad to see anything of Christ in any man ; but Thou hast come, O Saviour, not only that we might have life, but that we might have it more abundantly, so our prayer is that there may be abundance of life.

O make Thy people strong in the Lord, in the power of His might. Lord, we find when we walk close with God that we have no desire for the world. When we get away altogether from the things that are seen and temporal, and live upon the invisible and eternal, then we shall have angels' food ; nay, better than that, the food of Christ Himself, for his flesh is meat indeed, and His blood is drink indeed. Then have we meat to eat that the world knoweth not of. We pray Thee raise all our brothers and sisters in Christ into the high and heavenly frame of mind in which they shall be in the world and not be of it.

Whether they have little or much of temporal things, may they be rich in Thee and full of joy in the Holy Ghost, and so be blessed men and women. We pray for some of Thine own people who seem to be doing very little for Thee, Lord, have mercy upon those whose strength runs towards the world, and who give but little of their strength to the spread of the Gospel and the winning of souls. O let none of us fritter away our existence ; may we begin to live since Christ hath died ; may we reckon that because He died, we died to all the world, and because He lives, we live in newness of life. Lord we thank Thee for that newness of life.

We praise Thy name for a new heaven and a new earth ; we bless Thee that we now see what we never saw before, and hear what we never heard before. Oh ! that we might enter into the very secret place of this inner life. May we have as much grace as can be obtained; may we become perfect after the manner of Thy servant Paul, but still press forward, seeking still to be more and more conformed to the image of Christ.

Lord, make us useful. Oh let no believer live to himself. May we be trying to bring others to Christ. May our servants, and work-people, and neighbours all know where we live; and if they do not understand the secret of that life, yet may they see the fruit of that life, and may they ask, "What is this?" and enquire their way to Christ that they may be sanctified too. O Lord, we pray Thee visit Thy Church. May none of us imagine that we are living aright unless we are bringing others to the cross. Oh! keep us from worldliness; keep us much in prayer; keep us with the light of God shining on our forehead.

May we be a happy people, not because screened from affliction, but because we are walking in the light of God. Again we offer prayer for the many efforts that are scattered abroad to-day. May they be good wherever they are. We pray for all churches; Lord, revive them all. Wherever Christ is preached, may it be proved that He draws all men unto Him. May the preaching of Christ to-day be peculiarly efficacious. Oh that Thou wouldst raise up many that would preach Christ, simply, boldly, and with the Holy Ghost sent down from heaven. Send us better days ; send us days of refreshing from the presence of the Lord.

Lord, shake the earth with the power of God. Oh ! that the heathen lands may hear the Word of God and live. But first convert the Church, and then Thou wilt convert the world. Oh deal with those that depart from the faith and grieve Thy Holy Spirit. Bring them back again to their first love, and may Christ be fully and faithfully preached everywhere to the glory of His name. Now forgive us every iniquity; now lift us beyond the power of every sin; now lift us to pray and praise ; now make the home full of sacred power, and, last of all, come, Lord Jesus. This is the great wish of our souls. Even so, come quickly, come quickly, Lord Jesus. Amen and Amen.

BLESSED art Thou, O God; teach us Thy statutes! Because Thou art the infinitely blessed One, Thou canst impart blessing, and Thou art infinitely willing to do so, and therefore do we approach Thee with great confidence, through Jesus Christ Thy Son, whom Thou hast made blessed for evermore.

Oh hear Thou the voice of Thy servants this day, and according to Thine infinite love and wisdom answer Thou us ; according to Thy riches in glory, by Christ Jesus.

First we would confess before Thee, O God, the sin we have committed, mourning over it. Touch each one's heart now with tenderness that everyone of us may lament that Thou shouldst even have a few things against us, if they be but few, for in the great love of our blessed Master He said to His churches, "Nevertheless, I have a few things against Thee." O Lord, if Thou hast so kept us by Thy grace that there have been but a few things against us, yet help us to bewail them much. O, Infinite Love, can we sin against Thee at all? How debased is our nature then! Forgive, sweet Saviour, forgive sins against Thy love and blood, against Thy wounds and death, and give us Thy Spirit, O Saviour, more fully, that we may live Thy life while we are here among the sons of men, for as Thou art, even so also are we in this world, and we wish the parallel to become more close and perfect every day!

Forgive those who have never felt the guilt of sin, who are living in it, who are carnally minded, who are therefore dead. O, quicken by Thy divine Spirit; take away the pleasure which they feel in sin; deliver them from being the bond slaves of it. Alas we know the sorrow of sometimes being captured by it, but still we are not yet slaves. The Spirit, the life of God, in Jesus Christ, hath made us free from the law of sin and death. O, deliver others; bring them up out of the horrible pit of sin. Deliver them from the death of their natures and save them by the Spirit of the living God, and apply the precious blood of Jesus to their hearts and consciences.

And, Lord, hear us who are Thy children, in whom the Spirit beareth witness with our spirit, that we are the children of God. Hear us while we bring before Thee our daily struggles. Blessed be Thy name ; there are some sins which Thou hast helped us to overcome, and now they are. trodden beneath our feet with many a tear that we ever should have been in bondage to them. And O there are rebellions within our nature still. We think that we are getting holy, and behold we discover that we are under the power of pride, that we are self-conceited about ourselves. Lord help us to master pride.

And then when we try to be humble before Thee we find ourselves falling into inaction and supineness. Lord, slay sloth within us, and never let us find a pillow in the doctrines of grace for ease while yet a single sin remains. Besides, great God, the raging lusts of the flesh will sometimes pounce upon us like wild beasts. Help us to- be very watchful lest by any means we be torn and rent by them. O keep us, we beseech Thee, Lord, for without Thy keeping we cannot keep ourselves. Alas we are even sometimes subject to unbelief. If trials come which we expected not, or if the body grows faint, how liable we are to begin to doubt the faithful promise, and so to grieve the Holy Spirit. Lord, we cannot bear this ; we. cannot bear this ; it is not enough for us that our garments are clean, and that we walk uprightly before men ; we long to walk before Thee in such a way that there will be nothing to grieve Thy Spirit, nothing to vex the tender love of our Beloved. O, come, Divine Spirit, and exercise Thy cleansing power upon it according to Thy promise, "I will cleanse Thy blood which I have not cleansed, saith the Lord, that dwelleth in Zion."

O that everything might help us towards purity, for we crave after it; we mind the things of the Spirit, and there is groaning within us to be utterly delivered from the things of the flesh, that we may in spirit, soul, and body, be a cleansed temple fit for the indwelling of the Holy One of Israel. Lord help us, we pray Thee, in our daily life, to be as Christ was. If we are men of sorrows, may there be that luster about our sorrow which there was about His in patience and holy submission to the Divine law. If we are men of activity may our activity be like His, for he "went about doing good." May we seek in all ways the good of our fellow-men and the glory of our God.

We wish that the zeal of Thine house would eat us up; that we should be full of sacred warmth; that our lips were touched with the live coal so that there be fire in us perpetually flaming and burning, and ourselves a living sacrifice unto God. Bless us, we pray Thee, as to our example and influence. May it always be of a salutary kind; may there be sweetness and light about us which all must be obliged to perceive. Not for our honour would we crave this, but that our light may so shine before men that they may "see our good works and glorify our Father which is in heaven." The Lord grant us this!

We beseech Thee, bless the unconverted among us; bring them in, dear Saviour, bring them in. Help the living among us to compel them to come in that Thy house may be filled; may something of a sacred compulsion be used that they may not be left outside to starve in the highways and hedges, but be brought in to the Gospel feast. The Lord bless our country at this time.

Wilt Thou be gracious unto those who have the helm of affairs that in the midst of great difficulty they may be wisely and graciously directed. God bless the Sovereign with every mercy, and let all that are in authority share the Divine favour. Bless other countries, too, for whom we do most earnestly pray, especially for our brethren in Christ across the Atlantic, blessing and praising Thee that we have so many there that are not only of our own kin by nationality, but also kin in Christ. God bless them and those in the Southern seas. The Lord bless the Church of Christ there, nor do Thou fail to remember the struggling ones on the Continent of Europe, and all the missionaries that are labouring in the foreign field.

O, Saviour, let Thy kingdom come. When will this earth be delivered from the incubus of superstition and of infidelity? O that Thou wouldst hear creation's groans and come quickly. O Thou great Deliverer, joy of the earth art Thou, the expected of the tribes of Israel still; come, we beseech Thee, Thou absent love, Thou dear unknown. Thou fairest of ten thousand fair; come a second time to earth and to the sons of men, and specially to Thy Bride, the Church. Even so come quickly, Lord Jesus. Amen.

OUR Father, Thou dost hear us when we pray. Thou hast provided an advocate and intercessor in heaven now ; we cannot come to Thee unless Thy Holy Spirit shall suggest desire, and help us while we plead. We would ask that the subject which caused such conflict to Paul may be beyond conflict with us; may we know the Christ and have Him to be our all in all. We would have the conflict about others, but may we be past it for ourselves. He is everything to us; more than all in Him we find.

We do accept Thee, Lord Jesus, to be made unto us wisdom, righteousness, sanctification, and redemption. We will not look outside of Thee for anything, for everything is in Thee. Our sin is pardoned, our sinful nature is subdued ; we have a perfect righteousness; we have an immortal life ; we have a sure hope; we have an immovable foundation. Why should we look beyond Thee? Why should we look within to ourselves, knowing that Thou shalt be the only well from which we will draw the living water, the only foundation upon which we will be built. We would thrust out new rootlets this day, can take fresh hold on the blessed soil in which grace has planted us. O Saviour, reveal Thyself anew, teach us a little more, help us to go a little deeper into the divine mystery. May we. grip Thee and grasp Thee;

may we suck out of Thee the nutriment of our spirit; may we be in Thee as a branch is in the stem, and may we bear fruit from Thee. Without Thee we can do nothing. Forgive, we pray Thee, Thy servants, any wanderings during the past. If we have forgotten Thee, forget not us; if we have acted apart from Thee, forgive the act. Blot out the sin. Help us in the future to live only as we live in Thee, to speak, and even to think, as in union with our living Head. Take away from us all life which is contrary to the life of Christ; bring us into complete subjection in Him, until for us to live shall be Christ in every single act of life. May we walk humbly with God in joyful faith in the finished work of Christ. Saviour, look on Thy beloved ones, and give blessings according to our necessities. We cannot pray a prayer that would comprise all, but Thou canst, Great

Intercessor, plead for each one, and get for each one of us the blessing wanted. Are we depressed? Give us stronger faith. Have we become worldly?

Pardon this great offence and lead us more into spiritual things. Have we become joyous, but have forgotten the Source of Joy? Lord, sweeten and savour that joy with the sweet perfume of Thine own presence. Have we to preach, and do we feel weak? Oh! be our strength. Are we engaged in the Sunday-school, and have we seen little success? Lord, teach us how to teach; give us our boys and girls to be our spiritual reward. Are we sickly? Have we those that vex us because they are unholy and un- godly? This, indeed, is a terrible trial to many; Lord, help them, both in their personal sickness and in this great spiritual trouble. Have we dear ones whom we love with all our hearts, who pine before our eyes ? Lord, have pity upon them and restore them, and give them patience to bear pain ; and give us resignation to Thy will in this matter.

Whatever the trial of Thy servants, make a way of escape that we may be able to bear it. Our great concern, however, is to grow in grace and to become like our Master.

We struggle and we struggle, but how small our progress! Lord, help us in any matter in which we have felt defeated. If we have been betrayed through want of watchfulness. Lord forgive and help another time. If any of Thy servants have lost the brightness of their evidence, give them to come to Christ as sinners if they cannot come as saints. And if through Satan's temptation any are sorely put to it even to keep their feet, hold them up; and if any have fallen, help them to say, "Rejoice not against me, O, mine enemy; when I fall I shall arise." Now look in great mercy upon those who are unconverted; Lord save them. Some are quite careless; Lord, they are dead; come and quicken them. We cannot see, but Thou canst.

Oh that some of the most obdurate and hardened might be softened by the touch of Thy Spirit this very day; and may others who are not careless, but who are even seeking after eternal life, but who are going- the wrong way to work, may they be shown their error, may they be led in the way by Thee, may they look, and, looking, live. We know how many of them are wanting to be this and that before they take Christ to be all in all; may they cease their seeking by finding everything in Christ. As Thou art a prayer-hearing God, and a God of pardon, issue many a pardon from Thy heavenly court to-day, sealed with the Redeemer's blood, signed with the Father's name. Oh today, Lord, ere men grow old in sin, ere they die in their sins, save them with an everlasting salvation.

God bless our country and our Sovereign; God bless this city ; may there be no disquietude between the different orders of men; the employer and the employed; but may there be a general spirit of goodwill given to- the people of this city, and do Thou prosper us. Remember all people, especially the poor, the widows and the fatherless, and any that are depressed in spirit, whose depression tends to the failure of reason; the Lord restore them, and such as are dying. O Lord, let them not die without hope, and may Thy believing people learn to pass away without even tasting the bitterness of death. May they enter into rest, each one walking in his own uprightness.

Save this age from its own intellectual pride; give back the spirit of simple faith in Christ, for we desire His glory. "

For Thine is the kingdom, and the power, and the glory, for ever and ever. Amen."

O LORD, many of us feel like the lame man at the Beautiful Gate of the temple. Come by this way and make the lame ones perfectly sound. O Lord, Thou canst do by Thy servants today what Thou didst by them in the olden time. Work miracles of mercy even upon outer court worshippers who are too lame to get into the holy place. But there are many who feel like that man when he was restored. We would follow our Restorer, the Prince of Life, into the temple, leaping and walking and praising God. He has gone into the temple in the highest sense, up to the throne of God. He climbs, and we would follow, up the steps of the temple one by one, made meet. We would come nearer and nearer to the throne of God.

O Lord, Thou hast done such great things for us that we feel the drawings of Thy love. "The Lord hath appeared of old unto me, saying:

Yea, I have loved Thee with an everlasting love, therefore with lovingkindness have I drawn Thee." Draw us nearer, Lord, draw us into the inner Sanctuary ; draw us within the place which once was hidden by the veil which Christ has rent ; bring us right up to the throne of grace, and there beholding the glory of God above the Mercy Seat may we have communion with the Most High. Heal all our diseases and forgive us all our trespasses. Still, Lord, though healed of a former lameness so that now we have strength, we need a further touch from Thee ; we are so apt to get dull and stupid ; come and help us. Lord Jesus. A vision of Thy face will brighten us ; but to feel Thy Spirit touching us will make us vigorous. Oh! for the leaping and the walking of the man born lame. May we today dance with holy joy like David before the Ark of God.

May a holy exhilaration take possession of every part of us; may we be glad in the Lord; may our mouth be filled with laughter, and our tongue with singing, "for the Lord hath done great things for us whereof we are glad." Today help Thy people to put on Christ. May we live as those who are alive from the dead, for He is the quickening Spirit ; and may we feel Him to be so. Is any part of us still dead. Lord quicken it. May the life which has taken possession of our heart take possession of our head; may the brain be active in holy thought ; may our entire being, indeed, respond to the life of Christ, and may we live in newness of life.

We would fain fall down on our faces and worship the Son of God today. It is such a wonder that He should have loved us; and He has done such wonderful things for us and in us that we may still call Him God's unspeakable gift. He is unspeakably precious to our souls. Thou knowest all things, Lord ; Thou knowest that we love Thee.

May that love bubble up to-day like a boiling cauldron, may our hearts overflow; and if we cannot speak what we feel, may that holy silence be eloquent with the praise of God. Lord, send Thy heart throughout the entire Church. Lord, visit Thy Church, restore sound doctrine, restore holy and earnest living. Take away from professors their apparent love for frivolities, their attempts to meet the world on its own ground, and give back the old love to the doctrines of the cross, the doctrines of the Christ of God; and once more may free grace and dying love be the music that shall refresh the Church, and make her heart exceeding glad. Just now when the earth is waking up to life, Lord, wake up dead hearts; and if there are seeds of grace lying dormant in any soul may they begin to bud, may the bulb down at the heart send forth its golden cup and drink in of the light, the life of God. Oh! save to-day.

"Thy King in the midst of Thee is mighty : He will save." Our very heart is speaking now much more loudly and sweetly than our lips can speak. Lord save sinners; great High Priest have compassion on the ignorant and such as are out of the way. Great Shepherd of the sheep gather the lambs within Thine arm ; find out the lost sheep; throw them on Thy shoulders and bring them home rejoicing.

We ask that everywhere there may be great numbers added to the Church. Thou who didst bring in five thousand so soon, bring in five thousand in many and many a place. We read the statistics of Thy Church with great sorrow; how small an increase! Lord multiply us with men as with a flock; increase the people, and increase the joy. Make us to joy before Thee as the joy of harvest. Lord, we pray for our country with all our heart; and as Thou biddest us we pray for those in authority, for the Sovereign as supreme,

for the Court of Parliament, for all magistrates and rulers. We pray also for the poorest and the down-trodden. The Lord look upon the poor of this world, and make them rich in faith, and comfort them in heart by the Holy Ghost. The Lord save the nation. Let Thy light and Thy truth go forth to the most distant parts of the earth; "let the people praise Thee; O God let all the people praise Thee." Give us the times of refreshing. May we have a visit from Christ by the power of His Spirit; and until He come may there be a blessed halcyon time of peace and salvation.

" Thy kingdom come, Thy will be done, on earth, as it is in heaven." And do Thou come Thyself, great King. May our eyes, if it please Thee, behold Thee on earth; but if not, if we fall asleep ere that blessed array, we can say, "I know that my Redeemer liveth ; and though after my skin worms destroy this body, yet in my flesh shall I see God."

Bless every Sunday-school teacher, every tract distributor, every open-air preacher. Bless, we pray Thee, all Bible-women and nurses, deacons and missionaries of the City Mission, Bible readers and all others who in any way seek to bring men to Christ O God the Holy Ghost, work mightily, we pray Thee ; flood the world with a baptism of Thy power, and "let the whole earth be filled with a knowledge of the Lord as the waters cover the sea." We ask all in that dear name which made the same man whole, which is sweet to God in heaven and dear to us below ; and unto Father, Son and Holy Ghost be glory, world without end. Amen.

O GOD our Father, we do remember well when we were called to Thee ; with many sweet and wooing voices we were bidden to return. Thou didst Thyself hang out the lights of mercy that we might know the way home, and Thy dear Son himself came down to seek us. But we wandered still. It brings the tears to our eyes to think that we should have been so foolish and so wicked, for we often extinguished the light within and conscience we tried to harden, and we sinned against light and knowledge with a high hand against our God.

Thou hast often brought us very low even to our knees, and we cried for mercy, but we rose to sin again. Blessed was that day when Thou didst strike the blow of grace, the effectual blow. Then didst Thou wither up our comeliness and all our perfection was rolled in the dust. We saw ourselves to be slain by the law, to be lost, ruined, and undone, and then we rolled to and fro in the tempests of our thoughts and staggered like drunken men, and were at our wits' end — then did we cry unto Thee in our trouble, and blessed be Thy name for ever, Thou didst deliver us.

O happy day that sealed our pardon with the precious blood of Jesus accepted by faith. We would recall the memory of that blessed season by repeating it. We come again now to the cross whereon the Saviour bled; we give another look of faith to Him. We trust we never take away our eyes off Him, but if we have done so we would look anew; we would gaze into the body of the Son of God, pierced with nails, parched with thirst, bleeding, dying, because "it pleased the Father to bruise Him; He hath put Him to grief."

Lord God, we see in Thy crucified Son a sacrifice for sin ; we see how Thou hast made Him to be sin for us that we might be made the righteousness of God in Him; and we do over again accept Him to be everything to us. This is the victim by whose blood the covenant is made through faith ; this is that Paschal Lamb by the sprinkling of whose blood all Israel is secured; for Thou hast said, "When I see the blood I will pass over you."

This is the blood which gives us access into that which is within the veil; this is the blood which now to our souls is drink indeed, and we do rejoice in the joy which this new wine of the covenant hath given unto our spirits. We would take afresh the cup of salvation and call upon the name of the Lord We would pay our vows now in the midst of all the Lord's people and in the courts of His house; and this is a part payment of our vow that we bless the Lord Jesus who hath put away our sin. We bless Him that He hath redeemed us unto Himself not with corruptible things as silver and gold, but with His own precious blood; and we do avow ourselves today to be the Lord's.

We are not our own; we are bought with a price. Lord Jesus, renew Thy grasp of us, take us over again, for we do even with greater alacrity than ever before surrender ourselves to Thee, and so "bind the sacrifice with cords, even with cords to the horns of the altar." O Lord, I am Thy servant, and the son of Thine handmaid. Thou hast loosed my bonds. The Lord liveth and blessed be my Rock. Henceforth within that Rock I hide myself. For Him I live. The Lord enable all His people with sincere hearts, with undivided hearts, thus again to give themselves up to Jesus, and do Thou set in them anew the marks and tokens of Thy possession till every one of us shall say as many of us can say, "From henceforth let no man trouble me; for I bear in my body the marks of the Lord Jesus Christ."

We bless Thee, Lord, for that mark to which some of us can look back with much joy. It is not in our hand, nor in our forehead, nor on our foot, nor on our heart alone; our whole body has been buried with Christ in baptism unto death, and now the whole body, soul and spirit, by our willing consecration, belong unto Christ henceforth and forever. Our Father, there is one prayer which has kept rising to our lip even while we have been thus speaking to Thee. It comes from our very heart. It is: Bring others to Thyself. Hast Thou not said, O God of Jacob, "Yet will I gather others unto Him that have not been gathered?" Hast Thou not given to Thy Son the heathen for His inheritance, and the uttermost parts of the earth for His possession? Lord, give Thy Son the reward of His travail; give Him a part of that reward this day wherever He is preached. Oh! That some might be moved with the love of Christ.

Lord, some know not who Thou art; convince them of Thy Deity and Thy power to save. Lord, many of them do not think; they live as if they were to die, and there would be an end of them. O Divine Spirit, convince them of judgment to come. Set before each careless eye that day of terrible pomp when for every idle word that men shall speak they must give an account. O Divine Spirit, teach unreasonable men true reason; teach the obdurate sensitiveness; look upon them, Jesus, just as Thou didst on those of the synagogue, not with anger, but still being grieved because of the hardness of their hearts. "Father, forgive them, they know not what they do," and bring many, many, many this very day to the dear feet that were nailed to the cross. Oh! how we long for it.

Deny us what Thou wilt, only bring sinners to Thyself. Lord Jesus, Thou art gone from us. We rejoice that this is the fact, for Thou hast taught us that it is expedient for us that Thou shouldest go, and that the Comforter should be with us ; but, oh let us not miss that promised presence of the Comforter. May He be here to help and succour in all works of faith and labours of love, and may we feel that He has come among us and is dwelling with us because He is convincing the world of sin, of righteousness and of judgment to come.

O Spirit of God, bring men to accept the great propitiation, to see their sin washed away in the purple flood whose fount was opened when the heart of Christ was pierced, and may blood-washed sinners begin to sing on earth that everlasting anthem which shall be sung by all the redeemed in heaven. We beseech Thee now, Lord, to look upon all

Thy people, and grant everyone a blessing. Some are in great trouble. Deliver them, we pray Thee.

Others may be in great peril, though they have no trouble. The Lord save His people from the evils of prosperity. It may be some of Thine own people find it hard to worship because of cares ; may they be able, like Abraham, when the birds came down upon the sacrifice, to drive them away.

O Spirit of God, make us all more holy. Work in us more completely the image of Christ. We do long to be as the Lord Jesus Christ in spirit and temper, and in unselfishness of life. Give us the character of Christ, we pray Thee. Redemption from the power of sin is purchased with His blood, and we crave for it, and pray that we may daily receive it. Let the whole militant Church of Christ be blessed; put power into all faithful ministries; convert this country; save it from abounding sin ; let all the nations of the earth know the Lord, but especially bless those nations that speak our own dear mother tongue, where our same Lord and Christ is worshipped this day after the same fashion.

The Lord bless His people. Bring the Church to break down all bonds of nationality, all limits of sects, and may we feel the blessed unity which is the very glory of the Church of Christ; yea, let the whole earth be filled with His glory. Our prayer can never cease until we reach this point : " Thy Kingdom come, Thy will be done, on earth as it is in heaven." Nothing less than this can we ask for.

And now hear us as we pray for the Sovereign and all in authority, and ask Thy blessing to rest upon this land, and let Thy blessing extend over all the family of man. We ask it for Christ's sake. Amen.

O GOD! We would not speak to Thee as from a distance, nor stand like trembling Israel under the law at a distance from the burning mount, for we have not come unto Mount Sinai, but unto Mount Sion, and that is a place for holy joy and thankfulness, and not for terror and bondage. Blessed be Thy name, O Lord! We have learnt to call Thee "Our Father, which art in heaven"; so there is reverence, for Thou art in heaven; but there is sweet familiarity, for Thou art our Father.

We would draw very near to Thee now through Jesus Christ the Mediator, and we would make bold to speak to Thee as a man speaketh with his friend, for hast Thou not said by Thy Spirit, " Let us come boldly unto the throne of the heavenly grace." We might well start away and flee from Thy face if we only remembered our sinfulness. Lord! we do remember it with shame and sorrow ; we are grieved to think we should have offended Thee, should have neglected so long Thy sweet love and Tender mercy; but we have now returned unto the "Shepherd and bishop of our souls." Led by such grace, we look to Him whom we crucified, and we have mourned for Him and then have mourned for our sin.

Now, Lord, we confess our guilt before Thee with tenderness of heart, and we pray Thee seal home to every believer here that full and free, that perfect and irreversible charter of forgiveness which Thou gavest to all them that put their trust in Jesus Christ. Lord! Thou hast said it: "If we confess our sins. Thou art merciful and just to forgive us our sins and to save us from all unrighteousness."

There is the sin confessed: there is the ransom accepted: we therefore know we have peace with God, and we bless that glorious one who hath come "to finish transgression, to make an end of sin," to bring in everlasting righteousness, which righteousness by faith we take unto ourselves and Thou dost impute unto us. Now, Lord, wilt Thou be pleased to cause all Thy children's hearts to dance within them for joy?

Oh help Thy people to come to Jesus again today. May we be looking unto Him to-day as we did at the first. May we never take off our eyes from His Divine person, from His infinite merit, from His finished work, from His living power, or from the expectancy of His speedy coming to "judge the world in righteousness and the people with His truth." Bless all Thy people with some special gift, and if we might make a choice of one it would be this: "Quicken us, O Lord, according to Thy Word." We have life; give it to us more abundantly. Oh, that we might have so much life that out of the midst of us there might flow rivers of living water. The Lord make us useful. Do, dear Saviour, use the very least among us; take the one talent and let it be put out to interest for the great Father. May it please Thee to show each one of us what Thou wouldest have us to do. In our families, in our business, in the walks of ordinary life may we be serving the Lord, and may we often speak a word for His name, and help in some way to scatter the light amongst the ever-growing darkness; and ere we go hence may we have sown some seed which we shall bring with us on our shoulders in the form of sheaves of blessing. O God! Bless our Sunday-schools, and give a greater interest in such work, that there may be no lack of men and women who shall be glad and happy in the work of teaching the young.

Do impress this, we pray Thee, upon Thy people just now. Move men who have gifts and ability also to preach the Gospel. There are many that live in villages, and there is no gospel preaching near them. Lord! set them preaching themselves. Wilt Thou move some hearts so powerfully that their tongues cannot be quiet any longer, and may they attempt in some way, either personally or by supporting someone, to bring the gospel into dark benighted hamlets that the people may know the truth. O Lord! stir up the dwellers in this great, great city. Oh! arouse us to the spiritual destitution of the masses. O God, help us all by some means, by any means, by every means to get at the ears of men for Christ's sake that so we may reach their hearts.

We would send up an exceeding great and bitter cry to Thee on behalf of the millions that enter no place of worship, but rather violate its sanctity and despise its blessed message. Lord wake up London, we beseech Thee. Send us another Jonah ; send us another John the Baptist. Oh that the Christ Himself would send forth multitudes of labourers amongst this thick standing corn, for the harvest truly is plenteous, but the labourers are few. O God save this city; save this country; save all countries; and let Thy kingdom come; may every knee bow and confess that Jesus Christ is Lord.

Our most earnest prayers go up to heaven to Thee now for great sinners, for men and women that are polluted and depraved by the filthiest of sins. With sovereign mercy make a raid amongst them. Come and capture some of these that they may become great lovers of Him that shall forgive them, and may they become great champions for the cross.

Lord, look upon the multitudes of rich people in this city that know nothing about the gospel and do not wish to know.

Oh ! that somehow the poor rich might be rich with the gospel of Jesus Christ. And then, Lord, look upon the multitude of the poor and the working classes that think religion to be a perfectly unnecessary thing for them. Do, by some means we pray Thee, get them to think and bring them to listen that faith may come by hearing, and hearing by the Word of God.

Above all, O Holy Spirit, descend more mightily. Would, God, Thou wouldest flood the land till there should be streams of righteousness; for is there not a promise, " I will pour water upon him that is thirsty and floods upon the dry ground." Lord, set Thy people praying; stir up the Church to greater prayerfulness. Now, as Thou hast bidden us, we pray for the people among whom we dwell. We pray for those in authority in the land, asking every blessing for the Sovereign, and Thy guidance and direction to the Parliament, Thy benediction to all judges and rulers as also upon the poorest of the poor and the lowest of the low. Lord, bless the people; let the people praise Thee, O God ! yea, let all the people praise Thee, for Jesus Christ's sake. Amen and Amen.

OUR Father, which art in heaven, our hearts are full of gratitude to Thee for Thy We bless Thee that we have it in our houses, that Thou hast given to many of us to understand it and to enjoy it. Although as yet we know not what we shall know, yet have we learned from it what we never can forget, that which has changed our lives has removed our burdens, has comforted our hearts, has set our faces like flints against sin and made us eager after perfect holiness.

We thank Thee, Lord, for every leaf of the Book, not only for its promises which are inexpressibly sweet, but for its precepts in which our soul delights, and especially for the revelation of Thy Son, our Lord and Saviour Jesus Christ. O God, we thank Thee for the manifestation of Him even in the types and shadows of the Old Testament. These are inexpressibly glorious to us, full of wondrous value, inexpressibly dear because in them and through them we see the Lord. But we bless Thee much more for the clear light of the New Testament, for giving us the key to all the secrets of the Old Testament, for now, reading the scriptures of the new covenant, we understand the language: of the old covenant and are made to joy and to rejoice therein.

Father, we thank Thee for the Book, we thank Thee for the glorious Man, the God whom the Book reveals as our Saviour ; and now we thank Thee for the Blessed Spirit, for without His light upon the understanding we should have learned nothing. The letter killeth, it is the Spirit that giveth life. Blessed are our eyes that have been touched with heavenly eye-salve. Blessed are the hearts that have been softened, that have been made ready to receive the truth in the love of it ! Blessed be the sovereign grace of God that hath chosen unto Him a people who delight in His Word and who' meditate in it both day and night! Our hearts are full of praises to God for this Man of Truth, for this unmeasured wealth of holy knowledge. Lord make us to enjoy it more and more. May we feed upon this manna; may we drink from this well of life ; may we be satisfied with it, and by it be made like to the God from whom it came.

And now, Lord, our prayer is to Thee at the mention of Thy sacred Book, that Thou wouldst write it upon the fleshy tablets of our heart more fully. We want to know the truth that the truth may make us free. We want to feel the truth that we may be sanctified by it.

Oh let it be in us a living seed which shall produce in us a life accept- able before God, a life which shall be seen in everything that we do unto the living God, for we remember that Thou art not the God of the dead but of the living.

Lord, we ask that Thy Word may chasten us whenever we go astray, may it enlighten us whenever for a moment we get into darkness. May Thy Word be the supreme ruler of our being. may we give ourselves up to its sacred law to be obedient to its every hint, wishing in all things, even in the least things, to do the will of God from the heart and having every thought brought into captivity to the mind of the Spirit of God.

Bless Thy people; bless them in this way by saturating them with the Word of Thy truth. O Lord, they are out in the world so much. Oh grant that the world may not take them off from their God. May they get the world under their feet ; let them not be buried in it, but may they live upon it, treading it beneath their feet, the spiritual getting the mastery always over the material. Oh that the Word of God might be with us when we are in the midst of an ungodly generation. May the Proverbs often furnish us with wisdom, the Psalms furnish us with comfort, the Gospels teach us the way of holiness, and the Epistles instruct us in the deep things of the kingdom of God.

Lord educate us for a higher life, and let that life be begun here. May we be always in the school, always disciples, and when we are out in the world may we be trying to put in practice what we have learned at Jesu's feet. What He tells us in darkness may we proclaim in the light, and what He whispers in our ear in the closets may we sound forth upon the housetops. Oh dear, dear Saviour, what could we do without Thee.

We are as yet in banishment, we have not come into the land of light and glory; it is on the other side the river, in the land where Thou dwellest, Thy land of Immanuel, and till we come thither be Thou with us. We have said unto ourselves, How shall we live without our Lord; and then we have said unto Thee, " If Thy Spirit go not with us, carry us not up hence." Oh be to us this day as the fiery cloudy pillar that covered all the camp of Israel. May we dwell in God; may we live and move m God; may we be conscious of the presence of God to a greater extent than we are conscious of anything else.

Bless the churches. Look on them, Lord; cast an eye of love upon the little companies of the faithful wherever they may be and help them and their pastors, and may the churches be in every place a light in the midst of this crooked and perverse generation. O God, we are waiting and watching for a display of Thy great power among the people. It is an age of great luxury and great sin and gross departures from the truth ; we beseech Thee defend Thine own. When Thine ark was carried captive among the Philistines and set up in the temple of Dagon, Dagon fell before it, then didst Thou smite Thine adversaries in the hinder parts and put them to a perpetual reproach, and Thou canst do the like again, and we pray it may be so. Oh for the stretched out hand of God.

We are longing to see it in the conversion of great multitudes by the gospel, that those who have said, "Aha, aha, the gospel has lost its power," may be made foolish by the wisdom of the Most High, even as Jannes and Jambres were made foolish when they could not do so with their enchantments, but God was with His servant.

O, Jehovah, Thou art the true God, God of Abraham, of Isaac, and of Jacob, this God is our God for ever and ever; He shall be our guide even unto death. Thou who spakest by the apostles speak still by Thy servants, and let Thy Word be with as much power as when Thou saidst, "Let there be light, and there was light." Oh! For the lifting up of Thy voice! Let confusion and darkness once again hear the voice of Him that makes order and that giveth life. Oh! how we would stir Thee up, Thou gracious God. Our prayers would take the form of that ancient one, "Awake, awake, put on Thy strength." Art Thou not He that cut Egypt and wounded the crocodile? Hast Thou not still the same power to smite and to vindicate Thine own truth and deliver Thine own redeemed?

O Lamb, slain from before the foundation of the world. Thou art still to sit upon the throne, for He that is on the throne looks like a Lamb that has been newly slain. O Jesus, we beseech Thee take to Thyself Thy great power ; divide the spoil with the strong ; take the purchase of Thy precious blood and rule from the river even unto the ends of the earth. Here we are before Thee; look on us in great pity. Lord, bless Thine own people. With favour do Thou compass them as with a shield. Lord, save the unsaved. In great compassion draw them by the attractive magnet of the cross, draw them to Thyself, compel them to come in that the wedding may be furnished with guests.

With one heart we put up our prayer on the behalf of the teachers of the young. We thank Thee, Lord, that so many men and women are ready to give their Sabbath's rest to this important service. Oh grant that zeal for teaching the young may never burn low in the church.

May any that are taking no part in it and who ought to be, be aroused at once to commence the holy effort. Bless the teachers of the senior classes; may their young men and women pass into the church; may there be no gap between the school and the church. Bridge that distance by Thy sovereign grace. But equally bless the teachers of the infants and of the younger children. May conversion go on among the young. May there be multitudes of such conversions. In effect, we would pray that no child may leave the schools unsaved. Oh! Save the children, great Lover of the little ones. Thou who wouldst have them suffered to come to Thee, Thou wilt not forget them, but Thou wilt draw them and accept them. Lord! save the children. Let all the schools participate in the blessing which we seek, and by this blessed agency may this nation be kept from heathenism; this city especially be preserved from its dogged disregard of the Sabbath, and its carelessness about the things of God. Oh bless the Sabbath-school to London, to every part of it, and let Jesus Christ be glorified among the little ones, and again may there be heard loud in the streets of Jerusalem from the babes and sucklings out of whose mouths Thou hast ordained strength. The Lord be with these dear workers throughout to-day and make it a high day, a festival of prayer and faith, a time when Jesus the Lord shall especially meet with them and bless them.

God bless our country! God save our Sovereign! Grant guidance at this time to all with regard to the political affairs of this nation. Grant Thy blessing to all ranks and conditions of men, and let every nation call Thee "blessed." Let all tongues speak the name of Jesus and all men own Him as Lord and King. We ask it in His name. Amen.

OUR Father, we have listened to Thy gracious words. Truly Thy paths drop fatness. Wherever Thou art, mercy abounds. Before Thy feet rivers of grace spring up. When Thou comest to man it is with the fullness of pardoning love. Thou hast bidden us come to Thee and seek Thee while Thou mayest be found. We would come now. May Thy holy Spirit help us! May Jesus lead the way and be our Mediator now! Blessed be Thy name; there are many who sought Thy face many years ago. We have since then tasted that Thou art gracious, and we know by a delightful experience that Thou dost indeed give milk and honey to such as trust Thee. Oh! we wish we had known Thee earlier. Lord, Thou hast been full of truth and faithfulness to us throughout every step of our journey, and though Thou hast not withheld the rod of the covenant from us, we are as grateful for that this morning as for the kisses of Thy lips. Thou hast dealt well with Thy servants according to Thy Word. Blessed be Thy name for ever and ever. But there are some who have never come to Thee ; they are hearers, but hearers only ; they have hastened to gracious invitations thousands of times, but they have never accepted them. Say unto them, " Thereto hast thou gone, but no further shalt thou proceed in thy carelessness and trifling. Here shalt thou stay and turn unto Thy God."

O Saviour, Thou hast all power in heaven and earth, therefore Thou canst through the preaching of Thy Word influence the hearts of men. Turn them, and they shall be turned. Oh do it this day. We would now in our prayers come ; as we came at first would we come again; we would renew our vows, we would again repeat our repentance and our faith, and then look at the brazen serpent and touch but the border of Thy garment. We would begin again. O, Lord, help us to do it in sincerity and truth. And first we do confess that we are by nature lost and by practice ruined. We are altogether as an unclean thing, and all our righteousnesses are as filthy rags. We would lie at those dear pierced feet bleeding at heart because of sin, wounded, mangled, crushed by the fall and by our own transgression. We confess that if Thou shouldst number our sins upon us and deal with us accordingly we should be sent to the lowest hell. We have no merit, no claim, no righteousness of our own. Oh! now, dear Saviour, we look up to Thee. Oh ! that some might look for the first time, and those of us that have long looked would fix our happy gaze again upon that blessed substitutionary sacrifice wherein is all our hope. Dear Saviour, we do take Thee to be everything to us, our sin bearer and our sin-destroyer. We have not a shadow of a shade of a hope anywhere but in Thyself, Thy life. Thy death, Thy resurrection, Thine ascension, Thy glory, Thy reign. Thy second advent; these are the only stars in our sky.

We look up to Thee and are filled with light. But O Thou dear, dear Saviour, we dare not turn to ordinances, we dare not turn to our own prayers, and tears, and almsgivings, we dare not look to our own works, we only look to Thee; Thy wounds, Immanuel, these bleed the balm that heals our wounds, Thy crowned head once girt with thorns, Thy body once laid in the silent tomb, Thy Godhead once covered and concealed from man, but now resplendent amidst triumphant hosts. If we can perish trusting in Thee we must perish, but we know we cannot, for Thou hast bound up our salvation with Thy glory, and because Thou art a glorious Saviour forever, none that trust in Thee shall ever be confounded. But we do trust Thee now. If all our past experience has been a mistake, yet we will begin at the cross today; or if we have never had any experience of Thee before we would begin today. Oh hear Thou, hear Thou the prayer: " Dear Saviour, draw reluctant hearts, To Thee let sinners fly." By His agony and bloody sweat, by His cross and passion, by His precious death and burial, we beseech Thee hear us now! We plead with Thee for some that are not pleading for themselves. O Spirit of God, let it not be so any longer. Now sweetly use Thy key to open the fast-closed door, and come into men's hearts and dwell there that they may live. We have a thousand things to ask. We should like to plead for our country and for all countries; we should like to plead with Thee for the sick and for the. dying, for the poor and for the fatherless. We have innumerable blessings to ask, but somehow they all go away from our prayer just now, and this is our one cry: Save, Lord, we beseech Thee, even now send salvation! Come Holy Spirit to open blind eyes and unstop deaf ears and quicken dead hearts.

Father, glorify Thy Son that Thy Son may glorify Thee. Holy Spirit, do Thine office and take of these things of Christ and reveal them unto us. We gather up all our prayers in that salvation through the blood of the Lamb. Amen.

O GOD, let us not be formalists or hypocrites at this time in prayer. We feel how easy it is to bow the head and cover the face, and yet the thoughts may be all astray, and the mind may be wandering hither and thither, so that there shall be no real prayer at all. Come, Holy Spirit, help us to feel that we are in the immediate presence of God; and may this thought lead us to sincere and earnest petitioning. There are some who know not God; God is not in all their thoughts ; they make no reckoning of Thee, Thou glorious One, but do their business and guide their lives as if there was no God in heaven or in earth. Strike them now with a sense of Thy presence.

Oh that Thine eternal power might come before their thoughts, and now may they join with Thy reverent people in approaching Thy mercy seat. We come for mercy, great God; it must always be our first request, for we have sinned, sinned against a just and holy law of which our conscience approves. We are evil, but Thy law is holy and just and good. We have offended knowingly; we have offended again and again; after being chastened we have still offended, and even those of us who are forgiven, who' through Thy rich love have been once for all washed from every stain, yet have we sinned grievously ; and we confess it with much shame and bitter self-reproach that we should sin against such tender love, and against the indwelling of the Holy Spirit, who is in His people; and who checks them and quickens their con sciences; so that they sin against light and knowledge when they sin.

Wash us yet again. And when we ask for this washing it is not because we doubt the efficacy of former cleansing. Then we were washed in blood. Now, O Saviour, repeat upon us what Thou didst to the twelve when Thou didst take a towel and basin and wash their feet. And when that was done Thou didst tell them that he who had been washed had no need save but to wash his feet. After that was done he was clean every whit. Oh let Thy children be in that condition this morning — clean every whit — and may they know it; and thus being clean may they have boldness to enter into the Holy of Holies by the blood of Christ; and may they now come and stand where the cherubim once were, where the glory still shines forth. And may we before a blood-besprinkled mercy seat, ourselves washed and cleansed, pour out our prayers and praises.

As for those that never have been washed, we repeat our prayer for them. Bring them, oh bring them at once to a sense of sin. Oh that we might see them take their first complete washing, and may they become henceforth the blood washed and blood redeemed consecrated ones, belonging forever unto Him who has made them white through His atoning sacrifice. And, blessed Lord, since Thou dost permit Thy washed ones to come close to Thyself we would approach Thee now with the courage which comes of faith and love, and ask of Thee this thing. Help us to overcome every tendency to evil which is still within us, and enable us to wear armour of such proof that the arrows of the enemy from without may not penetrate it, that we may not be wounded again by sin. Deliver us, we pray Thee, from doubts within and fears without, from depression of spirit, and from the outward assaults of the world.

Make us and keep us pure within, and then let our life be conducted with such holy jealousy and watchfulness that there may be nothing about us that shall bring dishonour to Thy name. May those who most carefully watch us see nothing but what shall adorn the doctrine of God our Saviour in all things. Lord help Thy people to be right as parents. May none of us spoil our children; may there be no misconducted families to cry out against us. Help us to be right as masters; may there be no oppression, no hardness and unkindness. Help us to be right as servants; may there be no eye service, no purloining, but may there be everything that adorns the Christian character. Keep us right as citizens; may we do all we can for our country, and for the times in which we live.

Keep us right, we pray Thee, as citizens of the higher country; may we be living for it, to enjoy its privileges, and to bring others within its burgess-ship, that multitudes may be made citizens of Christ through our means. Lord help us to conduct ourselves aright as Church members; may we love our brethren; may we seek their good, their edification, their comfort, their health. And oh! may such of us as are called to preach have grace equal to that responsibility. Lord make every Christian to be clear of the blood of all those round about him. We know that there are some who profess to be Thy people, who do not seem to care one whit about the souls of their fellow men. God forgive this inhumanity to men, this treason to the King of kings. Rouse the Church, we pray Thee, to a tenderness of heart towards those among whom we dwell. Let all the churches feel that they are ordained to bless their neighbours. Oh, that the Christian Church in England might begin to take upon itself its true burden.

Let the Church in London especially, with its mass of poverty and sin round about it, care for the people and love the people; and may all Christians bestir themselves that something may be done for the good of men, and for the glory of God Lord, do use us for Thy glory. Shine upon us, O Emmanuel, that we may reflect Thy brightness; dwell in us, O Jesus, that out of us may come the power of Thy life. Make Thy Church to work miracles, because the miracle-worker is in the midst of her. Oh send us times of revival, seasons of great refreshing; and then times of aggression, when the army of the Lord of Hosts shall push its way into the very center of the adversary, and overthrow the foe in the name of the King of kings.

Now forgive Thy servants all that has been amiss, and strengthen in Thy servants all that is good and right. Sanctify us to Thy service, and hold us to it. Comfort us with Thy presence; elevate us into Thy presence. Make us like Thyself; bring us near Thyself, and in all things glorify Thyself in us, whether we live or die. Bless the poor, remember the needy among Thine own people; help and succour them. Bless the sick, and be very near the dying. The Lord comfort them.

Bless our country. Let every mercy rest upon the Sovereign; send peace to disquieted districts; give wisdom to our senators in the making and in the seeing to the keeping of the law. And may Thy kingdom come not here only, but in every land and nation. Lands across the flood remember with the plenitude of Thy grace. Let the whole earth be filled with Thy glory. We ask it for Jesus' sake. Amen,

O JEHOVAH, our God, Thou lovest Thy people. Thou hast placed all the saints in the hand of Jesus, and Thou hast given Jesus to be to them a leader, a commander and a husband; and we know that Thou delightest to hear us cry on the behalf of Thy Church for Thou carest for Him, and Thou art ready to grant to Him according to the covenant provisions which Thou hast laid up in store for Christ Jesus. Therefore would we begin this prayer by entreating Thee to behold and visit the vine and the vineyard which Thy right hand hath planted.

Look upon Zion the city of our solemnities; look upon those whom Thou hast chosen from before the foundation of the world, whom Christ hath redeemed with blood, whose hearts He has won and holds, and who are His own though they be in the world. Holy Father, keep Thy people, we beseech Thee, for Jesus' sake.

Though they are in the world let them not be of it, but may there be a marked distinction between them and the rest of mankind. Even as their Lord was holy, harmless and undefiled, and separate from sinners, so may it be with believers in Christ. May they follow Him and may they not know the voice of strangers, but come out from the rest that they may follow Him without the camp. We cry to Thee for the: preservation of Thy Church in the world, and especially for her purity. O, Father, keep us, we beseech Thee with all keeping, that the evil one touch us not. We shall be tempted, but let him not prevail against us. In a thousand ways he will lay snares for our feet; but, oh deliver us as a bird from the snare of the fowler. May the snare be broken that we may escape. Let not Thy Church suffer dishonour at any time, but may her garments be always white. Let not such as come in among her that are not of her utterly despoil her.

O Christ, as Thou didst groan concerning Judas, so. may Thy children cry to Thee concerning any that have fallen aside into crooked ways, lest the cause of Christ in the earth should be dishonoured. O, God, cover, we beseech Thee, with Thy feathers, all the people of Christ, and keep Thy Church even until He shall come Who, having loved His own that were in the world, loveth them even to the end. We would ask just now that we may be washed as to our feet; we trust Thou hast bathed us once for all in the sin-removing fountain. Thou hast also washed us in the waters of regeneration and given us the; renewing of our minds, through Jesus Christ; but O for daily cleansing. Dost Thou see any fault in us? Ah! we know that Thou dost. Wash us that we may be clean. Are we deficient in any virtue? Oh supply it that we may exhibit a perfect character to the glory of Him who has made us anew in Christ Jesus. Or is there something that would be good if not carried to excess?

Be pleased to modify it lest one virtue should slaughter another, and we should not be the image of Christ completely.

O Lord and Master, Thou who didst wash Thy disciples' feet of old, still be very patient toward us, very condescending towards our provoking faults, and go with us, we pray Thee, till Thy great work shall be completed and we shall be brethren of the First Born, like unto Him. Gracious Master, we wish to conquer self in every respect; we desire to live for the glory of God and the good of our fellow men; we would have it true of us as of our Master, " He saved others. Himself He cannot save." Wilt Thou enable us especially to overcome the body with all its affections and lusts; may the flesh be kept under; let no appetite of any kind of the grosser sort prevail against our manhood, lest we be dishonoured and unclean.

And let not even the most refined power of the natural mind be permitted to come so forward as to mar the dominion of the Spirit of God within us. Oh help us not to be so easily moved even by pain, may we have much patience, and let not the prospect of death ever cause us any fear, but may the spirit get so much the mastery of the body that we know nothing can hurt the true man. The inner newborn cannot be smitten, nor is it to die; it is holy, incorruptible, and liveth and abideth forever in the life that is in Christ Jesus.

Oh for a complete conquest of self. Especially render us insensible to praise, lest we be too sensitive to censure. Let us reckon that to have the approbation of God and of our own conscience is quite enough; and may we be content, gracious God, to bear the caviling of unreasonable men; yea, and to bear the misrepresentations of our own brethren.

Those that we love, if they love not us, yet may we love them none the less, and if by mistake they misjudge us, let us have no hard feelings towards them, and God grant we may never misjudge one another. Doth not our Judge stand at the bar? Oh keep us like little children who do not know, but expect to know hereafter, and are content to believe things which they do not understand. Lord keep us humble, dependent, yet serenely joyful. May we be calm and quiet even as a weaned child, yet may we be earnest and active.

O Saviour, make us like Thyself. We wish not so much to do as to be. If Thou wilt make us to be right we shall do right. We find how often we have to put a constraint upon ourselves to be right, but, oh ! that we were like Thee, Jesus, so that we had but to act out ourselves, to act out perfect holiness.

We shall never rest till this is the case, till Thou hast made us ourselves to be inwardly holy, and then words and actions must be holy as a matter of course. Now, here we are, Lord, and we belong to Thee. Oh it is because we are Thine own that we have hope. Thou wilt make us worthy of Thee. Thy possession of us is our hope of perfection. Thou dost wash our feet be- cause we are Thine own. Oh! how sweet is the mercy which first took us to its heart and made us all its own and now continues to deal tenderly with us, that being Christ's own we may have that of Christ within us which all may see proves us to be Christ's own!

Now we would bring before Thee all Thy saints and ask Thee to attend to their trials and troubles. Some we know are afflicted in person, others are afflicted in their dear friends, some are afflicted in their temporal estate and are brought into sore distress.

Lord, we do not know the trials of all Thy people, but Thou dost, for Thou are the Head, and the pains of all the members are centered in Thee. Help all Thy people even to the end. Now we pray Thee to grant us the blessing which we have already sought, and let it come upon all the churches of our beloved country. May the Lord revive true and undefiled religion here and in all the other lands where Christ is known and preached, and let the day come when heathendom shall become converted, when the crescent of Mohammed shall wane into eternal night, and when she that sitteth on the Seven Hills and exalteth herself in the place of God shall be cast down to sink like a mill-stone in the flood. Let the blessed Gospel of the eternal God prevail, let the whole earth be filled with His glory. Oh that we may live to see that day. The Lord bless our country; have pity upon it. God bless the Sovereign with every mercy and blessing.

Grant that there may be in Thine infinite wisdom a change in the state of trade and commerce, that there may be less complaint and distress. Oh let the people see Thy hand, and understand why it is laid upon them, that they may turn from wrong- doing and seek righteousness and follow after peace. Then shall the blessing return. The Lord hear us as in secret we often cry to Thee on behalf of this misled land. The Lord deliver it, and lift up the light of His countenance upon it yet again, for Jesus' sake. Amen.

GOD of Israel, God of Jesus Christ, our God for ever and ever! Help us now by the sacred Spirit to approach Thee aright with deepest reverence, but not with servile fear ; with holiest boldness, but not with presumption. Teach us as children to speak to the Father, and yet as creatures to bow before our Maker.

Our Father, we would first ask Thee whether Thou hast ought against us as Thy children? Have we been asking somewhat of Thee amiss, and hast Thou given us that which we have sought? We are not conscious of it, but it may be so, and now we are brought as an answer to our presumptuous prayers into a more difficult position than the one we occupied before. Now it may be that some creature comfort is nearer to us than our God ; we had better have been without it and have dwelt in our God and have found our joy in Him. But now. Lord, in these perilous circumstances give us grace that we may not turn away from Thee. If our position now be not such as Thou wouldst have allotted to us had we been wiser, yet nevertheless grant that we may be taught to behave ourselves aright even now lest the mercies Thou hast given should become a cause of stumbling, and the obtaining of our hearts' desire should become a temptation to us. Rather do we feel inclined to bless Thee for the many occasions in which Thou hast not answered our prayer, for Thou hast said that we did ask amiss and therefore we could not have, and we desire to register this prayer with Thee that whensoever we do ask amiss, Thou wouldst in great wisdom and love be pleased to refuse us.

O, Lord, if we at any time press our suit without a sufficiency of resignation do not regard us, we pray Thee, and though we, cry unto Thee day and night concerning anything, yet if Thou seest that herein we err regard not the voice of our cry, we pray Thee. It is our hearts' desire now, in our coolest moments, that this prayer of ours might stand on record as long as we live, not as I will, but as Thou wilt. But, O Lord, in looking back we are obliged to remember with the greatest gratitude the many occasions in which Thou hast heard our cry.

We have been brought into deep distress, and our heart has sunk within us, and then have we cried to Thee and Thou hast never refused to hear us. The prayers of our lusts Thou hast rejected, but the prayers of our necessities Thou hast granted Not one good thing hath failed of all that Thou hast promised.

Thou hast given to us exceeding abundantly above what we asked or even thought, for there was a day when our present condition would have been regarded as much too high for us ever to reach, and in looking back we are surprised that those who did he among the pots of Egypt should now sit every man under his vine and fig tree, that those who wandered in the wilderness in a solitary way should now find a city to dwell in, that we who were prodigals in rags should now be children in the Father's bosom ; that we who were companions of swine should now be made heirs of God and joint heirs with Christ.

Oh what encouragement we have to pray to such a prayer-hearing God who far exceeds the request of His children. Blessed be the name of the Lord forever, our inmost heart is saying. Amen, blessed be His name. If it were only for answered prayer or even for some unanswered prayers we would continue to praise and bless Thee as long as we have any being. And now. Lord, hasten to the voice of Thy children's cry. Wherever there is a sincere heart seeking for greater holiness answer Thou that re- quest, or wherever there is a broken spirit seeking for reconciliation with Thyself be pleased to answer it now. Thou knowest where there is prayer, though it be unuttered, and even the lips do not move. Oh ! hear the publican who dares not lift his eye to heaven. Hear him while he cries, " God be merciful to me a sinner."

Hear such as seem to themselves to be appointed unto death. Let the sighing of the prisoner come before Thee! Oh that Thou wouldst grant peace and rest to every troubled spirit all over the world who now desires to turn his face to the cross and to see God in Christ Jesus.

O Lord, if there are any of Thy servants exercised about the cases of others we would thank Thee for them. Raise up in the Church many intercessors who shall plead for the prosperity of Zion, and give Thee no rest till Thou establish her and make her a joy in the land. Oh there are some of us that cried to Thee about our country. Thou knowest how in secret we groaned and sighed over evil times, and Thou hast begun to hear us already, for which we desire to praise and bless Thy name. But we would not cease to pray for this land that Thou wouldst roll away from it all its sin, that Thou wouldst deliver it from the curse of drunkenness, rescue, it from infidelity, from popery, from ritualism, from rationalism and every form of evil, that this land might become a holy land.

O, Lord, bring the multitudes of the working men to listen to the gospel. Break in, we pray Thee, upon their stolid indifference. Lord, give them a love of Thy house, a desire to hear Thy gospel, and then wilt Thou look upon the poor rich who so many of them know nothing about Thee and are worshipping their own wealth. The Lord grant that the many for whom there are no special gospel services, but who are wrapped up in self- righteousness, may be brought to hear the gospel of Jesus that they also, as well as the poor, may be brought to Christ. God bless this land with more of gospel light, and with more of gospel life and love. Thou wilt hear us, O Lord.

Then would we pray for our children, that they might be saved. Some of us can no longer pray for our children's conversion, our prayers are heard already. But there are others who have children who vex them and grieve their hearts. O God, save sons and daughters of godly people. Let them not have to sigh over their children as Eli did and as Samuel did, and may they see their sons and daughters become the children of the living God. We would pray for our servants, for our neighbours, for our kinsfolk of near or far degree, that all might be brought to Jesus. Do Thou this, O God, of Thine infinite mercy. And as we are now making intercession we would, according to Thy Word, pray for all kings, such as are in authority, that we may lead quiet and peaceable lives. We pray for all nations also-. O Lord, bless and remember the lands that sit in darkness, and let them see a great light, and may missionary enterprise be abundantly successful. And let the favoured nations where our God is known, especially this land and the land across the mighty ocean that love the same Saviour and speak the same tongue, be always favoured with the Divine presence and with abundant prosperity and blessing.

O Lord, Thou hast chosen this our race and favoured it and multiplied it on the face of the earth, and whereas with this staff it crossed this Jordan it hath now become two great nations. Lord be pleased to bless the whole of the race and those absorbed into it, and then all other races that in us may be fulfilled the blessing of Abraham, "I will bless you and ye shall be a blessing."

And now, Father, glorify Thy Son ! In scattering pardons through His precious blood glorify Thy Son ! In sending forth the Eternal Spirit to convince men and bring them to His feet, Father glorify Thy Son!

In enriching Thy saints with gifts and graces, and building them up into His image, Father glorify Thy Son! In the gathering together of the whole company of His elect and in the hastening of His kingdom and His coming. Father glorify Thy Son! Beyond this prayer we cannot go: "Glorify Thy Son that Thy Son also may glorify Thee," and unto Father, Son and Holy Spirit be glory for ever and ever. Amen.

O Lord, if some of us began to doubt Thee we should begin to doubt our senses, for Thou hast done such wonderful things for us., Thou hast done more for us than Thou didst for Thomas. Thou didst allow Thomas to thrust his finger into Thy wounds; but Thou hast often thrust Thy finger into our wounds, and healed them. THOU who art King of kings and Lord of lords, we worship Thee. "Before Jehovah's awful throne We bow with sacred joy." We can truly say that we delight in God. There was a time when we feared Thee, O God, with the fear of bondage. Now we reverence, but we love as much as we reverence. The thought of Thine Omnipresence was once horrible to us.

We said; "Whither shall we flee from His presence? "and it seemed to make hell itself more dreadful, because we heard a voice, " If I make my bed in hell, behold, Thou art there." But now, O Lord, we desire to find Thee. Our longing is to feel Thy presence, and it is the heaven of heavens that Thou art there. The sick bed is soft when Thou art there. The furnace of affliction grows cool when Thou art there, and the house of prayer when Thou art present is none other than the house of God, and it is the very gate of heaven. AMEN

Come near, our Father, come very near to Thy children. Some of us are very weak in body and faint in heart. Soon, O God lay Thy right hand upon us and say unto us, "Fear not." Peradventure, some of us are alike, and the world is attracting us. Come near to kill the influence of the world with Thy superior power. Even to worship may not seem easy to some. The dragon seems to pursue them, and floods out of his mouth wash away their devotion. Give to them great wings as of an eagle, that each one may fly away into the place prepared for him, and rest in the presence of God today. AMEN

Our Father, come and rest Thy children now. Take the helmet from our brow, remove from us the weight of our heavy armour for awhile, and may we just have peace, perfect peace, and be at rest. Oh help us, we pray Thee, now. As Thou hast already washed Thy people in the fountain filled with blood and they are clean, now this morning wash us from defilement in the water. With the basin and with the ewer, O Master, wash our feet again. It will greatly refresh; it will prepare us for innermost fellowship with Thyself.

So did the priests wash ere they went into the holy place. Lord Jesus, take from us now everything that would hinder the closest communion with God. Any wish or desire that might hamper us in prayer remove, we pray Thee. Any memory of either sorrow or care that might hinder the fixing of our affection wholly on our God, take it away now. What have we to do with idols anymore? Thou hast seen and observed us. Thou knoweth where the difficulty lies. Help us against it, and may we now come boldly, not into the Holy place alone, but into the Holiest of all, where we should not dare to come if our great Lord had not rent the veil, sprinkled the mercy seat with His own blood, and bidden us enter. AMEN

O LORD God, help us now really to worship Thee. We would thank Thee for this occasion. We bless Thy name for setting- apart this hallowed season. Lord, wilt Thou shut the door upon the world for us ? Help us to forget our cares. Enable us to rise clean out of this world. May we get rid of all its down-dragging tendencies. May the attractions of these grosser things be gone, and do Thou catch us away to Thyself. We do not ask to be entranced nor to see an angel in shining- apparel, but we do ask that by faith we may see Jesus, and may His presence be so evidently realized among us that we may rejoice as well as if our eyes beheld Him, and love Him and trust Him and worship Him as earnestly as we should do if we could now put our fingers into the print of the nails. Amen.

O Thou precious Lord Jesus Christ, we do adore Thee with all our hearts. Thou art Lord of all. We bless Thee for becoming man that Thou mightest be our next of kin, and being next of kin we bless Thee for taking us into marriage union with Thyself and for redeeming us and our inheritance from the captivity into which we were sold. Thou hast paid Thy life for Thy people; Thou hast ransomed Thy folk with Thy heart's blood. Be Thou, therefore, forever beloved and adored. And now Thou art not here for Thou art risen. Our souls would track the shining way by which Thou hast ascended through the gate of pearl up to Thy Father's throne. We seem to see Thee sitting there, man, yet God, reigning over all things for Thy people, and our ears almost catch the accents of the everlasting song which rolls up at Thy feet:

Worthy is the Lamb that was slain to receive honour, and power, and glory, and dominion, and might for ever and ever." Lord, we say, "Amen." From the outskirts of the crowd that surround Thy throne we lift up our feeble voices in earnest "Amens," for Thou wast slain and hast re- deemed us to God by Thy blood and hast made us kings and priests unto God, and we shall reign with Thee, for though far off by space, we know that we are very near to Thy heart. Thou lookest over the heads of the angelic squadrons to behold us, and Thou dost hear the praises — aye, and the groans of Thy well-beloved, for are not we most near Thee, Thy flesh and Thy bones? We know we are. We feel the ties of kinship within us.

We our best Beloved's are, and He is ours, and we are longing to get through the crowd that surround Him, and to get to the forefront, and there to bow prostrate at the dear feet that were nailed to the tree for us, and worship the Lamb Who liveth for ever and ever, Who has prevailed to take the book and loose the seven seals thereof, to Whom be glory, world without end. Hallelujah! AMEN

O, Saviour, accept these our poor praises. They come from those Thou lovest, and as we prize any little things that come from those we love, so do we feel that Thou wilt accept the thanksgiving, the reverential homage of Thy people, redeemed ones who are a people near unto Thee, whose names are graven on the palms of Thy hands, of whom Thou art the active head and for whom Thy heart beats rue and full of love e'en now. Oh, we can say we love Thee; we wish we loved Thee more; but Thou art very dear to us. There is naught on earth like Thee. For the love of Thy name we would live and die. If we think we love Thee more than we do, we pray that we may yet love Thee more than we think. Oh, take these hearts right away and unite them with Thine own, and be Thou heart and soul and life and everything to us; for whom have we in heaven but Thee, and there is none upon earth we desire beside Thee. We worship the Father, we worship the Son, we worship the Holy Ghost with all the powers of our being. We fall prostrate before the awful yet glorious throne of the Infinite Majesty of heaven. The Lord accept us since we offer these praises in the name of Jesus. AMEN

And now most blessed Lord, look down upon those who do not love Thee. O Redeemer, look upon them with those eyes of Thine which are as flames of fire. Let them see how ill they treat Thee. May they consider within themselves how dire is the ingratitude which can be negligent of a Saviour's blood, indifferent from a Saviour's heart. Oh, bring the careless and the godless to seek for mercy. Let those that are postponing serious things begin to see that the very thought of postponement of the claims of Christ is treason against His Majesty. O Saviour, dart Thine arrows abroad and let them wound many that they may fall down before Thee and cry out for mercy. But there are some who are wounded; broken hearts that seek peace, men and women, like Cornelius, that want to hear the words which God commands. Oh, come Divine Physician, and bind up every broken bone. Come with Thy sacred nard which Thou hast compounded of Thine own heart's blood, and lay it home to the wounded conscience, and let it feel its power. Oh! Give peace to those whose conscience is like the troubled sea which cannot rest. AMEN

LORD, we would come to Thee, but do Thou come to us. Draw us and we will run after Thee. Blessed Spirit, help our infirmities, for we know not what we should pray for as we ought. Come, Holy Spirit, and give right thoughts and right utterance that we may all be able to pray in the common prayer, the whole company feeling that for each one there is a portion.

We are grateful as we remember that if the minister in the sanctuary should not be able to pray for any one of us there is One who bears the names of all His redeemed upon His breast, and upon His shoulder, who will take care with the love of His heart and the power of His arm to maintain the cause of all His own. Dear Saviour, we put ourselves under Thy sacred power this day, yea, make intercession for the transgressors. AMEN

We desire to praise the name of the Lord with our whole heart, so many of us as have tasted that the Lord is gracious. Truly Thou hast delivered us from the gulf of dark despair, wherein we wretched sinners lay. Thou hast brought us up also out of the horrible pit and out of the miry clay, Thou hast set our feet upon a rock, and the new song which Thou hast put into our mouths we would not stifle, but we would bless the Lord whose mercy endureth forever. We thank Thee, Lord, for the love without beginning which chose us or ever the earth was, for the love without measure which entered into covenant for our redemption, for the love without failure which in due time appeared in the person of Christ and wrought out our redemption, for that love which has never changed, though we have wandered; that love which abideth faithful even when we are unfaithful.

Now, we have come close up to Thyself, to the light that shineth between the wings of the Cherubim, and we speak with Thee now as a man speaketh with his friends. Our God, we are Thine. Thou art ours. We are now concerned in one business, we are leagued together for one battle. Thy battle is our battle, and our fight is Thine, Help us, we pray Thee.

Thou who didst strengthen Michael and his angels to cast out the dragon and his angels, help poor flesh and blood that to us also the word may be fulfilled: "The Lord shall bruise Satan under your feet, shortly." Our Father, we are very weak. Worst of all we are very wicked if left to ourselves, and we soon fall a prey to the enemy. Therefore help us, We confess that sometimes in prayer when we are nearest to Thee at that very time some evil thought comes in, some wicked desire. Oh ! what poor simpletons we are. Lord help us. We feel as if we would now come closer to Thee still, and hide under the shadow of Thy wings. We wish to be lost in God. We pray that Thou mayest live in us, and not we live, but Christ live in us and show Himself in us and through us. Lord sanctify us. Oh! That Thy spirit might come and saturate every faculty, subdue every passion, and use every power of our nature for obedience to God. AMEN

Come, Holy Spirit, we do know Thee; Thou hast often overshadowed us. Come, more fully take possession of us. Standing now as we feel we are right up at the mercy seat our very highest prayer is for perfect holiness, complete consecration, entire cleansing from every evil. Take our heart, our head, our hands, our feet, and use us all for Thee. Lord take our substance, let us not hoard it for ourselves, nor spend it for ourselves.

Take our talent, let us not try to educate ourselves that we may have the repute of being wise, but let every gain of mental attainment be still that we may serve Thee better. May every breath be for Thee ; may every minute be spent for Thee. Help us to live while we live and while we are busy in the world as we must be, for we are called to it, may we sanctify the world may we be lumps of salt in the midst of society.

May our spirit and temper as well as our conversation be heavenly; May there be an influence about us that shall make the world the better before we leave it Lord hear us in this thing. And now that we have Thine ear we would pray for this poor world in which we live. We are often horrified by it. O, Lord, we could wish that we did not know anything about it for our own comfort. We have said, "Oh for a lodge in some vast wilderness." We hear of oppression and robbery and murder, and men seem let loose against each other. Lord, have mercy upon this great and wicked world. What is to be done with these millions ? What can we do ? At least help every child of Thine to do his utmost. May none of us contribute to the evil directly or indirectly, but may we contribute to the good that is in it. Amen.

We feel we may speak with Thee now about this, for when Thy servant Abraham stood before Thee and spake with such wonderful familiarity to Thee, he pleaded for Sodom; and we plead for London. We would follow the example of the Father of the Faithful and pray for all great cities, and indeed for all the nations. Lord let Thy kingdom come. Send forth Thy light and Thy truth. Chase the old dragon from his throne, with all his hellish crew.

Oh! That the day might come when even upon earth the Son of the woman, the Man-child, should rule the nations, not with a broken staff of wood, but with an enduring scepter of iron, full of mercy, but full of power, full of grace, but yet irresistible. Oh! that that might soon come, the personal advent of our Lord ! We long for the millennial triumph of His Word.

Until then, O Lord, gird us for the fight, and make us to be among those who overcome through the blood of the Lamb and through the word of our testimony, because we " love not our lives unto the death." We lift our voice to Thee in prayer ; also, for all our dear ones. Lord bless the sick and make them well as soon as it is right they should be. Sanctify to them all they have to bear. There are also dear friends who are very weak ; some that are very trembling. God bless them. While the tent is being taken down may the inhabitant within look on with calm joy, for we shall by-and-by "be clothed upon with our house that is from heaven." Lord help us to sit very loose by all these things here below. May we live here like strangers and make the world not a house but an inn, in which we sup and lodge, expecting to be on our journey tomorrow. Amen.

Lord save the unconverted, and bring out, we pray Thee, from among them those who are converted, but who have not confessed Christ. May the Church be built up by many who, having believed, are baptized unto the sacred name. We pray Thee go on and multiply the faithful in the land. Oh! That Thou wouldst turn the hearts of men to the gospel once more. Thy servant is often very heavy in heart because of the departures from the faith. Oh! bring them back; let not Satan take away any more of the stars with his tail, but may the lamps of God shine bright. Oh! Thou that walketh amongst the seven golden candle- sticks trim the flame, pour forth the oil, and let the light shine brightly and steadily. Now, Lord, we cannot pray any longer, though we have a thousand things to ask for. Thy servant cannot, so he begs to leave a broken prayer at the mercy seat with this at the foot of it: We ask in the name of Jesus Christ Thy Son. Amen.

Teresa of Avila *(28 March 1515 – 4 October 1582) Teresa Sánchez de Cepeda y Ahumada was a part of the Counter Reformation. As a young teen she became conscious of her own impotence in confronting sin, and the necessity of absolute subjection to God. She founded a reformed Carmelite order. Teresa traveled to establish cloisters for her order. Eventually she was persecuted by those within the greater Carmelite order who did not wish to take vows of poverty or go shoeless (take off your shoes you are on holy ground.) which was a part of Teresa's reforms. She wrote extensively in her seclusion.*

O my God! Source of all mercy! I acknowledge Your sovereign power. While recalling the wasted years that are past, I believe that You, Lord, can in an instant turn this loss to gain. Miserable as I am, yet I firmly believe that You can do all things. Please restore to me the time lost, giving me Your grace, both now and in the future, that I may appear before You in "wedding garments." Amen

Let nothing upset you, let nothing startle you. All things pass; God does not change. Patience wins all it seeks. Whoever has God lacks nothing:

God alone is enough. Amen.

If, Lord, Thy love for me is strong as this which binds me unto Thee, what holds me from Thee Lord so long, what holds Thee Lord so long from me? O soul, what then desirest thou? Lord I would see Thee, who thus choose Thee. What fears can yet assail Thee now?

All that I fear is but lose Thee. Love's whole possession I entreat, Lord make my soul Thine own abode, And I will build a nest so sweet It may not be too poor for God. A soul in God hidden from sin, What more desires for Thee remain, Save but to love again, And all on flame with love within, Love on, and turn to love again. Amen.

Majestic sovereign, timeless wisdom, Your kindness melts my hard, cold soul. Handsome Lover, selfless Giver, Your beauty fills my dull, sad eyes. I am Yours, You made me. I am Yours, You called me. I am Yours, You saved me. I am Yours, You loved me. I will never leave Your presence.

Give me death, give me life. Give me sickness, give me health. Give me honor, give me shame. Give me weakness, give me strength. I will have whatever you give. Amen.

Give me the grace to recollect myself in the little heaven of my soul where You have established Your dwelling. There You let me find You, there I feel that You are closer to me than anywhere else, and there You prepare my soul quickly to enter into intimacy with You…Help me O Lord, to withdraw my senses from exterior things, make them docile to the commands of my will, so that when I want to converse with You, they will retire at once, like bees shutting themselves up in the hive in order to make honey. Amen

O Lord of heaven and earth! Is it possible, while we are still in this mortal life, for us to enjoy You with such special friendship? Oh! The joys which You bestow on souls who give themselves entirely to You! For the love of the Lord, my soul, wake out of this sleep and remember that God does not keep you waiting until the next life before rewarding you for your love of Him. Your recompense begins in this life.

They that really love You, my Good, walk safely on a broad and royal road. They are far from the precipice. Hardly have they begun to stumble when You, Lord, give them Your hand. One fall is not sufficient for a person to be lost nor are many, if they love You and not the things of the world. They journey in the valley of humility. I cannot understand what it is that makes people afraid of setting out on the road of perfection. May the Lord, because of who He is, give us understanding of how wretched is the security that lies in such manifest dangers as following the crowd and how true security lies in striving to make progress on the road of God. Let them turn their eyes to Him and not fear the setting of this Sun of Justice, nor, if we don't first abandon Him, will He allow us to walk at night and go astray.

O Lord, who could describe how great a gain it is to cast ourselves into Your arms and make an agreement with You; You take care of my affairs and I of Yours....For what am I Lord without You?

What more do I want in this life than to be so near you that there is no division between You and me. O Lord of my life, draw me to Yourself, but do it in such a way that my will may ever remain so united to You that it shall be unable to leave You.

O Lord, how true that all harm comes to us from not keeping our eyes fixed on You; if we were to look at nothing else but the way, we would soon arrive. But we meet with a thousand falls and obstacles and lose the way because we don't keep our eyes—as I say—on the true way. It seems so new to us that you would think we had never walked on it. It's certainly something to excite pity, that which sometimes happens. Teach me, my God, to suffer in peace the afflictions which You send me that my soul may emerge from the crucible like gold, both brighter and purer, to find You within me.

My God, I want nothing but Your will, submission to it has such power over me that my soul desires neither death nor life. But then, if it be Your will, I desire to live, in order to serve You better.

If, through my intercession, I could do anything to make a single soul love and praise You more, and that only for a short time, it would seem to me of greater moment than my being in glory. Grant, that our love may never be small, but always most ardent, like a great fire that cannot but shine brightly.

No, my God, love does not consist in shedding tears, in enjoying consolations and that tenderness which for the most part we desire and in which we find comfort, but in serving You with righteousness, fortitude of soul, and humility. The other seems to me to be receiving rather than giving anything.

O Lord, grant that my love be not the fruit of my imagination but be proved by works. What can I do for You who died for us and created us and gave us being, without counting myself fortunate in being able to repay You something of what I owe you? Well do I know, my Lord, of how little I am capable. But I shall be able to do all things provided You do not withdraw from me. Amen.

O my soul: Consider the great delight and great love the Father has in knowing His Son and the Son in knowing His Father; and the enkindling love with which the Holy Spirit is joined with them; and how no one of them is able to be separate from this love and knowledge, because they are one. These sovereign Persons know each other, love each other, and delight in each other. Well, what need is there for my love? Why do You want it, my God, or what do You gain?

Oh, may You be blessed! May You be blessed, my God, forever! May all things praise You, Lord, without end, since in You there can be no end. Amen.

Be joyful, my soul, for there is someone who loves your God as He deserves. Be joyful, for there is someone who knows His goodness and value. Give thanks to Him, for He has given us on earth someone who thus knows Him, as His only Son. Under this protection you can approach and petition Him, for then His Majesty takes delight in you. Don't let any earthly thing be enough to separate you from your delight, and rejoice in the grandeur of God; in how He deserves to be loved and praised; that He helps you to play some small role in the blessing of His name; and that you can truthfully say: My soul magnifies and praises the Lord. Amen.

Francis Xavier (*April 7, 1506-December 3, 1552)Francis Xavier born Francisco de Jasso y Azpilicueta, was from the Basque region between France and Spain. He was a founder of the Society of Jesus and a friend of Ignatius of Loyola. Francis Xavier had a burden for missions and traveled to India, Ceylon, Japan and China to evangelize. He is said to have been an athlete and a high-jumper. He died in China at the age of 46.*

Eternal God, Creator of all things remember that You alone hast created the souls of unbelievers, which You have made according to Your image and Likeness. Behold, O Lord, how to Your dishonor many of them are falling into Hell. Remember, O Lord, Your Son Jesus Christ who so generously shed His blood and suffered for them.

Do not permit that Your Son Our Lord, remain unknown by unbelievers, but with the help of Your saints and the Church, the Bride of Your Son, remember Your mercy, forget their idolatry and infidelity, and make them know Him, Whom You have sent, Jesus Christ, Your Son, Our Lord Who is our salvation, our life, and our resurrection, through Whom we have been saved and redeemed, and to Whom is due glory forever. Amen

My God, I love Thee; not because I hope for heaven thereby, nor yet because who love Thee not are lost eternally. Thou, O my Jesus, Thou didst me upon the cross embrace; for me didst bear the nails and spear, and manifold disgrace and griefs and torments numberless and sweat of agony; even death itself, and all for one who was Thine enemy. Then why, O blessed Jesus Christ should I not love Thee well? Not for hope of winning heaven or of escaping Hell. Not with the hope of gaining aught, nor seeking a reward, but as Thyself hath loved me, O ever-loving Lord!
Even so I love Thee, and will love and in Thy praise will sing, solely because Thou art my God, and my eternal King. Amen.

O my Lord Jesus! Teach me to be generous; teach me to serve Thee as Thou deservest; to give, and not to count the cost; to fight and not to heed the wounds; to toil and not to ask for rest; to labor, seeking no reward, save that of knowing that I do Thy will. Amen.

Not with the hope of gaining aught, not seeking a reward; but as Thyself hast loved me, O ever-loving Lord. E'en so I love Thee, and will live, and in Thy praise will sing; solely because Thou art my God and my eternal King. Amen.

Soli Deo Gloria

INDEX

AETHELWOLD OF WINCHESTER P 43
ALCUIN OF YORK P 43
AMBROSE OF MILAN P 44
ANDREWES, LANCELOT P 49
ANGELA DI FOLIGNO P 59
ANSELM OF CANTERBURY 60
ANTIOCHUS OF PALESTINE P 80
AQUINAS, THOMAS P 82
ASSISSI, FRANCIS OF P 88
AUGUSTINE OF HIPPO P 89
BASIL OF CESAREA P 91
BENEDICT OF NURSIA P 93
CALVIN, JOHN P 93
CATHERINE OF GENOA P 102
CATHERINE OF SIENA P 109
CLEMENT OF ALEXANDRIA P 112
COLUMBA P 114
CHRYSOSTOM, JOHN P 114
DONNE, JOHN P 116
EPHREM THE SYRIAN P147
IGNATIUS OF LOYOLA P 149
JEROME P 151
KEMPIS THOMAS A' P 152
LISIEUX, THERESE OF P 156
LUTHER MARTIN P 158
MACARIUS OF EGYPT P 160
MACDONALD, GEORGE P 160
MAGDEBURG, MECHTHILD OF P 166
MURRAY, ANDREW P 166
ORIGEN P 192
PATRICK P 192
SALES, FRANCIS DE P 193
SPURGEON, CHARLES H. P 195
TERESA OF AVILA P 310
XAVIER, FRANCIS P 315

ABOUT THE AUTHOR

Doug Whitley grew up in eastern North Carolina. At the age of four he came in childlike faith to Jesus Christ. He dedicated his life to Christ while on a church camp-out at the age of eleven. Doug spent three summers on staff at a Christian camp. He traveled to Mexico twice on short-term mission trips. Doug has worked as a sponsor to both Junior and Senior High young people. He has coached state championship soccer teams and conference championship teams on the college level and took one team to the finals on the national level. Doug's experience with Christian drama began in high school when he traveled for three years with a Christian drama team. It was during this time that the impact of drama became evident in its ability to reach souls and change hearts as he witnessed the effects on the lives of congregations. Mr. Whitley holds a B.A. in speech and an M.A. in dramatic production. He has been a college speech department chairman a director of special programs at Southside Christian School. He has appeared in four Christian films, various TV and radio programs. His acting credits include many Shakespearean roles as well as Biblical roles. Mr. Whitley is the author of eight Christian plays, several short stories and he has co-authored an Easter Cantata.

Doug began his present ministry in August of 1990 after breaking his arms while wiring a friend's barn. It was during this time that God strengthened his faith to begin this full-time drama evangelism ministry. Doug and his wife, Cheri, travel together trusting the Lord to meet their needs. The ministry has taken them from coast to coast, North to South and literally around the world presenting God's Truth through the lives of these heroes of the faith. In portraying the lives of these men, Doug feels not only their burden for others, but the burden of portraying men who were giants of the faith. Each man's testimony continues to challenge Doug's own heart and life to be a better servant of God.

www.preachersofthepast.com

A Sweet Smelling Savor

Made in the USA
Columbia, SC
26 November 2017